VIRTUAL HALLYU

Korean Cinema of the Global Era

Kyung Hyun Kim

DUKE UNIVERSITY PRESS *Durham & London 2011*

© 2011 Duke University Press

All rights reserved

Printed in the United States of America on acid-free paper ∞

Designed by Jennifer Hill

Typeset in Chaparral Pro by Tseng Information Systems, Inc.

Library of Congress Cataloging-in-Publication Data appear on the
last printed page of this book.

To all filmmakers, critics, teachers, festival programmers, cinephiles, and policymakers—who helped make Korean cinema during the first decade of the 2000s a globally recognized phenomenon.

CONTENTS

Martin Scorsese

To find a filmmaker or group of filmmakers with a new approach to film language, new answers to the question of what a movie *is* and what it *can* be . . . it's one of the most rewarding aspects of movie culture. The pictures coming out of Iran and Taiwan in the 1990s, for example, required an adjustment. I remember watching them for the first time, seeing that they were urgent, passionately made, and I quickly understood that I would have to let the pictures themselves guide me, teach me their grammar, show me the way to their secrets, *and* to the cultural experiences and givens shared by the different filmmakers.

The great Korean cinema of the late 90s and the 2000s crept up on me, slowly and without warning. Hong Sang-soo's *The Day a Pig Fell into the Well* was a deceptively unassuming picture, made with great assurance. The narrative was intricate, but not in a manner that drew attention to itself—it was only as the movie unfolded that you came to understand how complex it was. The settings seemed banal, the concerns of the characters life-size, the focus uncomfortably intimate. The film left me unsettled—what had I just *seen*?

I was intrigued. I saw some pictures by another Korean filmmaker named Bong Joon-ho—a completely different approach, more overtly comic in his first feature, *Barking Dogs Never Bite*, but the comedy was savage and merciless. In *Memories of Murder* and *The Host*, I saw a clear link to American genre filmmaking, but it was interpreted and felt in a completely new way. *The Host* was fun, complex, rich, and panoramic, but in its own way it was just as troubling as the Hong film.

Park Chan-wook's *Sympathy for Mr. Vengeance*, like his subsequent pictures *Lady Vengeance* and *Old Boy*, seemed to come out of a different strain in genre filmmaking—American drive-in movies, J-horror, Shaw Brothers martial arts epics. But the violence and action and chaos became expressive instruments, and the films were as ferocious as a great Eric Clapton guitar solo. But lingering in the background was that same unease and melancholy that I recognized in the other pictures.

The unease and melancholy took front and center in Lee Chang-dong's *Green Fish* and *Peppermint Candy*. These pictures were designed as ambitious portrayals of an entire society filtered through the experience of a few characters, devoted to giving you the *texture* of life, the dreams and the cold hard realities, the habits and prejudices, the different ways of living.

As the years went by, I realized that I was slowly becoming absorbed in Korean cinema and its development, and I became more absorbed with each new picture from these directors and others, like *The President's Last Bang* by Im Sang-soo, *Camel(s)* by Park Ki-young, *Breathless* by Yang Ik-joon, *Never Forever* by Gina Kim, and *Jealousy Is My Middle Name* by Park Chan-ok, an extremely subtle and emotionally complex film; and then in older pictures by filmmakers like Im Kwon-Taek, Park Kwang-su, and the late, great Kim Ki-young. I was actually introduced to *The Housemaid*, one of Kim's most disturbing pictures, by the author of this book, and it became one of the first restorations undertaken by The World Cinema Foundation when it was formed in 2007.

Following these films and filmmakers over the years has shown me just how vital a role cinema can play in the life of a culture, no matter how "challenging" the movies are considered, how much or how little money they make, how large or small a public they find either inside or outside the country. The categories that many resort to when they judge movies nowadays—"entertaining" vs. "difficult," "fast-paced" vs. "slow moving," "short" vs. "long," "fun" vs. "art"—have very little to do with the movies themselves or how they affect viewers who come to them with an open mind. The films of Hong, Lee, Bong, Park, and their fellow filmmakers speak of, to, and from their culture, sometimes critically but never indifferently or disinterestedly—for that reason, they are genuine cultural ambassadors.

Kyung Hyun knows this. He knows that vital works of art *never* sit easily within the society they come out of. And he helps to explain, in this fine book, how the give and take between those filmmakers and their country actually functions. He enlarges our vision of one of the great national cinematic flowerings of the last decade.

Immediately after the release of Kim Jee-woon's *The Good, the Bad, the Weird* (*Choŭn nom, nappŭn nom, isanghan nom*) in July 2008, I had a chance to talk to its producer, Choi Jae-won. This Korean macaroni Western about three outlaws, set in colonial Manchuria during the 1930s, had just opened in theaters throughout South Korea. On its opening day, *The Good, the Bad, the Weird* occupied 949 of the country's approximately 2,000 screens and was on its way to selling over seven million tickets (for a gross of over $43 million). That would not break the box office record set two summers earlier by Bong Joon-ho's *The Host* (*Koemul*), which had sold a whopping 13.19 million tickets on 620 screens.[1] But selling seven million tickets for *The Good, the Bad, the Weird* was, I thought, not a small feat considering that South Korea has a population of only forty-nine million.[2] Everywhere you went in Korea that summer, you heard the film's theme song, a remake of the Animals' "Don't Let Me Be Misunderstood," blaring on the radio and saw ads for the movie whizzing by on buses. The faces of the film's three main actors—Song Kang-ho, Jung Woo-sung, and Lee Byung-hun, who played three outlaw gunmen—looped endlessly on various television commercials selling notebook computers and credit cards. Yet this summer blockbuster hit—a pastiche of global appropriations and reappropriations, in particular Sergio Leone's 1966 *The Good, the Bad, and the Ugly* and Lee Man-hŭi's 1971 local Manchurian Western *Cut the Chain* (*Soesasŭl ŭl kkŭnŏra*)—had, according to Choi, "failed to overwhelm the BEP [break-even point]." Choi bemoaned the film's lackluster returns: "How is it possible that the bestselling summer blockbuster of the year cannot even break even?" To his dismay, I retorted, "Wasn't the movie shot almost entirely in Korean?" At a time when the novelty of hallyu (the wave of Korean exports in popular music, film, and television dramas) had waned, I thought that mainstream audiences outside Korea would be very unlikely to go see a Korean-language film, which prominently featured the comic gags of local star Song Kang-ho and consequently was largely incomprehensible to viewers beyond a hard-core constituency.

1   Poster for *The Good, the Bad, the Weird*.

Only about eighty million people, worldwide, speak Korean, and this figure includes twenty million North Koreans, who cannot legally consume South Korea's cultural products. Even though the live action films made in South Korea at the peak of the hallyu era generally delivered the high visual production value and spectacle that the market demanded, they were largely dependent on wit derived from the unique and ironic use of the Korean language.[3] Beyond the Korean Peninsula, only the small Yanbian Autonomous Prefecture in the northeastern region of China uses Korean as the official language. Though *han'gŭl*, the Korean alphabet, is a uniquely efficient writing system made up of fourteen consonants and ten vowels, Korean is considered a difficult language[4] and is largely inaccessible to nonnative speakers. Despite the popularity of hallyu in China, Japan, Vietnam, and other neighboring countries over the past decade, fluent speakers of Korean are still difficult to find beyond Korean diasporic communities. When hallyu finally began showing signs of stagnation in Japan in 2006, films with expensive price tags—such as *The Good, the Bad, the Weird*, starring two of Korea's brightest hallyu stars, Jung Woo-sung and Lee Byung-hun—were unable to immediately find buyers in Japan, previously the biggest importer of hallyu products. By 2007, Korean film export sales to Japan had sputtered to a dismal $ 3.3 million, about the same as in the pre-hallyu days, merely two years after Korean film exports to Japan had hit a record $ 60.3 million.

Things got even worse for *The Good, the Bad, the Weird*. Piracy had caused the collapse of the market for ancillary products (DVD rentals and sales, view on demand, and television broadcast rights) in Korea, and the film could not make any substantial profit in these secondary markets. Also, in 2009, after having a difficult time finding a Japanese distributor, *The Good, the Bad, and the Weird* finally opened in Japan—only to flop badly. Therefore, the film's investors—who had put up $25 million, including $18 million for production and approximately $5 million for advertising—earned less than $20 million after splitting the gross local theatrical proceeds of $43 million with distributors and theaters. Almost all of the proceeds came from the Korean box office. *The Good, the Bad, the Weird*, Korea's bestselling film in 2008, which outsold even Hollywood competitors such as *Kung Fu Panda* and *Mama Mia* by a two-to-one ratio, unfortunately found itself in the loss column. Although the price of producing and publicizing a blockbuster film had climbed from $2 million in 1999 (*Shiri*) to $25 million in 2008 (*The Good, the Bad, the Weird*), the demand for these products had actually shrunk.

By calling this book *Virtual Hallyu*, I hoped to achieve an ironic effect. Though cinema did play a critical part in hallyu, most recent scholarship on the Korean wave of exports typically places K-drama and K-pop at hallyu's fulcrum. By designating the Korean cinema of the past decade as "virtual"—which intriguingly etches the signifiers "artificial" and "spectral" over its original meaning of "truthful" and "potential"—I wanted to remind readers that cinema's modernist ambitions played a subconscious, if not unconscious, role in hallyu's proliferation. Though hallyu is more familiar through popular films like Kwak Jae-yong's *My Sassy Girl* (*Yŏpki jŏk in kŭnyŏ*, 2002) and Yi Chae-han's *A Moment to Remember* (*Nae maum sok ŭi chiukae*, 2004), these productions failed to establish an aesthetic standard in the local film culture the way the films of Bong Joon-ho, Park Chanwook, Hong Sang-soo, or Lee Chang-dong did throughout the 2000s. *Virtual Hallyu*, consequently, is a reflection of *both* the modernist ambition to engage cinema as a technological tool that could challenge language and literature as the principal mode of creative expression *and* the postmodern failure to extend cinema's power beyond populist entertainment.[5] Throughout the book, I evaluate how Korean cinema during this period included not only independently produced, anti-establishment *tayangsŏng* (diverse) films made possible by subsidies from the Korean Film Council (KOFIC), but also a sizable film industry with annual box office sales of $1 billion (1.15 trillion won in 2010), led by several *chaebŏl* groups such as CJ, Lotte, and Tongyang (Showbox), which cultivated a culture of near total disregard for the modernist productions featured in film festivals.[6] The "virtual" that I invoke in these pages is consequently both a celebration and a mourning of the nascent blossoming of Korean modernity in a global age that has sought to nip it in the bud and to transform it into a postmodern production.

Specifically, this book celebrates and mourns the supersized Korean cinema produced during the days of hallyu. I began teaching Korean film in 1996 at the University of California, Los Angeles (UCLA), and I now teach it at the University of California, Irvine. Every year, in spite of my familiarity with Korean film texts, I am confronted with the unfamiliar, with its attendant requirements for renewed identification and negotiation. Writing this book during the hallyu period was like being inside a house that was constantly being refurbished. Korean cinema in many ways engineered hallyu, which in a real sense revealed a shift—however fleeting—in the American perception of Korea, thus rendering possible a magical and virtual identity for myself as well. Although I have now written two books and innumerable numbers of articles on Korean film, I am still unsure how to answer the following questions: Did the Korean films produced during the first decade of the twenty-first century constitute a countercinema that, even at a subconscious level, sought to resist American cultural hegemony? Or was it primarily a cinema that effectively danced to the tunes of Hollywood, which always requires an Asian sidekick: Akira Kurosawa in the 1970s, John Woo and Tsui Hark in the 1980s and the 1990s, and Park Chan-wook in the 2000s?

"We cannot tell from the mere taste of wheat who grew it" is one of Marx's mottos that still remains in vogue.[7] After all, a capitalist product is evaluated by how well it can camouflage who the real producers are (for example, Third World sweatshop labor). And if a hallyu comedy can provide just as good a chuckle as an American film for only a fraction of the distribution fee that Hollywood studios charge, is there even a need to check the tag at the back of the neck or (in this case) sit around until the end credits roll in order to identify the country of origin? Most films made during the hallyu era, including those of Park Chan-wook, Bong Joon-ho, and even

Hong Sang-soo (inspired by the works of Luis Buñuel, Robert Bresson, and Eric Rohmer), did not completely depart from the stereotypical image that made-in-Korea cultural products had previously established—cheap imitation films collectively known as "Copywood," essentially no different from the inferior counterfeit products that imitate designer clothes for only a fraction of the price of the original. During the writing of my previous book and this one, and the producing of three feature-length films over the past ten years (*Invisible Light* in 2003, *Never Forever* in 2006, and the remake of *The Housemaid* in 2010), I was consequently plagued by the following assertion: Korean cinema is just another name for a late-capitalist cultural revolution that unseated Hong Kong in a rotating chair, but will soon inevitably be gobbled up and spat out by Hollywood when its replacement is found. It is not a genuine national cinema that could be a model for other nations because of the uncreative way it uses the universal language of Hollywood while neglecting the local history and experiences that contribute to its effect and pathos.[8] And yet. And yet. If postmodern mimicry of Hollywood is something no national cinema or media industry of the twenty-first century can avoid, shouldn't the success of the Korean cinema of the past decade be perceived as the best exemplary vision of a national cinema of our time? I also remain convinced that Korean cinema's critical and commercial achievements over the last ten years amounted to substantially more than just a handful of actors who generated tens of thousands of obsessive fans in neighboring countries, overused buzzwords fraught with nationalist (*sijang jŏmyuryul*, or domestic market share) and capitalist (*sonik punkijŏm*, or break-even point) overtones, or a handful of titles that were sold for remake adaptation rights in Hollywood. The made-in-Korea content and style over the past decade, however short-lived, did have an impulsive natural spontaneity that created a cross-cultural appeal in a region still grieving over the atrocities Japan had committed against China and Korea during World War II that happened seventy years earlier. This is the reason I dedicate this book to all the people—filmmakers, critics, teachers, festival programmers, cinephiles, and liberal policymakers— who helped make Korean cinema during the first decade of the 2000s a globally recognized phenomenon.

I wish to gratefully acknowledge the help of the Korea Foundation, which provided me with an Advanced Research Grant that made possible a leave from teaching from January to December of 2008. The Korean

Film Archive and its then director Cho Sun-hee, with her colleagues Cho Jung-hyung and Chung Chong-hwa, made me feel welcome at the archive during a six-month stay in Seoul in 2008. My parents, Byung Kon Kim and Yeon-sup Lee, also provided home-cooked meals, a comfortable bed, and emotional support each time I flew to Korea for research, to deliver talks, and to teach. A timely grant from the Academy of Korean Studies, "Curriculum Development for Teaching Contemporary Cultural Topics in Korean Studies" allowed me to complete this manuscript in 2010–11. The Humanities Center at the University of California at Irvine provided further research funds for travel and other miscellaneous expenses. My department chairs, Ted Fowler (former) and Martin Huang (present), and my dean Vicki Ruiz, allowed me to concentrate on my research; had it not been for their forbearance, this book could not have been written in a timely manner. Mindy Haekyung Han and Francine Shapiro Jeffrey, who work in the department's front office, patiently accommodated most of my many unreasonable requests. David E. James has been an amazing intellectual inspiration since I started my graduate work at the University of Southern California (USC) in 1992. Nancy Abelmann, Rey Chow, Carter Eckert, and Kim U-chang have guided my studies since I left USC, and I am grateful to have them as mentors. Dudley Andrew, Charles Armstrong, Youngmin Choe, Kyeong-Hee Choi, Steven Chung, James Fujii, Takashi Fujitani, Alex and Mieke Gelley, Kelly Jeong, Jonathan M. Hall, Earl Jackson Jr., Joseph Jonghyun Jeon, Kyu Hyun Kim, Soyoung Kim, Aaron Magnan-Park, Hyangjin Lee, Sohl Lee, Young-Jun Lee, Walter K. Lew, Akira Lippit, Anne McKnight, Albert Park, Hyunseon Park, Sunyoung Park, Michael Raine, James Steintrager, Bert Scruggs, Serk-bae Suh, and Rei Terada were all wonderful colleagues who brought me joy and relief during an often tedious and forlorn process of writing and editing. Writing essays in Korean and communicating some of my ideas to Korean readers also helped me to form the main ideas behind this book. In this regard, I thank my Korean colleagues in the fields of film, literary, and cultural criticism who have tirelessly listened to me babble about Korean films over the years: Baek Moon-im, Chung Sung-Il, Han Suk-jeong, Huh Moon-young, Hwang Ho-duk, Hwang Jong-yeon, Kim Hang, Kim Young-jin, Lee Young-jae, and Seo Young-chae. Many filmmakers—including Choi Dong-hoon, E J-yong, Hong Sang-soo, Im Chan-sang, Im Kwon-Taek, Jang Sun-woo, Gina Kim, Lee Chang-dong, Park Kwang-su, and Martin Scorsese—were also great companions. And they offered unique insights that could not be simply gotten from websites. As in my first book, I tried my best here to analyze their wonderful films after sometimes countless viewings, but I know that my discussions will never match the rigor and labor with which they were created. Dear friends Sunyoung Lee and Michelle Cho, as proofreaders, and Jeanne Ferris, as copyeditor, offered many thoughtful insights while scrupulously going through what must have been a book with which they could not easily agree. Sohl Lee provided last minute help with indexing. I was given opportunities to discuss various sections of this book at the following institutions: Columbia University, Dong-A University (Pusan, Korea), Duke University, Hanyang University (Seoul, Korea), Harvard University, the Korean National University of Arts (Seoul, Korea), the University of Iowa, Lincoln Center's Film Society, the University of Minnesota (Twin Cities), Oberlin College (my alma mater), the University of Rochester, the Smithsonian Institution's Freer and Sackler Galleries, Stanford University, UC Berkeley, UC Davis, the University of Southern California, the University of Texas (Austin), the University of Washington (Seattle), and Yonsei University (Seoul, Korea). In spite of my flaws and shortcomings, the generous organizers, patient audiences, and their constructive feedback made this book infinitely better. Last but not least, Courtney Berger, my fabulous editor at Duke University Press, and her associate Christine Choi, made the entire process a painless one.

Portions of chapter 1 were derived from an early work, "The Blockbuster Auteur in the Age of *Hallyu*: Bong Joon-ho," which was published in *Hallyu: Korean Media Influence in Asia and Beyond*, edited by Do Hyun Kim, 181–201 (Seoul: Seoul National University Press, 2011). Portions of chapter 5 appeared, in different forms, as *"Turning Gate"* in *Film Quarterly* 57, no. 4 (summer 2004): 35–41; "The Awkward Traveller in *Turning Gate*," in *New Korean Cinema*, edited by Chi-yun Shin and Julian Stringer, 170–79 (New York University Press, 2005); and "Death, Eroticism, and Virtual Nationalism in the Films of Hong Sangsoo," in *Azalea: Journal of Korean Literature and Culture* 3 (2010): 135–69. An earlier version of chapter 7 was published as "'Tell the Kitchen That There's too much *Buchu* in the Dumpling': Reading Park Chan-wook's 'Unknowable' *Oldboy*," in *Horror to the Extreme: Changing Boundaries in Asian Cinema*, edited by Jinhee Choi and Mitsuyo Wada-Marciano, 179–98 (Hong Kong: Hong Kong University Press, 2009).

Korean names in this manuscript are transliterated according to Korean standards, with the surname first. Most libraries and Korean studies scholars in the United States conform to the romanization system that is known as the McCune-Reischauer system. I have attempted to use that romanization system for Korean names, terms, and titles, except for those names that have their own divergent orthography, especially in English-language subtitles. I have also retained the preferred names of certain directors whose works have been released in the United States, such as Hong Sang-soo (Hong Sang-su in the standard romanization), Park Chan-wook (Pak Ch'an-uk), and Im Kwon-Taek (Im Kwon-t'aek).

Virtual Hallyu

Something odd and unexpected took place during the last *fin de siècle*: South Korean cultural products that had previously attracted very little interest beyond Korea and the Korean diasporic communities scattered around the world suddenly became "cool." The worldwide appetite for Korean cultural content from the late 1990s to 2007 or 2008 was impressive. Korean television dramas, films, music, fashion, and even cuisine — all marketed under the banner of hallyu (韓流) or the "Korean wave" — became wildly popular in areas such as the Pacific Rim and western China. Several Korean stars past their primes in their homeland emerged as overnight sensations in Japan;[1] an entire floor of a glitzy Beijing shopping center was redone according to a hallyu theme;[2] and remote rural locales in Korea, long forgotten by even those who lived nearby, became tourist attractions.[3] Even academics began to take notice. First came an avalanche of English-language books on the subject of the New Korean Cinema during the first few years of the twenty-first century,[4] followed almost immediately by several anthologies and special volumes written mostly by media and communications scholars on the success of Korean TV dramas all across Asia.[5] "Hallyu," a term coined by Chinese journalists in the late 1990s that punned the pronunciation of two characters for Korea (韓) and wave (流) with another compound expression, "cold current" (寒流), rapidly became a household and critical academic term, particularly in East and Southeast Asia.[6]

Box Office Rules

Aided by the intensification of the media's globalization, Korea's 1980s democratization movement and subsequent status as the best-wired nation in the world,[7] and the strengthened pan-Asian consciousness resulting from the 1997 Asian economic crisis, hallyu started its surge in the years immediately after the Asian economic crisis hit Korea. Its popularity caught the new liberal Korean government of Kim Dae-jung by surprise. The Korean wave arguably began to ripple when Kang Che-gyu's *Shiri* (1999), a spy thriller exploiting Korea's North-South division, miraculously reached the top of Japan's box office in January 2000. *Shiri* was not only the first Korean film to reach the top in Japan, it was the first to crack the top ten. This film predated the massive success of the Korean television drama *Winter Sonata* (*Kyŏul yŏnga*) by four years and eventually grossed more than $10 million in Japan alone. *Shiri*, which cost only $2 million to make, eventually became one of the most profitable Korean films ever. Park Chan-wook's *JSA: Joint Security Area* (2000) and Kwak Jae-yong's *My Sassy Girl* (*Yŏpgijŏk in kŭnyŏ*, 2001)—both of which also preceded *Winter Sonata* and the runaway popularity of its middle-aged heartthrob, Bae Yong-jun—succeeded *Shiri* as successes in Japan.[8]

Following the success of *Shiri* and *JSA*, two stories that pivoted around North Korean terrorists and soldiers and the Cold War division of the peninsula between the Communist North and the Capitalist South, Park Chan-wook's *Oldboy* (2003), *My Sassy Girl*, Yi Chae-han's *A Moment to Remember* (*Nae maŭm sok ŭi chiukae*, 2004), and Hur Jin-ho's *April Snow* (*Oech'ul*, 2005) achieved overseas box office success and drove the pan-Asian appetite for the hallyu in the early years of the century. These films featured easily digestible plotlines and hallyu stars like Jeon Ji-hyun and Bae Yong-jun. However, by the end of the decade, the Asian public quickly lost interest in these films. As I stated in the preface, not even *The Good, the Bad, the Weird*—an expensive blockbuster Western featuring some of the best-known pan-Asian stars—could save hallyu from its rapid decline in cinema. This sudden decline in the popularity of the Korean wave since 2007 is just as inexplicable as its emergence. Perhaps Edward Said put it best: "Why do wigs, lace collars, and high buckled shoes appear, then disappear, over a period of decades?"[9] Even the most comprehensive answer to this question may not be satisfying, because history itself is written and reconstructed by people who tend to assign meanings to past events that "acquire objective validity only *after* the assignments are made [Said's emphasis]."[10]

By the time the Korean government had begun spending millions of dollars in public funds to effectively protect, subsidize the production of, and market hallyu, overseas interest in the phenomenon had already dwindled.[11] The heavy reliance on a Cold War theme derived from Korea's division, coupled with the Korean film industry's failure to develop multilingual content or an international star system—or to expand its roster of stars beyond a couple of actors—ended up limiting the potential of Korean film and television products, eventually precipitating hallyu's demise. So serious was the downward spiral of hallyu in 2009 that Hallyuwood, a $250 million complex in Koyang (adjacent to Seoul)—slated to open in 2013 with a theme park, hotel, and media facilities—changed its name to Korea World from one that was quickly losing cultural cachet. Many construction projects eventually halted completely because of delinquent payments and lawsuits over breach of contracts between the city and the developers.[12] Furthermore, the conservative government led by President Lee Myung-bak began in 2008 to pursue policies in cinema that attempted to close off many of the paths to success that the Korean film industry had been following during the liberal government rule that lasted from 1998 to 2007.[13]

The popularity of hallyu coincided with the ten-year period during which two liberal presidents, Kim Dae-jung and Roh Moo-hyun, presided over the country before conservatives retook control of the presidency in 2007's landslide election. It would be a mistake to deny any kinship between hallyu and the liberal sociopolitical mood that fostered it. However, just as increased government subsidies around 2005 could not slow hallyu's rapid decline, attempting to explain a body of work that essentially relied on creative aesthetic expressions by examining state policies and socioeconomic factors alone would not yield satisfying results. It would be an exaggeration to elevate hallyu to the pantheon of celebrated aesthetic movements such as the modernist literature that blossomed in Paris during the early part of the twentieth century, or the Italian neorealist cinema of the period after the Second World War. Nonetheless, hallyu's legitimate place in history can be discovered only when we ask how it stylistically and thematically addressed "values that belong to a bourgeois world on the wane," to borrow a phrase from Terry Eagleton.[14]

Precisely what values would be on the wane in a country that had never gone through the kind of indigenous industrial revolution and modernization processes experienced by the West or Japan? If new kinds of aesthetic movements take form in opposition to preexisting establishments, what images and icons gave a sense of coherent identity to what we now know as hallyu, and to the Korean cinema that played such a crucial part in it? And if modernism can be described as a mixture of mourning and revolt directed against the waning national bourgeoisie, can hallyu be described as being motivated by postmodernism, an aesthetic sensibility that celebrates newly minted moneyed classes of dubious origins as well as the revival of conservative neoliberal values? Hallyu was and perhaps still is a cultural phenomenon that collapses the gap between modernism, an aesthetic auteurist revolt against both the waning nationalist (*minjok-juŭi*) forces and authoritarian (*kwŏnŭi-juŭi*) legacies that drove Korea throughout much of the latter part of the twentieth century, and postmodernism, typified by lavishly produced multi-genre pan-Asian blockbusters targeting pan-Asian audiences—for example, the television series *Taejanggŭm* (*Jewel in the Palace*) or a monster film like *The Host*.

Though scholarship on hallyu has proliferated in the past few years, even in English language, most of the essays featured in special volumes and anthologies on hallyu have placed an excessive emphasis on data that range from numbers of foreign tourists to various annual figures from the entertainment industry, as well as quotes from random pan-Asian consumers of hallyu products and contents.[15] What is largely absent thus far from hallyu scholarship is a critical engagement with the question of how and why the viewer processes new screen figures such as the protofeminist Chosun-era female doctor Jang-geum from *Taejanggŭm* or the monster (half fish, half dragon) that lives in the River Han from *The Host* as embodiments of modern, hybrid, and even global desires. Textual discussions of forms that express the global era's anxieties are imperative in order to assert hallyu's role in the protonationalist, neoliberal enterprise. Not atypical, for instance, is a point raised by Doobo Shim, who—while attempting to debunk the notion of "globalization" as either an outgrowth of "cultural imperialism" or "workings of the project of modernity"—flatly dismisses what he calls the "from modernity to postmodernity; from capitalism to late capitalism" argument made by Marxist literary critics. Shim states that "political economists critique this notion by arguing that the conflation of modernity with capitalism is wrong," before adding that "the notion of globalization as an outcome of modernity . . . tends to provide an aura of 'inevitability' to the rise of neoliberalism and concentrated corporate control (and hypercommercialization) of the media in the present era."[16] In other words, according to Shim, Marxist critics such as David Harvey and Fredric Jameson have misled us, making us think that modernity—or modernism—is not only a capitalist invention but also an affirmation of inescapable neoliberalism or total corporate control. Such positions by media studies scholars on modernist literary or film theory tend to reduce any serious attempt to disentangle the ideological complexities of textual matters to supercilious and overdetermined articulations of trenchant Marxist principles.[17] Though I am in agreement with many communications scholars that various hallyu entertainment contents, media, and art have engineered intercultural flows in and out of Asia, and have thereby constituted hybrid persuasions and forms that are neither authentically Korean nor appropriations of Hollywood pastiche, I remain wary of a scholarship that completely avoids analyzing the forms, structures, and ideals of hallyu. Screen subjects, whether in film or on television, are products of fantastic, elusive, and even erratic identifications; a cultural critic's function is to unveil the latent meanings beneath the sometimes seemingly placid, conservative or liberal textual surfaces. Though it is tempting to dismiss all hallyu products, including blockbuster films, as necessary ideological affirmations of laissez-faire values, that dismissal would only accept the totalizing claims made by *both* Marxist critics and media scholars. Therefore, this book proposes to explain how contemporary Korean cinema, caught between the conflicting interests of the modernist affection for the sublime induced by the auteur cinema and its postmodern invalidation necessitated by chaebŏl-driven multiplex market forces, continues to negotiate with both real and monstrous cinematic representations of what I am calling virtual hallyu.

Virtual Hallyu allows us to think about Korean cinema over the past decade in the midst of: (1) the faltering of grand ideologies—such as democracy, socialism, and antiglobalization—that gave way to parochial nationalism, local product consumerist protection, and Internet activism; (2) the reduction of the image, removing any impression, metaphor, or allegory of socially symbolic acts; (3) the meaninglessness of the distinction between realism, modernism, and postmodernism, since they simply cannot provide anything new in the critical methodologies of visual cultures given that—as I will explain below—the boundary between "the way things are remembered" and the "way things really were" has been crossed through the massive repository of images collected over the past decade; and (4), as mentioned above, the blurring of the boundaries between Hollywood and the generic conventions of non-Hollywood products that have generated hybrid, mutating, transnational forms of every kind of genre possible in Korean cinema, including Westerns, eco-disaster, and science fiction once very specific to American cinematic mythologies.

In other words, this book is an attempt to think about how recent cinema in South Korea has produced subjects that extend far beyond standard models of semiotics or Cold War political allegories. Some of the figures to be analyzed are: the monster that pops out of the River Han (*The Host*); a schizophrenic Korean doctor during the Japanese colonial period (*Epitaph*); an impulsive pimp servicing an aging dictator (*President's Last Bang*); decadent libertine intellectuals (*Woman Is the Future of Man*); a schizo man who refuses to grow up (*Oasis*); and a salary man as vengeful fighting machine (*Oldboy*). By invoking a unique yet centripetal quality with appeal beyond the national, these protagonists escape from the particular brands of sublimity or affect (for instance, torn flags, women's tears, youthful revolt, or religious themes) that had served as metonyms of national spirit. In analyzing these figures, I insist that these recent films challenge traditional boundaries: urban versus provincial, nationalists versus collaborators, and Communist North versus capitalist South.

Virtual-Actual

Yi Sang's "Lingering Impressions of a Mountain Village" bears witness to the "relentless defamiliarization of the familiar" and the critical role the landscape plays in that process:

> They say there are roe deer and wild boar over there on P'albong Mountain. And some even say they've seen a "bear" that comes down to catch crayfish in the gully where they used to hold rituals to pray for rain. I continually suffer from the *delusion* [my emphasis] that these animals, which I have only seen in zoos, have not been captured from these mountains and put in zoos, but rather have been taken from zoos and put in these mountains. When night falls, just as men retire to their chambers, P'albong disappears into the lacquer-black, moonless night.[18]

As early as 1935, Yi Sang, the young, ailing poet who had never before lived outside Seoul, had found full expression of his interiority by bringing a new mode of landscape into being. Both the nocturnal disappearing act performed by P'albong Mountain and Yi Sang's imagining that animals have been placed in these mountains after being taken from a zoo play pivotal roles in reconstructing an indelible image of the threatened P'albong. The irony here is that bears can no longer be spotted in Korea's mountains, and the only way wild bears could be restored would be to take them from a zoo and place them in the mountains. In other words, Yi's 1935 "delusion" has become today's nightmarish reality. By stripping the awe from wild animals, he forces the mountain to lose its novelty. Mountain P'albong, which he later compares to the Paramount Pictures logo[19] can no longer sustain the image of infinity, divinity, and unpredictable wildlife. Consequently, the intensity of the rural landscape's sublimity also immeasurably decreases. What Yi calls modern "delusion" lays bare the foundation on which the virtual-actual subjects, following the theories of Gilles Deleuze and Félix Guattari, come into being.

If modern writing—as evidenced here by Yi Sang, who writes about the impending horror of disappearing mountains and wildlife—presented the opening of the unconscious by first figuring a virtual system of possibilities through language, cinema in the era of late capitalism has further expanded this condition of possibilities through figurations of elements that are beyond the field of representation in literature. "Virtual-actual" is the concept through which Deleuze sought to move visual theory, especially film theory, beyond the representational.

In this regard, Deleuze's theories about "virtual" and "actual" become even more intriguing. Consistent with his other concepts, what Deleuze does is to unhook the virtual from its classic configuration of an ontological entity split between truth and falsehood, remapping it instead within a terrain somewhere between a creative process and something already created. Surely, the virtual technically distinguishes itself from the actual by being the constituent, whereas the actual is positioned as the constituted. But rest assured—the virtual alone does not mean much without the actual, and vice versa. In this regard, the virtual is consistent with other key concepts of Deleuze—such as the anti-Oedipal schizo, the nomad, and the body-without-organs—that aim to question the stability of "fixed truth" and seek to problematize how truth in the traditional Western metaphysics has evolved through the putative neutrality of image. This is precisely the reason why he ambitiously took up the question of cinema in his two volumes, *Cinema 1: Movement-Image* and *Cinema 2: Time-Image*. Since the present is always a fleeting peak composed of multilayered sheets of the past and can never be fully grasped without the past, while the past can never completely sever itself from the present, the virtual is always realized within a fragment of memory that is both solid and transient. So, from this perspective, however faithful a representation of history might be to its origin, it can never be permanently situated within the domain of the nonvirtual. The difference between the way things are remembered and the way they really were is then jettisoned for the creative purpose of *virtually* transforming elements from history in order to pave a third path or indexicality and produce an *actual* image—in this case, cinema.[20]

To claim that any past or historical remembrance possesses a virtual quality usually invites infuriating responses from those who fail to grasp the subversive potential of Deleuze's counterfactual virtuality. What I would like to emphasize is the fact that to recognize the virtual status of the past is not to completely deny everything that has happened.[21] The virtual-actual of Deleuze refigures the classic ontological relationship that insists on distinguishing between the way things appear and the way they really are, taking that relationship somewhere else. Where to? An alternative third path, where the difference between true and false is nullified, power is difficult to reach, and the nomad, schizo, or desiring machine is reconstituted through art and artists. Deleuze's contribution to the virtual must be understood within a creative field where any kind of being has to be located within a plane of becoming that is somewhere between virtual and actual. And once actual cinema is constituted, it sets off again to realize the possibility of the virtual through imaginative spectatorship.

More than any other concept, the virtual-actual remains contemporaneous with recent Korean cinema due to Korea's late arrival at both its capitalist wealth accumulation and national cinema stardom. The self-referential mechanism of cinema that documents live action for twenty-four frames per second and then projects them at a later date—after the initial film stock has been processed, edited, most often CG rendered, and color corrected; and music, dubbing (automated dialogue replacement, or ADR), and sound effects separately designed, recorded, and added—complicates the question of what is real and what is unreal. Here the fissure between empirical representations and their transcendental possibilities is broadened, for cinema constantly shuffles its meaning not only between frames, but also between shots that often defy continuity. In other words, because of the technologically arduous and elaborate process of narrative feature films, which also presents a radical departure from the direct representation of linear time, each film effectively reinvents an affective visual and auditory landscape. In effect, truth is fundamentally eschewed, despite our perception of film as the art form that most closely approximates reality.

The documentary film scholar Bill Nichols has said that "the distinction between fact and fiction blurs" whenever a film is projected.[22] But even as frames of film are projected before our eyes, often leaving a lasting impression on our synapses, we are faced with the question of whether these particular frames will enter into our minds as a vibrant, multidimensional Bergsonian *durée* that will endure as a virtual entity and also have an actual impact. Deleuze seeks to perceive sensual experiences somewhere between the Kantian sublime, which ultimately can never be represented or copied, and the Benjaminian sense of post-auratic affectation in the age of simulacra and mechanical reproduction. Nothing can better underscore the virtual-actual that Deleuze has delineated than the apparatus of cinema, which is reliant on the mechanism that spits out twenty-four frames per second. Having long been consumers of movies and avid readers of cinematic language, we can generally anticipate the visual figuration of any film image's subsequent shot because of the various patterns forged between the present shot and the one that preceded it. Ironically, in the first decade of the twenty-first century, South Korea—a nation that had not been either culturally or sociopolitically independent throughout the previous century—articulated this virtual potential in cinema better than any other country.

Planet Hallyu

Not since the late 1500s and the early 1600s, when a massive number of Korean potters were forcibly abducted to Japan to engineer the birth of the Japanese Imari porcelain tradition, have Korean cultural products exerted so much influence in countries outside Korea. In 2005 South Korea earned almost $200 million for its exported films and other mass media. Both television programs ($123.5 million) and cinema ($76 million) registered record sales during that year (see table 1).[23] Though Korea's export figures are a paltry sum compared to the international box office figures for Hollywood films, which in 2006 grossed about $16.3 billion outside the United States,[24] the $76 million reported export figure for Korean films was nevertheless a monumental number; representing the first time the Korean film industry had erased its annual trade deficit since such data began being recorded in the 1970s. Korean films made during much of the first decade of the 2000s had healthy, long "legs" that stretched beyond Korea's borders. As a result, international critics and industry experts[25] have pointed to the Korean case as a surprising anomaly in the phenomenon described by Franco Moretti as "Planet Hollywood," where every industrialized country sustains a major trade deficit with the United States because of an imbal-

Table 1. Estimated annual Korean film export earnings

	2002	2003	2004	2005
Total sales	$14,952,089	$30,979,000	$58,284,600	$75,994,580
Contracted figure	$14,952,089	$30,979,000	$58,284,600	$75,994,580
Additional income from sales of previous years	NA	NA	NA	NA
Compared to previous year	+33%	+107%	+88%	+30%
Export titles	133	164	194	202
Per title sale price	$112,422	$188,896	$300,436	$376,211

Source: 2010 data from KOFIC.
Note: Contracted figure includes minimum guarantee, flat sales, and other miscellaneous ancillary market (television, video, online demand, remake rights, etc.) deals.

ance that tilts heavily in favor of Hollywood products.[26] The fact that the Korean film industry managed to turn in annual export figures in the early twenty-first century that inched almost even with those of Korean import of Hollywood imports demonstrates that some concrete substance (at least in financial terms) lay behind the ballooned hype of hallyu.

Perhaps more surprising than the attraction of hallyu was the return of domestic audiences to Korean films.[27] The share of the domestic theatrical market held by Korean films, which had been whittled down to almost negligible percentages during the early 1990s,[28] suddenly exploded during the hallyu years. Moreover, Korean consumers were generally satisfied by their moviegoing experiences. Local products have proven to be utterly uncompetitive in almost every nation where the overwhelming majority of moviegoers attend American-style multiplexes,[29] which offer soft drinks and popcorn, comfortable sofa-like seats—costing $600 each—arranged in stadium rows, and satisfying projection of 35mm Hollywood prints.[30] Korea, along with India, has been a conspicuous anomaly. Korea's increasingly affluent[31] and culturally savvy youth, finally released from the authoritarianism of the past, continued to watch Korean movies at a surprisingly similar rate as, or at a slightly higher than, Hollywood products[32] (see table 2 in chapter 9). Korean films were successful not only at attracting overseas buyers, but also at cultivating their own domestic audience,

2006	2007	2008	2009	2010
$24,514,728	$24,396,215	$21,036,540	$14,122,143	$13,582,850
$24,514,728	$12,283,339	$20,541,212	$13,930,262	$13,166,280
NA	$12,112,876	$495,328	$191,881	$416,570
-68%	-1%	-14%	-33%	-4%
208	321	354	279	276
$117,859	$38,266	$56,901	$55,499	$47,704

whose members responded strongly to films that delivered dialogue in their native language.

If there was a difference between the Korean cinema of the hallyu period and other national cinema movements such as the New Latin American cinema of the 1960s or France's *nouvelle vague*, it was that Korean cinema built its international reputation not merely through auteur films like those by Hong Sang-soo or Im Kwon-Taek, but also through unabashedly commercial films such as *My Sassy Girl*, which made its heroine Jeon Ji-hyun an instant Pan-Asian superstar, and television dramas such as *Winter Sonata*, which had very little to do with formal experimentation. But even in these productions, the viewer becomes aware of cracks in the dominant ideologies. For instance, perhaps no moment in Korean cinema of the past decade better underscores the obsolete figure of anachronistic bourgeoisie than the scene from *My Sassy Girl* where the aging father of the title character, played by Jeon Ji-hyun, keeps falling asleep. The hallyu titles that garnered global recognition were unambiguously branded as comedy, romantic drama, action, and horror films. Ironically, the filmmakers who made their debuts in the 1990s had to package their films as multi-genre productions such as comic–family melodrama–monster (Bong Joon-ho's *The Host*), erotic–horror–crime mystery (Park Chan-wook's *Oldboy*), or comic–romantic–women's tearjerker (Lee Chang-dong's *Secret Sunshine*), which required audiences to use their intellectual acumen to decode their tightly sealed codes of social satire. By disguising social agendas and visual aspirations underneath the veneer of formulaic genre elements,[33] Korean cinema sought a path that slightly diverged from the commercial footsteps of the Hong Kong action and martial arts cinema of the 1980s.

Some of this was in many respects progressive and subversive, pulling together deep structures of modern mythologies and folklore against the backdrop of Korean cities, but much of it inevitably plunged into the unimaginative aesthetic that simply interpreted the postmodern closing of the gap between phenomenon and essence as a ceaseless series of thoughtless, empty images. However, the emphasis on high-production value and genre formulaic elements did create a film culture that restored the confidence of the local audience confidence. In turn, this helped Lee Chang-dong, Hong Sang-soo, Kim Ki-duk, Im Kwon-Taek, Bong Joon-ho, E J-yong, and Park Chan-wook find financing throughout the decade for the ambitious film projects they wrote and directed. Also, Korean cinema was able to technologically and aesthetically mobilize visuality with astounding speed so as to become competitive in megaplexes, giving even sci-fi films such as Choi Dong-hoon's *Jeon Woo-chi: The Taoist Wizard* (*Chŏn U-ch'i*, 2009) box office success. This affirmed the critic Chris Berry's wry proclamation that Korean cinema is a "full-service cinema."[34]

Because auteur cinema is conventionally considered to be the province of directors like Andrei Tarkovsky, Ingmar Bergman, and Abbas Kiarostami, whose works stand for a relentless and uncompromising vision of humanity and its fallibility,[35] it is sometimes difficult to determine whether or not genre formulas can successfully be incorporated into art-house films. However, in the case of Korean cinema, the rapid rise of exports, the increase of domestic film audiences, the rising visibility of Korean cinema in film festivals across the globe, and the emergence of Korean film stars as matinee idols across Asia—all achieved by about 2005—could not have been possible without the presence of savvy film directors who recognized the importance of both box office figures driven by blockbuster genre formulas and artistic ambitions driven by individual auteurs, who oversaw every creative part of filmmaking from the screenplay to the distribution and marketing campaign. Bong Joon-ho, Park Chan-wook, and Kim Jee-woon, Korea's blockbuster auteurs of the early twenty-first century, have attained their stardom by fully exploiting their love-hate relationship with the genre films from Hollywood, Japan, and Hong Kong with which they grew up. By fully embracing Hollywood, rather than rejecting it, their works display hybridity that equally engages both national identity and global aesthetics, art and commercialism, conformity and subversion, and narrative coherence and stylistic flair.

This is why Bong, Park, and Kim among others may be the true heirs of postmodern cinema, which arguably began when nouvelle vague directors started to make films in France in the late 1950s and the 1960s that parodied everything from American studio genre forms of the previous decades to postwar consumerist pop culture and austere political conventions of the day. The anxieties caused by the sociopolitical terror and violence that lasted for four decades after Korea's liberation from Japan in 1945 meant that until the 1990s, Korean cinema could not playfully exploit the formulaic genre forms, though Korean society thoroughly ingested American pop culture. For example, one of the bestselling hits of the early 1990s, Kang Woo-suk's *Two Cops* (1993), now seems terribly dated, as it is only a cheap, unauthorized remake—almost verbatim, shot by shot—of Claude Zidi's comedy *Part-Time Cops* (*Ripoux*, 1986); and it does not creatively redeploy genre forms. Only when it was released from the post-traumatic themes and formal constraints of realism during the late 1990s was Korean cinema finally able to cast a cold, objective eye on parochial identities from the vantage point of a distinctively amalgamated energy that fused globalization and cosmopolitanism.

The heyday of blockbuster auteurs actually was not the first time that Korean popular culture flirted with postmodernism. For over two generations, Korean popular cultural performers and icons skillfully formulated a hybrid identity between American and Korean. In addition to other more officially sanctioned routes, American popular culture had found its way into Korean homes through the American Forces Korea Network (AFKN) that ran both radio and television stations for the 37,000–50,000 American servicemen and women stationed in Korea.[36] Because KBS was not able to air its first television broadcast until 1960 and Korean radio stations resisted playing American popular music throughout much of the 1950s, AFKN generated a rapidly growing fan base among Korean youths. Roald Maliangkay writes that "of equal importance were live shows organized at military clubs and camps throughout the country"[37] that sprouted up after the American military occupation began in 1945. Most of the pioneers in Korean pop music—including the singers Patti Kim, Yun Pok-hŭi, and Hyŏn Mi and the composer and guitarist Shin Chung-hyŏn—started their careers performing for US servicemen and women in these clubs.[38] Considering the amount of Korean television and radio programming that had been carrying American popular music, since the late 1950s, and the number of movie theaters that heavily favored American content, the exposure of Korea to American products was perhaps as great as that of any other country in Asia. Though the democratization movement of the 1980s briefly flirted with ideas of decolonization, cultural independence, and sovereignty, no cultural alternatives could effectively challenge the hegemony of Hollywood until Korean commercial films—ironically, a Korean pastiche that emulated much of Hollywood's aesthetic—began to build its own audience base in the late 1990s. Even as we enter a post–Cold War era in which the ubiquity of postmodernism has meant the decline of models of national allegory, hallyu—whose very name, in the form of the character *han* (韓), denotes a still-intact national mark—proposed that the national cinema model still had some life left in it.

Cinema was the cultural medium through which Korea sought to establish itself as a new global standard. As Chris Berry argues, the Korean film industry helped to divide the existing US-centric system of blockbusters by making them more local.[39] Ironically by localizing and developing its own blockbuster films, which required that the films raise production values, place more emphasis on publicity, and incorporate genre formulas, Korean cinema during the early years of the century produced star directors like Lee Chang-dong, Park Chan-wook, Kim Jee-woon, and Bong Joon-ho, who were in great demand not only at international film festivals but also in Hollywood.[40] Also, the overseas successes of two television dramas, *Winter Sonata* and *Taejanggŭm* were unprecedented. These successes satisfied the postdemocratization fervor for national recognition of Korea's traditions (including culinary tastes, picturesque sites, costumes, and Confucian values), a showcase for popular stories in high taste, and also broad acceptance of local stars on the world stage. In its pursuit of this standardization of local products, however, hallyu largely neglected innovations in forms and genres, instead settling on narrative negotiations between a national aesthetic pathos and a postmodern image culture born out of consumption-led capitalism.[41]

Perhaps hallyu's success could be attributed to nothing more significant than the rise of nightlife in urban, suburban, and even provincial centers, which in turn led to the sprouting up of shopping malls and multiplex theaters. In 1982 South Korea officially lifted the midnight curfew that the

American military government first imposed in 1945. By the mid-1990s, bright lights in major marketplaces throughout the nation celebrated both the country's new economic prosperity and the much-improved political security that had resulted from democratization and reconciliation with North Korea. The streetlights of the Myongdong and Dongdaemun market districts would have humbled even Philippe Lebon, the inventor of the gaslights of Paris. As affirmed by brilliantly lit noir films such as Lee Myung-se's *Nowhere to Hide* (*Injŏng sajŏng Polkŏt ŏpta*, 1999) and Kim Jee-woon's *A Bitter Sweet Life* (*Talk'omhan insaeng*, 2005), much of Seoul looks better at night than it does in broad daylight. In those areas of the city where sleep never seems permitted before dawn, shops, restaurants and cafes, motels that rented rooms by the hour, and theaters offered up the "capacity of being nowhere," constituting what Paul Virilio calls the "dream décor of oblivion."[42] The high-speed Internet boom that took place in Korea after the late 1990s ironically meant that Korea's urban youth rarely needed to venture beyond their schools, homes, and offices. If they did choose to go outdoors, it was to the theater, where a different kind of cavernous hole awaited them. Between 1997 and 2007, Korea's annual per capita cinema admissions grew exponentially, from 0.68 to 3.22, while the figure changed little in most other major markets in the world.[43] The riotously colorful lobbies and the hypnotic cinematic experiences that multiplex theaters offered were as alluring as the dazzling array of shops that never seemed to close.[44] Such commercial institutions were no longer a privilege, but rather a prerequisite in the new era of cosmopolitanism marked by a mature democracy, revamped nationalism that kept pace with the growing nationalist movements in Japan, China, and North Korea, and expanding Internet technologies. However, much of Korea's moviegoing public remained loyal to its national appropriation of global cinematic standards by preferring to watch local disaster movies like Yoon Je-gyun's *Haeundae* (2009) or local action movies like Kang Je-gyu's *Taegukgi* (2005) that mimicked Hollywood films, instead of Hollywood originals that displayed far more expensive pyrotechnics and special effects. Just as many Americans resist engagement with cosmopolitanism by choosing not to watch movies with subtitles, Korean youth culture similarly disassociated itself from diverse cultural possibilities by consuming only films from Hollywood or Korea.[45]

It was in this environment that several new genres of Korean entertainment were institutionalized, coming to be known overseas as hallyu. Several years before *Winter Sonata*, which originally appeared on KBS in 2002 and was broadcast on NHK in 2003 and 2004, *Shiri* surprisingly dominated Japan's box office, and *My Sassy Girl*, which starred Jeon Ji-hyun in the flamboyant title role, became an instant pan-Asian hit. With hallyu, the cultural grandiloquence of Korean cinema was revived for the first time since the 1960s.[46] The rapid decline of book sales and the closing of major and university bookstores in downtown Seoul[47] thus coincided with the proliferation of spectacular bodies—what Gilles Deleuze, with the aid of Félix Guattari, refers to as the "abstract machine of faciality"[48]—in advertisements on the covers and pages of popular magazines, on billboards, and on television and Internet screens. If the stars of the 1980s and 1990s such as Ahn Sung-gi were often associated with their verbal stammers, resulting from psychological trauma that was deeply rooted in political terror, the stars of the 2000s—Jeon Ji-hyun and Jang Dong-gun, for example—became known through their faces. As iconic images—enhanced by computer graphics—these stars underscored the excessive agencies that celebrated the country's remarkable economic recovery not only from colonialism and the Korean War of the distant past, but also from the "IMF crisis" of 1997, which forced Korea to accept the terms of the International Monetary Fund to bail out its economy and to undergo major restructuring of its banks and corporate culture.

"Writing has never been capitalism's thing. Capitalism is profoundly illiterate," write Deleuze and Guattari.[49] Instead of written and printed expressions, a capitalist landscape is crowded with phonic, graphic, gestural, nonsignifying language that comes in all shapes and forms. They ebb and flow along with efforts to dismantle the tyranny of the signifier—not through the insistence of alternative kinds of values, but through the erasure and rewriting of traces that reconfigure the multiple conditions of the past and render them virtual. If the term "affectivity" has caught the attention of many academics who describe the creative processes taking place within the fields of the humanities and the arts, it is because the emotions with which one responds to the real have been floundering in the wake of the growing popularity of reality TV and the Internet. Most films analyzed in this book, from a colonial-era film—*Spring of Korean Peninsula* (1941)—that was rediscovered only in 2006 to *Jeon Woo-chi: The Taoist Wizard* (2009), reauthorize image as something that no longer dwells on the difference between the way things appear and the way they really are, instead placing image in the opaque category where viewers simultaneously experience both the preserved past and the fleeting present. I remain drawn to this radical potential of cinema that challenges power by getting everything wrong by the new standards of realism set by reality TV.

The next chapter, "Virtual Landscapes," investigates the recent commercial success of Korean cinema, or hallyu, from an unusual perspective: the trope of landscape and its relationship with modernity. By analyzing landscapes depicted in Im Kwon-Taek's venerable *Sopyonje* (1993), Hong Sang-soo's *The Power of Kangwon Province* (*Kangwondo ŭi him*, 1998), and Bong Joon-ho's *The Host* (*Koemul*, 2006), this chapter argues that Korean cinema, as early as the pre-hallyu 1990s, had pulled away from language as the organizing creative principle, establishing in its place a new national model of virtual cinema according to which the image is merely that: an image. This image breaks free from Korean cinema's past framed by either *sinp'a* (melodrama) or politically allegorical impulses. By attempting analyses of films by three auteurs—Im Kwon-Taek, who is best known for his realist long takes; the modernist Hong Sang-soo, whose works usually sell fewer than 100,000 tickets in theaters; and Bong Joon-ho, whose *The Host* remains Korea's bestselling film to date, with more than 13 million tickets sold—I have attempted to grasp the current state of Korean cinema not by situating its style between realism, modernism, and postmodernism, but by establishing it as a cultural standard that frames our present visual culture.

Chapter 2 analyzes two Korean films: one, Yi Pyŏng-il's *Spring of Korean Peninsula* (*Pando ŭi pom*, 1941), from the colonial period; and the other, Jeong Beom-sik and Jeong Sik's *Epitaph* (*Kidam*, 2007), a contemporary horror film set during the colonial period. In order to better contextualize today's popular interest in the subject of colonial modernity, I begin by examining the figure of the *nuŭi tongsaeng* (younger sister) that sets the tone for the fraught contradictions of the nation as it is caught between the fear of contamination (loss of virginity by becoming a *kisaeng* or a courtesan) and the urge to modernize (earning income that supports modern luxuries) raised in earlier colonial-era films. This figure—and the anxieties it represents—calls for the nation to remasculinize to protect these sisters from the threat of deflowering. I argue that the bodies riddled with sickness depicted in these films are an amalgamation of several contradictory discourses around colonized subjugation (and perhaps even resistance): first, the practical necessity of mobilizing Korean subjects into the Japanese war effort, and therefore into the corporate body; second, popular images of Korean masculinity (swinging wildly between muscular mad men to feeble, bedridden men) in the literary and cinematic canons of colonial Korea (1910–45); and last, the heterogeneous space of the colony during the Second World War, where complicity and collaboration had as strong a presence as resistance. In thinking about colonial and postcolonial period films in tandem, I propose to show how various forms of illness that range from physical (tuberculosis) to mental (aphasia) can be interpreted as socially symbolic symptoms even in a postmodern environment.

Chapter 3 delves into two historical films, *The President's Barber* (2004) and *The President's Last Bang* (2005), both of which were inspired by actual historical events. *The President's Barber* features military coups, fraudulent elections, anti-Communist witch hunts, and other human rights abuses, while *The President's Last Bang* paradigmatically depicts October 26, 1979, the day Park Chung Hee was shot to death. This chapter suggests that these two films could be argued to be "simulations," to invoke a Baudrillardian term, that are "no longer that of a territory, a referential being or a substance."[50] However, the question remains: how can films that are part and parcel of an industry that is worth a billion dollars a year—and that promulgate images that never push our emotions beyond a shallow photographic surface—render an aesthetic that is still socially relevant? This chapter lays bare the difficulty faced by Korean cinema in this era of blockbusters: how to confront and renegotiate the historical in an environment where only ahistorical (that is, postmodern) films thrive.

Chapter 4 extends the discussion of race, nationhood, and gender, this time by looking at three films featuring North Korean women: Kwak Kyŏng-t'aek's *Typhoon* (*T'aep'ung*, 2005), Hwang Pyŏng-guk's *Wedding Campaign* (*Na ŭi kyŏlhon wŏnjŏnggi*, 2005), and Pak Yŏng-hun's *Innocent Steps* (*Taensŏ ŭi sunjŏng*, 2005). All three films depict North Korean women as being both unwavering in their goals and capable of redemption, and in the process establish a new stereotype of the North Korean and Yanbian (the Korean autonomous prefecture in Jilin Province, northeast China, that shares its border with North Korea) woman. What is apparent in these films is that the portrayal of North Korean women has become much deeper than the one-dimensional, fatalistic caricatures that previously typified South Korean depictions of North Koreans. Yet it is less easy to speculate whether this new liberal approach toward the North firmly inscribes an ideological shift in South Korean views of North Korea. Using three recent film texts, this chapter explores how the South Korean production of North Korean subjects continues to serve South Korea's attempt to come to terms with an internal crisis characterized by the cultural disenfranchisement of an anxious, narcissistic male Korean subject.

Chapter 5 elaborates on the ambiguities raised in Hong Sang-soo's three films, *Turning Gate* (*Saenghwal ŭi palgyŏn*, 2002), *Woman Is the Future of Man* (*Yŏja nŭn namja ŭi miraeda*, 2004), and *Tale of Cinema* (*Kŭkjangjŏn*, 2005). Hong has recently emerged as a distinctive figure in world cinema, who seeks to foreground the tension between the essential human impulse to strive for happiness and pleasure, the conditioning of reason, and the tyranny of social meaning. This chapter argues that his films explore a rotating wheel of desire, guilt, and denial that sustains a tripartite structure of eroticism, hypochondria, and death. Departing from epic dramas and entertainment genres, Hong's films propose instead a consideration of the everyday temporalities of cosmopolitanism and narcissism, despite the seeming contradictions inherent in such a pairing. The eroticism in Hong's three films demands that we consider the need for a libertine space after Korea's intense politicization during the 1980s. Into this postpolitical libertine life, however, enters what I call virtual nationalism—that is, Hong's unforgiving analysis of Koreans, both those who have never set foot abroad and those who have returned home from their studies abroad (*yuhaksaeng*).

Chapter 6 deals with two films by Lee Chang-dong, *Oasis* (2003) and *Secret Sunshine* (*Milyang*, 2007). It argues that these films depart from an earlier tendency evident in Lee's films to start from real events such as the razing of rural space, to create room for sprawling suburbs, and the 1980 Kwangju massacre. This chapter contends that though these new films continue to exploit the subject of trauma, they have successfully moved their subjects away from being allegories of the nation's trauma. Employing Gilles Deleuze's model of the schizo, my chapter also aims to frame Jong-du, the male subject of *Oasis*, as someone who has been spared symbolic castration. Meanwhile, *Secret Sunshine*'s heroine Shin-ae remains within the anachronistic arc of Freudian post-traumatic recovery. While applauding Jong-du in *Oasis* as that rare instance of the schizo who bolts out of the Freudian armchair, this chapter critiques Lee's maneuver of resuscitating hysteria and melancholia—pathological conditions that have characterized "fallen women" in the Western literary imagination (including in the works of Flaubert and D. H. Lawrence)—in order to claim the domain of Korean women in distress.

Chapter 7 engages with Park Chan-wook's popular "revenge" trilogy:

Sympathy for Mr. Vengeance (2002), *Oldboy* (2003), and *Lady Vengeance* (2005). This chapter explores the emergence of a postmodern attitude that not only points to the faltering of grand ideologies (humanism, democracy, socialism, and so on), but that also chooses to believe that the image is merely an image. "Image" here is not an impression of reality, but rather a perception of matter that approximates the verisimilitude of both space and time but that may not have anything to do with reality. This produces a sense of the unknowable. The chapter probes a number of elements that typify Park's films: the trope of revenge and its relationship to Nietzschean *ressentiment*, the stylized use of violence, the gap between representation and signification, and the various spatial, historical, and ontological markers of the unknowable. All of these issues are raised as a way to investigate, challenge, and contextualize recent Western criticism that Park's films fail to produce social criticism.

My last book on Korean cinema was published in 2004, at a time when Korean cinema was at its historical climax. It is perhaps not a coincidence that this book on hallyu-era films has been completed at the precise moment when hallyu has come to a rapid decline. Despite that precipitous decline, Korean cinema's proud use of a minor language in a global era where English has proven again and again that it reigns supreme—and, through that use, a fierce stand against Hollywood in an open market replete with multiplex theaters—is noteworthy. In the final chapter, I point to the renaissance of *sagŭk* (Korea's *jidai-geki*) in the beginning of the 2010s as a cautiously optimistic new "originary world"—to borrow a Deleuzian term—for Korean cinema, one that best fulfills the potential of its virtuality. If Deleuze's use of the term "virtual" refers to something that is not only a thing of the past, but of a past that coexists with the present and also of a truth that coexists with the false, perhaps no more apt example can be found in these new sagŭks.

Cinema in Korea, perhaps because it ceded to television dramas and popular music the main stage of the hallyu drive during the first decade of the century, is the only virtual medium that remains—albeit frustratingly at times, as well as cantankerously and flakily—truly capable of adhering to its modernist principles of interrupting the inflated symmetry between signifier and signified, which putatively conditions the visual culture of late capitalism, and of posing one of the only affective disturbances in a media culture that has all but capitulated to the prevailing neoliberal globalization drive. As explained in my preface, the "virtual" that I invoke in this book constantly looks beyond the "virtual" of cyberspace, which is interchangeable with artificial or less than real, and into the realm that is both real and dreamlike. The virtual is akin to what was intended by Walter Benjamin in his dream of Paris as a city that would communicate itself through the walking *flâneur*.[51] It is related to his often-invoked *virtuelle*,[52] which meant both truthful (powerful) and potential, thus suggesting the utopian imaginary invoked every time we watch a film. Thus, I have paid attention to the process in which Korean film today can be read as a reproducible relation of forces reimagined into what amounts to a virtual site— that is, an ironical screen where history and its social referents can return only in forms that are both truthful and fantastic. Cinema, as I hope the reader will agree, is the only virtual act in the age of hallyu.

Sopyonje, The Power of Kangwon Province, and *The Host*

The epoch in which man could believe himself to be in harmony with nature has expired.

—Walter Benjamin, "The Storyteller"

이산저산 꽃이 피니
분명코 봄이로구나
봄은 찾아왔건마는
세상사 쓸쓸하구나
나도 어제는 청춘일러니
오늘 백발 한심허다
내 청춘도 날 버리고
속절없이 가버렸으니
왔다갈줄 아는 봄을
반겨한들 쓸 데가 있나
봄아 왔다가 가려거든 가거라
니가 가도 여름이 되면
녹음방초 승화시라
옛부터 일러 있고
여름이 되고 가을이 된들
또한 경계 없을소냐
한로상풍 요란해도
제 절개를 굽히지 않는
황국단풍은 어떠허며
가을이 가고 겨울이 되면
각목한천 찬바람에
백설이 펄펄 휘날리어
월백설백 천지백허니
모두가 백발의 벗이로구나
봄은 갔다가 해마다 오건만
이내 청춘은 한번 가서
다시 올 줄을 모르네 그려
어화, 세상 벗님네야
인생이 비록 백년을 산데도
잠든 날과 병든 날과
걱정근심 다 제하면
단 사십도 못 살 우리 인생인줄
짐작하시는 이가 몇몇인고

Flowers blossom everywhere,
Spring has definitely come.
Though spring is here,
My life is lonesome.
Yesterday I had my youth
But today my white hair put me to shame.
My youth has deserted me,
Leaving me behind.
What is the purpose, even if
I were to welcome spring that comes and goes?
Spring! If you were to leave, then leave!
Even without you here, when if summer comes,
The forest will turn green; the fragrant plants will bloom.
It has often been told this way.
When summer comes and autumn follows
Wouldn't there still be scenic beauty?
Though frost and wind annoy,
How about those golden chrysanthemums and
Maple leaves that resist bowing?
After fall when winter comes,
Drop-leaf trees shudder in cold wind,
White snow falls;
Since the moon, the snow, and the earth turn white,
Now everyone is a pal of the white-haired I.
Spring leaves, but surely every year it returns.
And yet my youth, once it leaves,
Knows no path of return.
Listen my friends,
Even if you were to live a hundred years,
Take away the days when you were sick, asleep,
And obsessed with a worried heart,
How many out there can guess that
You are lucky to live till forty?

—Song of Four Seasons (Sach'ŏlga)

2　In *Sopyonje*, spring has betrayed a man, prompting him to take radical action.

I begin this chapter with the "Song of Four Seasons," featured right before the climax of *Sopyonje*, Im Kwon-Taek's 1993 film, as a departure point for a discussion of the importance of landscape in recent Korean cinema. This *minyo*, or peasant song—which dates back to the seventeenth or eighteenth century, in the Chosun Dynasty—is unusual because of its insistence on the separation of the individual (the "I") from nature, rather than on the harmony between humans and nature. As Walter Benjamin declares in the epigraph to this chapter, one of the symptoms of modernity is that man can no longer "believe himself to be in harmony with nature." What intrigues me about the song is that it already shows the irresolvable sense of melancholia that results from humanity's inability to fulfill its union with nature—something Benjamin understood to be the condition of the alienated modern self only in the twentieth century. The song climaxes in the eleventh line: "Spring! If you were to leave, then leave!" At this point in *Sopyonje*, Yu-bong, the stubborn protagonist feels that the cyclical nature of the landscape has always betrayed him because, while his "youth has deserted" him, spring always returns as if it has not aged at all. He seems to demand: why is it that you ask me to be a good Confucian and seek harmony with nature when nature has betrayed me, without any promise of eternal life? This scene takes place after Yu-bong has blinded Song-hwa, his adopted daughter, and—as seen in figure 2, which complements the "Song of Four Seasons"—he remains physically bound to her. Song-hwa may have her youth, but she is blind; Yu-bong may have his vision, but his body is frail. In part because they are both incapable of accepting stability, they must become drifters, nomads, and wanderers who must perform on the road and avoid the metropolis. Seoul becomes prominent in *Sopyonje* only through its absence. Earlier in the film, when Yu-bong is approached by his friends in a regional town after a *p'ansori* performance and is asked to return to Seoul, ending his exile, he refuses, opting instead to continue wandering through the countryside.

Again Im Kwon-Taek

This theme of the modern self's explorations remains relevant in *Sopyonje* when Yu-bong, the film's patriarchal figure, seeks to demystify and de-romanticize the landscape. The detailed depiction of landscape suggests the betrayal the narrator feels at the annual renewal of nature (in contrast with the irreversible aging process of the individual), a betrayal that leads him to become alienated—the prerequisite cognitive position of an arguably Cartesian or Marxist subjecthood, with its potential to revolt. We understand Yu-bong's song about the betrayal of spring as directed against the nation that has continually renewed itself through Japanese *enka*, American jazz, and other entertainment forms, while leaving behind the traditional artist like himself. Unable to transform the world around him, he protests, but in a twist on Oedipus's fate, he makes his beloved daughter blind—out of fear that she would face an even bigger betrayal if she were to see the changes the country is going through as the years pass. Only through this protest can he extend the expiration date on the inevitable vanishing of the p'ansori and minyo, which can no longer be pristinely inscribed onto Korea's landscape. In other words, the separation of the individual from the cyclical nature of his or her environment allows the narrator to cast a suspicious gaze at nature (and the nation), which is capable of renewing itself every season (unlike humans whose hair turns white as they age), earning for itself an immortal subjectivity and ultimately betraying any kind of lingering gesture toward Confucian principles of unity between humans and their natural environment. Instead, what takes place in this minyo from Cholla Province is what Karatani Kōjin called the "discovery of landscape," which visually addresses one critical aspect of modernity that has reshaped the sensibilities of the new self: the landscape. In his *Origins of Japanese Modern Literature*, Karatani writes:

I would like to propose that the notion of "landscape" developed in Japan sometime during the third decade of the Meiji period. Of course, there were landscapes long before they were "discovered." But "landscapes" as such did not exist prior to the 1890s, and it is only when we think it in this way that the layers of meaning entailed in the notion of a "discovery of landscape" become apparent.[1]

The transformation of the very structure of perception from premodern to modern has been identified by Karatani as the discovery of a landscape in literature through successive layers of what he calls *tenko* (轉向), or the "inversion of consciousness."[2] This requires the revelation of a close link between the literary depiction of landscape and an introverted, solitary situation, which Karatani termed the modern subjecthood of interiority. This unveiling of the new subject draws the reader of modern literature closer to representational truth and proposes a view that is based on "the relentless defamiliarization of the familiar."[3]

In this chapter, I argue how this "defamiliarization of the familiar" becomes the very site where contemporary audiences produce sensations, affects, and feelings that have very little to do with the actual vanishing of the rural landscape, but instead have to do with the postmodern pleasures induced by nostalgia that stimulates one of the most powerful melodramatic reactions. It is no coincidence that *Sopyonje*, a low-budget film featuring no stars and having no marketing campaign when it was first released, drove over a million viewers to the theater in 1993. This was perhaps the first instance in the history of Korean cinema where the rural landscape produced an affective nostalgia on the big screen that led to an overwhelming domestic box office sensation. Since then, Korean cinema has been characterized by its virtual landscapes, where realism, modernism, and postmodernism merge in the midst of the rapid democratization and globalization that began around the time of the 1988 Seoul Olympics. Throughout this schizophrenic socioeconomic process, Korea has embraced with open arms the era of technological reproducibility, in which aura has long since dissipated. The country has also witnessed, on the one hand, the decline of the traditional bourgeois subjects of early capitalist formation (Daewoo and many other chaebŏls during the IMF crisis of 1997, print media like the newspaper *Tong-A Ilbo*, and even the military junta that formed the powerful ruling bloc for several decades after the Korean War) and, on the other hand, often the increased power of the nontraditional media such as the cinema, Internet companies, and game industry. Such a cultural schematic, a byproduct of the curious function of the unconscious and of desire, moves beyond the socioeconomic paradigm set by Marx as the civilized person's struggle to "wrestle with Nature to satisfy his wants, to maintain and reproduce life," while "at the same time, do[ing] so in all social formations and under all possible modes of production."[4] No more apt example of this can be found than the media products of twenty-first-century Korea. It is still difficult to describe contemporary South Korea as a postcolonial, postmodern, industrialized First World nation even though, at the beginning of 2010, it is impossible to ignore its role in the world economy as a leader of information technology (IT), biomedical sciences, and entertainment. However, such rapid economic and cultural development could not have been achieved without various accidents and derailments. After all, according to Paul Virilio, "rapidity is always a sign of precocious death for the fast species . . . and the source of many physical traumatisms."[5] The amazing speed and mechanical overload through which industrialization in Korea was achieved inevitably resulted in crises every several years or so (the "IMF crisis" of 1997, the National Assembly's attempted impeachment of President Roh Moo-hyun in 2003, Hwang Woo-suk's stem-cell research controversy in 2005, and the global recession and credit market crash of 2008–9). Within each and every crisis, a scale of cultural intensity of an aesthetically rich nation discovers and recovers its own corresponding modern mass sensation. In this chapter, I propose to show how the attention that cinema paid to all forms of landscape—rural (Sopyonje), tourist (Kangwon Province), and ultra-urban (The Host)—allows speed to play an important function as a critique of Korea's rapid growth.

As noted in the introduction, Korea boasts the best rate among advanced nations (excluding the United States) of local consumption of domestic film products—a rate far better than that of any European country or Japan. Perhaps it is not a coincidence that one of the greatest anomalies in film history from the past hundred years was projected within the confined space of South Korea, where the coevalness of emergent and late capitalism, global and local forces, and cultural oscillation between modernist affectation of the sublime and its postmodern invalidation produced a desire to magnify the cultural significance of authentic cultural uniqueness and realistic representation—while continuing to disqualify and debunk the austere qualities of modernist and realist aesthetic principles for the purpose of maximizing the entertainment values of various simulacra that originated from Hollywood and other pop industries of the West. What I am arguing is that the cinemas of the realist Im Kwon-Taek, the modernist Hong Sang-soo, and the postmodernist Bong Joon-ho—who made their marks over the past two decades—could exist only in a mixture that represents Korea's unique crisis at the height of its transition to a late capitalist economy. The three films I will discuss—*Sopyonje*, Hong Sang-soo's *The Power of Kangwon Province* (*Kangwondo ŭi him*, 1998), and Bong Joon-ho's *The Host* (*Koemul*, 2006)—further expand this condition of possibility through figurations of visual elements that are beyond the field of representation in literature. I want to emphasize that in all three films, the landscape serves as a key chronotope, or spatiotemporal matrix, through which new cinematic subjecthood is both discovered and demystified, setting up a prerequisite for a new paradigm of modern subjectivity. This subjectivity also includes a virtual representation of both an essentially unrepresentable space, a fictive landscape set during the colonial and postcolonial 1950s and 1960s of Korea, and, as I will soon explain, the transformation of Korea's pristine landscape into a cinematic tour for contemporary urban audiences. It is in this process of discovery and rediscovery that I find the potential to read Korean landscape rendered in recent cinema as a virtual subject that satisfies the double meaning of virtual: that which is endowed by the modernist discourse of the virtuous, or full of potential, and that which is suggested by the postmodern term "virtual reality," which is hardly real. This to me is the site of "virtual hallyu."

I have long been fascinated by the new industrial wastelands—barren rice paddies and endless rows of apartment buildings—not as literary concepts, but as postmodern cinematic concepts. "Nature" and "societies" account for what Bruno Latour calls the "Premodern Overlap,"[6] which, for instance, underscores the irrevocable grief of the itinerant p'ansori musicians who forever wander through rural Korea in *Sopyonje*. But melancholia may not even be that genuine or authentic in the world of simulacral cinematic images in a melodramatic musical like *Sopyonje*. As David E. James notes in "Im Kwon-Taek: Korean Cinema and Buddhism," the "idealization of the Korean landscape is for the domestic spectator overdetermined by the industrialization and urbanization that (as at the inception of industrialization and modern landscape art in England at the end of the eighteenth century) cause the rural world to appear as the location not of agrarian labor or deprivation but of *recreation and spiritual renewal* [my emphasis]."[7] There was, as early as 1993 when *Sopyonje* took the domestic box office by storm, the formation of a mass audience that caused "the rural world to appear as the location . . . of recreation and spiritual renewal." This process is not dissimilar to what Youngmin Choe classifies as the "cinematic affect" that is complicit in drawing film texts—such as the immensely successful pan-Asian film *April Snow*, starring Bae Yong-jun, in tandem with the tourist site of Kangwondo's Samch'ŏk.[8] The intense sensation that produces grief about the vanishing landscape in a realist film by the 1990s generated a postmodern audience response that cannot be separated from what James calls the "imbrication of the cultural tourism of cinema with the global politics of the tourist industry, a *prostitution* of its spectacular natural landscape in which South Korea has conspicuously engaged in its attempt to attract international attention [my emphasis]."[9] *Sopyonje*'s "prostitution" of Korea's natural landscape and national art, I might add here, was an attempt to attract not only international audiences, but also domestic ones. Hong Sang-soo's films also try to reference their own processes of "prostituting" the rural landscape—not only for foreign tourists, but for domestic urban tourists as well—but Hong's subtle resistance against this very postmodern praxis of reducing landscapes into domestic tours and other forms of leisure and recreation cannot reverse the dominant trend. I will argue below that the varying perspectives of, for instance, landscapes drawn from such films as *The Power of Kangwon Province* and *The Host* stake out modernist and postmodernist aesthetic positions, without necessarily being trapped within these preexisting boundaries.

Because it was invented at the end of the nineteenth century, when a new traveling leisure class and an aesthetic appreciation of new exotic locations also emerged, cinema gave a new meaning to landscape. According to Sergei Eisenstein, cinematic landscape became a "complex bearer of the possibilities of a plastic interpretation of emotions."[10] According to Martin Lefebvre, Eisenstein wanted to imply that in narrative films, landscape distinguishes itself from a mere background that subordinates itself to the primacy of plotlines in narrative cinema; landscape invokes its own system of meanings and representations that build "something like the tension between it and narrative."[11] Even filmmakers—like Im Kwon-Taek—who are best known for their excellent command of storytelling, almost always exploit this tension between landscape and narrative to advance their art. Some of Im's most accomplished works, such as *Mandala* (1981), *Sopyonje*, and *Painted Fire* (*Chw'ihwasŏn*, 2002) will be remembered chiefly for their exquisite photography of the curves of Korea's snowy mountains, paddies, streams, and shorelines. Humans and their stories sometimes pale in comparison to these images of landscapes, only to emerge on top of them by the end. Im's landscapes render familiar spaces of Korea slightly uncanny, as they inspire feelings of melancholia and loss because of the devastating impact that industrialization has had on nature. What contemporary audiences find engaging in realist films is the fact that the real (the contaminated landscape) and the unreal (pristine nature that survives only in Im Kwon-Taek's immaculately photographed films) constantly switch places with each other, invoking the power of the virtual-actual. In other words, Korea's actual modern humans continually allow themselves in the space of a movie theater to be affected by the virtual site of the cinematic premodern landscape after designing the movie sets and shooting them (not unlike the two-way traffic of virtual-actual in James Cameron's *Avatar*).

Slightly smaller than the state of Ohio, South Korea's geographical dimensions are not vast, especially considering that the overwhelming majority of its land mass is mountainous. Though usually intimate in scale, Korea looks infinitely expansive during the winter season, when its mountains, roads, gullies, and paddies are covered in white. Snow was first effectively used in a film by Yi Man-hŭi, *The Road to Sampo* (*Samp'o kanŭn kil*, 1976), which follows the wanderings of a prostitute and two male workers in harsh winter conditions. In this film, Korea's sterility is projected through the body of the female prostitute—who cries at the end of the film while deceptively saying that she is capable of bearing a child—the high plains covered in snow, and abandoned industrialized sites like half-built concrete highways. Most of the road scenes in Im Kwon-Taek's *Mandala*—the story of two Buddhist monks, the orthodox Pŏb-un and the unruly and unprincipled Chi-san—take place in winter. At this film's end, ironically, it is Chi-san who reaches nirvana and freezes to death. In the startling scene where Chi-san reaches his peak of stillness, the ground is covered in snow, which obliterates everything else. When Pŏb-un builds a pyre and burns Chi-san's body, the spatiality that engenders the theme of Buddhist transcendence of worldly essences reaches new visual heights as red flames scorch the human flesh against the white mountainous landscape. In snow and windy conditions, human movement in both of Im Kwon-Taek's road movies, *Mandala* and *Sopyonje*, is slowed down as if we are watching slow motion. Because snow is piled deep, the characters sometimes literally crawl as if they are no longer humans, but animals unable to walk upright. Often the snow captured in Im Kwon-Taek's films is sublime, not only because of its aesthetically pleasing color and texture, but because of its capacity to raise the ontological question of what it means to be a human in such horrid conditions. Though not nearly as profound as the monks' journey in *Mandala*, the wandering of Yu-bong, with Song-hwa in tow, over snowy fields (and, in the film's finale, the scene of Song-hwa's daughter leading Song-hwa as snowflakes begin to fall) remains one of the most memorable navigations depicted in Korean cinema. A shot of characters walking in snow is both visually emblematic of Im Kwon-Taek's subtle protest against Korea's hurried pace of industrialization and the object of the fascinated gaze of postmodern audiences, who are familiar only with snowmobiles, ski boots, and sport parkas in winter.

Hong Sang-soo's The Power of Kangwon Province

During the hallyu period, cosmopolitanism, which often takes the form of a "modernist argument against the tyranny of 'tradition' as narrow parochialisms and ethnocentrism,"[12] emerged in Korea. It was accompanied by the desire to represent a diverse range of multi-ethnic and national groups and to provide some sort of alternative to local varieties of nationalism within the legal and ethical framework of neoliberalism. But cinema proved to be both the harbinger of cosmopolitanism and an impediment to it. Although many of the films made in this period sought to depict ethnic and national diversity, anticolonial and anti-American sentiments continued to inspire popular narratives that reimagined and celebrated Korean national ethos and pathos. Such antinomies — cosmopolitanism and ethnocentrism — were brought together not only through the content depicted in hallyu but also by the city of Seoul itself. Seoul was not yet a city that had begun to offer itself up to immigrants as a second home, and, like Paris in the twentieth century, "neither the pronounced xenophobia of its inhabitants nor the sophisticated harassment by the local police"[13] had really improved.[14] Because the interests amalgamated in cinema are tempered by both global and national feelings without being committed to either, the pronounced cosmopolitanism or internationalism in many Korean films was not without its own critical views on ethnic and gender inequality. Some of the best filmmakers from this period — Im Kwon-Taek, Hong Sang-soo, and Bong Joon-ho, for example — all made work that featured similar visions of Seoul as a place of nomads, dislocation, and extraterritoriality. Although Seoul's history goes farther back than that

3 In *April Snow*, two city dwellers find themselves in the countryside as reluctant drifters.

of New York, Tokyo, or other famous world capitals, the frenzied pace at which globalization took place there has transformed it into a seemingly nondescript, ahistorical setting. The anonymous features of Seoul (convenience stores, Starbucks, and residential and office building elevators) provide more incentives for its contemporary audiences to embrace virtual landscape as one of the primary modes of escapist entertainment.

Hur Jin-ho is a filmmaker who has emerged during the hallyu period and whose work is just as important in the assessment of Korean cinematic landscape as that of Im, Hong, and Bong. Hur's *Christmas in August* (*8-wŏl ŭi K'ŭrisŭmasŭ*, 1998), *One Fine Spring Day* (*Pom nal ŭn kanda*, 2001), *April Snow* (*Oech'ul*, 2005), *Happiness* (*Haengbok*, 2007), and *Hou Sijŏl* (*A Good Rain Knows*, 2009) were successes in both Korea and Japan. As Choe argues, "*April Snow* relies on body over words, and *Spring Day* silences words in favor of sounds."[15] Though I agree with Choe's poignant analysis of Hur Jin-ho's work, I would add that his films also mobilize visuality through sounds and images of landscape.

Unlike Hong Sang-soo's city dwellers, whose unemployment or uncertainties in the city often place them reluctantly in the countryside, Hur Jin-ho's nomadism juxtaposed against the rural landscape does not require his characters to be loafers or slackers. On the contrary, his characters (played by Yu Ji-tae in *Spring Day*, Bae Yong-joon in *April Snow*, and Hwang Jeong-min in *Happiness*) purposefully leave the city behind, not necessarily to drift—or, to use Guy Debord's term, to "*dérive*," which, according to Libero Andreotti, "entails playful constructive behavior and awareness of psychogeographical effects, which completely distinguishes it from the classical notions of the journey and stroll"—but in order to temporarily migrate to the rural towns because their work inevitably is linked to the countryside.[16] Yu Ji-tae's character in *Spring Day* is hired by a rural radio station to capture various local sounds of nature, and Bae Yong-joon's character in *April Snow* must spend countless days and nights in Samch'ŏk where he knows no one, because his wife has been in a car accident and lies in a coma in a rural hospital. Hur's characters—with the possible exception of Hwang Jeong-min's decadent character in *Happiness*, who needs to rehabilitate at a rural institution because of his serious liver condition due to late-night partying and heavy smoking—are not deviants in urban bourgeois society; they are ideal citizens and workers in the city. If Yu-bong in *Sopyonje* and—as I will explain in this section—Sang-gwon in *The Power of Kangwon Province* face crises when they are *not* on the road and feel aversion to certain stabilities of home, Hur Jin-ho's characters lament the impossibility of attaining freedom without family, home, and the physical and moral structures of neo-Confucian values. Thus, they lament the loss of barriers based on these values. This is a pan-Asian conservatism that works very well in Hur's films. *April Snow* remains one of the all-time bestselling Korean films in Japan, and *Spring Day* is perennially ranked high by critics and moviegoers in Korea.

In Hong Sang-soo's *The Power of Kangwon Province*, two lead characters, Sang-gwon and Jae-wan, take a trip to Kangwon Province, a region well known for its pristine beauty and majestic mountains. While waiting for their flight at a small local airport at Sokch'o, they engage in small talk. The two protagonists cannot help noticing that the mountains in front of them are hardly inhabited by people. Having been city dwellers all their lives, they feel estranged from the pastoral landscape before their eyes. Sang-gwon asks, "How many people do you think that one mountain can hold?" He answers his own question: "How about a million? If you serried them, it's possible . . . Then just fifty of these would be enough to hold our entire [South Korean] population." While the majestic mountain is incautiously reimagined as boxed dwelling spaces, we notice that this particular sequence is assembled from two consecutive shots of the same mountain before Sang-gwon begins his recollection of a past love affair.

The first shot of this series is composed through a fully framed two-shot on a medium long lens with the two characters talking in the foreground.

4 Sang-gwon asks Jae-wan: "how many people do you think that one mountain can hold?" *The Power of Kangwon Province.*

The actual mountain is positioned outside the frame, but we are able to get a glimpse of it reflected on the airport window in the frame's background. Sang-gwon and Jae-wan talk about the mountain as if it is about to face a complete makeover and development. The link between landscape and the human no longer reveals a sense of sublime awe. The mountains of Kangwon have attracted the attention of the city dwellers but no longer inspire what Karatani described as either an astounding bewilderment or an "inversion of consciousness." In addition, the mention of a specific number such as "a million" not only reconfigures the mountain in finite terms but also humanizes it: the number refers to a particular mass of people. This doubly articulate process of quantifying and humanizing nature by associating it with a specific number accomplishes three things. First, it takes away the sublime character of the mountain, which has already been stripped of its awesome power by being made easily accessible to tourists by a thirty-minute plane ride from Seoul. Second, it closes the gap between humans and nature to a point where the rupture between the two seems to have collapsed, an effect that is the inevitable byproduct of the industrialization and overdevelopment conducted over the past hundred years in Korea. And third, the scornful attitude of the city dwellers, which no

5 A mountain unhindered by humans? *The Power of Kangwon Province.*

longer embodies the early romantic view of nature, proclaims the present era as one where the power of modernity has waned. Here, instead of the landscape as a modern construct that has extended itself as the interiorization process of modern subjecthood, what becomes prominent is the re-imagination of rural landscape as an enclave of grotesque monstrosity, in which a million people are jammed into a space that is probably no larger than several football stadiums. The second shot of the same mountain— unhindered by humans' figures or voices, yet obstructed by a partial view of a parked car, power lines and a post, and buildings—amplifies this sense of the grotesque uncanny by once more reminding us how vulnerable pristine nature is to humans' cranes and bulldozers.

Hong Sang-soo's cynical depiction of the urban dweller's gaze at the rural landscape, which has been reduced to a subject for banter, subtly protests what James, as mentioned earlier, has described as Korea's "prostitution of its spectacular natural landscape." An intriguing predecessor of this mood, I have argued, exists in the modernist poetry of Yi Sang. As I noted in the previous chapter, Yi Sang, who professes to have seen animals only in zoos, finds it surprising that a wild bear could still be spotted in the mountain village of Sŏng-ch'an, in Pyŏng-an Province (now in North

Korea) and reports that he is "suffering from the delusion" that these wild animals must have been taken from the zoo and put in the mountains, and not the other way around. A similar fascinating reversal, expressed eighty years later, is remarked on Hong's film. Despite the different mediums of literature and cinema, Yi Sang's Sŏngch'an and Hong Sang-soo's Kangwon Province both no longer present the allure of the landscape, and so the mountains of Kangwon Province or P'yŏng-an Province are simply transformed into objects that prioritize human subjectification: matchbox-type apartment buildings, in the case of Hong Sang-soo, and zoo enclosures, in the case of Yi Sang. Modernization, initiated by desperate attempts to curtail the horrors that nature had previously wrought, has succeeded in bringing such violent sensations to an end through strangulation. If the sublimation of art is fundamentally based on the terrifying encounter of the human with an image of infinitude and divinity, then even the greatest, most beautiful mountains and the natural wildlife preserved in South Korea have lost their ability to inspire that very sense of the sublime. Any interiority that had been awakened by the inversion of consciousness has, therefore, dissipated.

I return to the example of *The Power of Kangwon Province* to underscore this point. I am interested not only in the first shot (see fig. 4), in which the dialogue takes place, but also in the subsequent one (see fig. 5), which unveils for the viewers what was registered in the previous shot only as the virtual figuration of the actual topic of conversation. A strategy of aestheticization is at work precisely in that construction of the rather lengthy subsequent shot of the mountain: its nakedness has restored the representational rather than the virtual-actual presence of the mountain that the first shot had achieved. Jean-Luc Nancy writes: "Now, if all there is is the finite—if the 'there is' [*il y a*] is finite—then everything is presented in it, but in a finite presentation which is neither *representation* nor *the presentation of something unpresentable*."[17] Does the truth (the existence of the bare mountain) slip at the point where it is featured twice (once hindered by two urbanites, and the other time without such hindrance), revealing to the audience an interiority marked by the monstrosity of modernization in a densely populated nation (the continual transformation of the natural environment into real estate for a million inhabitants)? One other useful way to address Nancy's concept of "finite presentation" is to reconsider how both "representation" (the mountain represented by the still shot cinematography) and "the presentation of something unpresentable" (the

6   A typical mountain in Seoul filled with people. Photo by Kyung Hyun Kim.

grotesque imagery inspired by the insistence that the same mountain can be filled with a million people, something that is actually imaginable looking at the landscape of Seoul) structure a condition of possibility within this film.

However feeble, the interiority remains intact, even after the abuse of nature and with humans' utter disregard for the landscape. But what hits the nail right on its head is the inevitability of the postmodern exposure, with its recognition of historicity's surfaces and subjectification, even in a country like Korea that only began its modernization process within the last century. The archetypal essence of the modern self is the reconstitution of subjectivity through the reawakening of what Kant has termed "supersensible," which weathers the shock and the terror of the sublime and can transform such exposure into an aesthetic *jouissance*. It is because of this instinctual reliance on reason that we continue to maneuver through our everyday lives, despite the revelation that God has become either irrelevant or, as Kafka believed, is simply having "a bad day."[18] The invention of film arrived at a time, we ought to remember, when "the alienation of men from one another [had reached its] maximum."[19]

Bong Joon-ho and the Postmodern Landscape

After having tasted the bitterness of failure in the commercial marketplace when his first feature, *Barking Dogs Never Bite* (*Pŭlandasŭ ŭi kae*, 2000), flopped at the box office despite critical acclaim, Bong returned in 2003 with the buddy-cop mystery thriller *Memories of Murder* (*Salin ŭi chuŏk*). This film drew some of the highest critical praise of the decade from both local and international critics[20] and became one of the highest grossing films of the year, selling more than five million tickets in Korea alone. *The Host*, a scary monster movie that also incorporates elements of eco-disaster, a parody of the SARS virus, and family comedy, followed in 2006. It set the box office record in Korea, selling thirteen million tickets in a nation that has a population of only forty-nine million; that record remains unbroken today. Bong's next film was *Mother* (2009), a hard-hitting Oedipal crime mystery–drama.

Bong is intrigued by the evolving landscape of Korea, which has been mauled by the hurried pace of industrialization and modernization, and fascinated by Korea's rapidly shrinking natural landscape. Mountains, rivers, farms, blue skies, and forests often occupy Bong's cinematic imagination. However, unlike Im Kwon-Taek's cinematic representation of landscape, which entertains today's audiences by depicting the declining condition of the pristine, Bong's portrayal of landscape often shows nature beyond repair. Countryside towns and farms are invaded by reckless golfers in their expensive cars and loud designer clothes (*Mother*); a wide-open vision of green forest is obstructed by *ap'atŭ tanji*, the rows of apartment buildings that are ubiquitous in Korea (*Barking Dogs*); the Han River is inhabited by a monster and threatened by the sprawling cityscape (*The Host*); and a mountain is razed by miners and builders who extract rocks from it (*Memories of Murder*) to make cement and other construction materials. In these landscapes can be found a schizo intellectual, an apartment superintendent with an appetite for canines, a serial killer who shoves peach slices into his victims' vaginas, and an obsessive mother who carries enormous acupuncture needles. Such visions of landscape have their kin not in the films of Im Kwon-Taek,[21] but in the postmodern genre films of the Coen brothers, for instance, who have meticulously photographed the desolate landscapes of the American Southwest and Midwest in bleeding, saturated colors (for example, in *Raising Arizona*, *Fargo*, and *No Country for Old Men* with their wide-angle lens). Ironically, Bong Joon-ho is a grandson of the novelist Pak T'ae-won, whose work during the colonial period such as *Sosŏlga Kubo ssi ŭi haru* (*Daily Life of Novelist Kubo*, 1934) and *Ch'ŏnbyŏn p'unggyŏng* (*Landscape of Ch'ŏnbyŏn*, 1936), gave Korea its first literary images of *flânerie* as a member of *Kuinhoe* (the Group of Nine) along with Yi Sang. Extending the modernist agenda of his grandfather, who sought to defamil-

7 The novelist Pak T'ae-won (standing) with Yi Sang (left) and Kim So-un, a fellow writer (right), in 1936.

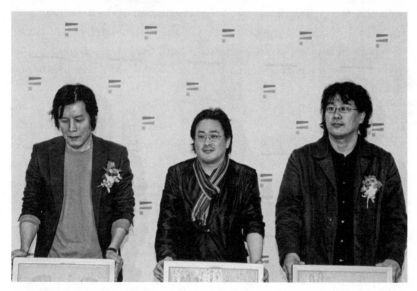

8 Lee Chang-dong (left), Park Chan-wook (middle), and Bong Joon-ho (right) are inducted into the Korean Film Archive Hall of Fame in 2008. Photo by Kyung Hyun Kim.

9 *Memories of Murder*'s typical use of a wide-angle lens. Bong's cinematography departs from Im Kwon-Taek's long-lens or medium-lens depiction of landscapes.

iarize everyday Seoul, then a colonial city, Bong's films depict the present global metropolis's parasitical dependence on nature and its destruction of ecological harmony.

This grotesque perversion of landscape accommodates Bong's postmodern vision of Korea, which arguably parallels Korean cinema's realism and modernism: it points the way past the lamentation of the deterioration of traditional values and the destruction of the natural landscape. Instead, these ruined landscapes are exploited as both the generic ingredients for his crime mystery, horror, and comedy films, and the affective sites of new virtuality.

One of the opening shots of *Memories of Murder* is a wide-angle shot of a farm on an autumn day in 1986. A farmer drives a tractor slowly along the narrow dirt road that splits a field. Several plainly dressed children shaking their butterfly nets follow the tractor, in whose trailer sits Pak Du-man, a local man with a crew cut, wearing a drab-colored light jacket. The golden rays of the sunset reflected on the lush, brown stalks of rice make the approaching harvest days seem warm and cheerful. This leisurely long shot, in which the frame is horizontally split by the earth and sky, may momentarily remind the viewers of the kinds of pastoral spaces so distinctively captured in the films of Im Kwon-Taek. However, when Pak, the local detective, squats down beside a cement drainage ditch next to the farm, the realist cinematic framework that aims to unite humans with nature sud-

10 An exhausted country cop needs more than fresh air to rehabilitate himself in
Memories of Murder.

denly dissipates. As Pak peers inside the ditch with the aid of a broken
mirror, a dead woman's almost naked body appears. The first thing to come
into view are her tightly bound hands behind her, covered in scum; this is
followed by a tight shot of her face. Her eyes are wide open and covered by
innumerable lines of black ants. The film has already shown the glories of
autumn, with its promise of a golden harvest. Yet if we comb through the
fields of reeds and forests, beyond the dried peppers in the front yards that
overlook the rice fields, and underneath the typically low mountain ridges
of Korea, we find the bodies of mutilated women.

Friedrich Engels wrote in *The Condition of the Working Class in England*:
"The greater the number of people that are packed into a tiny space, the
more repulsive and offensive becomes the brutal indifference, the unfeel-
ing concentration of each person on his private affairs."[22] One of the scenes
in *Memories of Murder* presages the concern in Bong's subsequent *The Host*
with the threat of highly communicable diseases in a rapidly changing
landscape where people are packed into "a tiny space": it is a scene that
takes place immediately after the leg of Pak's junior colleague has been infected with tetanus and must be amputated. Pak's nurse girlfriend phones
him to ask him for a date out by the deserted, barren farm by the river. In
a foreshadowing of his resignation from the police force—he goes on to
start a business selling health food—Pak receives a vitamin shot from his
girlfriend as they are seated in the open air. She has arranged this favor for

her exhausted boyfriend, who has been forced to serve double duty: as a criminal investigator who protects the public from a serial killer and as a riot policeman who endangers the public by firing tear gas at demonstrators and abusing police power during the late 1980s. Pak's arm, which is strapped to an IV bottle that dangles from one of the branches of a leafless tree by the river, eerily reminds the viewer that the relationship between nature and humans has entered an already virtual relationship in which artificially manufactured energy fluids, not oxygen naturally emitted by trees, must be injected into humans' veins in order to keep them healthy and alive—a lesson amply stressed in Bong's next film, *The Host*.

The Virtual-Actual City of *The Host*

Perhaps no other film reenacts South Korea's late modern impulses better than *The Host*, which—as noted above—holds the record for ticket sales in Korea. Some critics consider it to be only a lightweight film in which the traces of modern Korea's political past—such as the neocolonial US military occupation, the democratization movement of the 1980s, and the authoritarian government's disregard for civilian rights—appear only as postmodern appropriations drained of their previous vitalities. However, *The Host* is a visual text replete with metaphors (such as the half-fish, half-dinosaur monster), which require no interpretation, and national allegories (including a Molotov cocktail, women's archery, and a former student activist who has become a mobile phone company executive), which must be explained to become meaningful. In the film, the sensual subject that bears the meaning of the virtual is Seoul's urban landscape, which permits both historical density (for instance, its concrete sewers underneath riverbanks, skyscrapers belonging to a global mobile phone company, and the US military base in Yongsan) and the flatness of objects, pastiche, and smiling faces freed from traumas of the past.

What initially grabs the audience's attention in *The Host* are its reinscriptions of the elusive nature of cosmopolitanism, democratization, and globalization in an age of bizarre industrial accidents, nuclear proliferation (the North Korean threat), hype about lethal and highly contagious viruses (SARS, avian flu, mad-cow disease potentially breaking out in Korea through the Korea-U.S. Free Trade Agreement, and so on), and widespread *yŏpki* (perverted, bizarre) crimes. The film's postmodern narrative unpacks these crises into various scenarios ripe for a blockbuster. The

Host depicts hospital emergency rooms, an American military conspiracy, a hostage drama, a Godzilla-like monster disaster, protest rallies, and an urban proletariat that briefly pulls together the seams of what Fredric Jameson calls "social totality"[23] before it becomes inaccessible once again. What explicitly or implicitly becomes locked in the film's field of representation is the manner in which the ultimate significance of nature becomes part of an environmental problem that lies at the heart of social crisis and uncontrollable disaster—the first of its kind since industrialization took place along the Han River, the site of Korea's so-called economic miracle. In an age where the number of foreign workers in Korea has risen exponentially, the reintroduction of democratic elections in the late 1980s has forced even the political left to take volatile and unreliable popular opinions seriously, even if that means choosing free trade agreements with nations such as the United States instead of saving local farms and protecting the hygienic body of the nation.

In *The Host*, natural landscapes that had invited people's scorn after being stripped of their awesome impact by industrialization strike back in the form of a monster, which wields a power capable of destroying everything it encounters—humans, buildings, and other remnants of civilization. The birth of the monster is a reconstitution of the horror that declares that man and nature or nature and industry can no longer be distinguished. As Gilles Deleuze and Félix Guattari argue: "The human essence of nature and the natural essence of man become one within nature in the form of production or industry, just as they do within the life of man as a species."[24] Similarly, when industry extracts raw materials from nature and then sends its refuse into nature, this exchange belies the presumption that humans, nature, and industry are autonomous spheres. In Deleuze and Guattari's terms, the "glaring, sober truth that resides in delirium—is that there is no such thing as relatively independent spheres or circuits."[25] As a result, tales of early urbanization that feature *flânerie*, the arts, and the mythological tension between humans and nature are basically extinct. Therefore, the reappearance of monsters and creatures along the riverbanks of Seoul—a space where less than a century ago tigers descended from the mountains and terrified its residents—entertains us with its shock value.

The Host appropriates modernity's hurried present by assessing the shocking impact of its ability to destroy nature. If, in the work of cinematic predecessors of Im Kwon-Taek or Hong Sang-soo, the disappearance of the sublime potential of landscapes projected a sense of melancholia, here in the blockbuster disaster film, mourning and melancholia have been transformed into grotesque perversion. In other words, instead of "an inversion of consciousness," what remain are the vestiges of modernity in the empty form of prosaic shock and perversion. The monster of the Han River is surely both the allegory and the emblem of loss—of both national sovereignty and clean water. In the film's opening sequence, a Korean medical staff member at the US Eighth Army station in Seoul reluctantly dumps gallons of formaldehyde down a drain, as ordered by his American military superior. His protest that the toxic fluid (used to clean dead bodies in morgues) will eventually flow into the Han River, where it will find its way into the drinking water of Seoul's more than 10 million inhabitants, is to no avail. The American officer insists that the Han River is "very broad," and therefore one needs to be "broad-minded" about the drainage.[26] The monster that ultimately results from this toxic waste thus serves as an apocalyptic message about Korea's downward spiral, in terms of both environmental disasters and the country's continuing subordination by US military forces.

Much of the film centers on a father, Kang-du, who is desperately seeking his missing daughter, Hyeon-seo, who has been abducted by the monster. Hyeon-seo, initially thought dead, is alive in the creature's feeding pit—a concrete crevice under a bridge on the Han River. During this desperate search, Kang-du's family suffers its first casualty when Hyeon-seo's grandfather (Kang-du's father) is struck by a lethal swing of the monster's tail. But rather than settling for solemn and sober gestures of melancholia in the face of trauma, historic catastrophe, and national and familial loss, which had been typical in Park Kwang-su's and Jang Sun-woo's films about history made during the 1980s and 1990s, Kang-du and his siblings (Nam-il and Nam-ju) decide to confront the crisis. Much of the latter half of the film thus also focuses on the attempt to avenge the loss of the grandfather against this horrible half-dinosaur, half-fish creature. One of the most intriguing points in the film is that Kang-du is not a neurotic overworked father, a symptom of industrialization; instead he is a figure of post-industrial Korea who is initially inefficient, indolent, and therefore represented as lacking a phallus. It is only after being deemed guilty for having let go of Hyeon-seo's hand in the frenzied moment of the monster's attack and for miscalculating the number of bullets left in his rifle's chamber, which led to the death of his father, that Kang-du is given the key to

11   Stop running! Do you have the right girl, Kang-du? *The Host.*

restoring the social and moral order of both his family and the nation. Here the invocation of familial guilt is a deliberate slipping into the disjunctive synthesis of what Deleuze and Guattari call "desire-recording," which imposes on the subject the legal-ethical paradigm "that becomes identical with the form of triangulation: being daddy, mommy, or child."[27]

If the primary objective of *The Host* is to restore the stability of both the family and the nation, which Deleuze and Guattari—along with other critics, such as Foucault—have termed "oedipalized territorialities,"[28] then is the postmodern engagement of its director, Bong Joon-ho, something that aims at a conservative reaffirmation of "being daddy, mommy, or me"? And not something that takes on the deterritorialization that celebrates natural resistance through the schizo figures of the inefficient and sleepy Kang-du, or—to leave *The Host* for a moment—Jong-du (in Lee Chang-dong's *Oasis*) who remains completely outside the oedipalized circuit of flow,[29] for he recognizes neither the power of words (formalities) nor the phallus (his older brother's authority)? Is this the case only because *The Host* protests the hegemonic paradigm of the United States (the wealthy father who provides protection), South Korea (me), and North Korea (the Communist enemy) and so is able to avert a desire-recording that simply reproduces oedipalized desires that reimagine phallocentrism? In other words, isn't the vengeful Kang-du a body that manages to synthesize several deterritorialized flows amalgamated from ecological disaster, American military subordination, and familial fragmentation? Or is he simply a

Nietzschean man of *ressentiment* who is susceptible to the higher causes of nationalism and heroism that ultimately prevent the deterritorialized flows of desire and who instead aims to build another codified power structure of territoriality? It is almost impossible to find a satisfying answer to such questions, since *The Host* follows the mechanics of entertainment films by celebrating the remasculinization of Kang-du, even as it consciously recognizes the impossibility of narrative closure by having his heroic triumphs fall hopelessly short of saving his daughter from the monster. Having learned his lesson from the death of his father, where he was unable to muster much resistance, Kang-du reclaims his masculinity by lowering his body—without any assistance—into the creature's feeding pit in order to complete his search for his missing daughter.

However, just as Kang-du arrives at the dungeon, the monster snatches Hyeon-seo and another child survivor, Se-ju, with his cavernous mouth and leaps away. The Korean government, in order to battle the creature, has acquired from the American military a poisonous chemical called "Agent Yellow"—a substance unabashedly modeled after Agent Orange, a powerful contaminant that the United States had massively sprayed as a defoliant during the Vietnam War that led to major health complications for American veterans and Vietnamese civilians. The creature momentarily loses consciousness when it is exposed to the poisonous gas, which has been dispersed despite the protests of environmental groups along the riverfront. Taking advantage of this momentary lapse by the creature, Kang-du pries from its mouth his daughter and Se-ju. Se-ju miraculously survives, but this time Hyeon-seo is not as fortunate.

The Host's inability to close the quest-romance narrative with a happy ending reminds us of *Sopyonje*.[30] *Sopyonje* actually delivers a narrative arc that is eerily close to that of the monster film. In that epic, which spans four decades, Tong-ho spends his adult life combing Korea's countryside for any trace of his father, Yu-bong, and sister, Song-hwa, from the 1970s. Eventually Tong-ho learns that his father died long before and his sister is now blind. The suturing of the family, normally the final resolution of most genre films, is defamiliarized again at the end of *Sopyonje*, when Tong-ho finally meets with his sister but both suppress their feelings for each other. Soon after the "Song of Four Seasons" ends, and Yu-bong dies in this story within the story, Tong-ho, a retired drummer, accompanies Song-hwa as she takes the viewer through the vocal performance of the Korean classic *Sim Ch'ongjŏn* (*Tale of Sim Ch'ong*). This suppression of emotions in *Sop-*

yonje's anticlimactic climax underscores both Korean cinema's affirmation of and disengagement from "being daddy, mommy, or me." Tong-ho, who has been wandering on his own through the countryside and has been reintegrated into nature, has mastered the meaning of Koreans' equivalent of the *Anti-Oedipal* sentiment, called *han*, which aims to overcome grief. Tong-ho departs without even exchanging a kind word with his sister. With equal equanimity, Kang-du, after having slain the monster, prepares a meal in the final scene of *The Host* for Se-ju, an orphaned nomad he has apparently adopted, instead of his own daughter.

The nature without people—or the ability to articulate this space in modern writing, crucially defined as the self's interiorization—acquires a new meaning in *The Host*. One fascinating note about *The Host* is its portrayal of a virtual-actual city drained of crowds, as a result of both the monster's attack and the threat of a highly contagious virus. The masses of people who normally crowd the banks of the Han River are absent. This vacancy does not restore nature, but it certainly elicits in the viewer a phantasmagoric state that, according to Chris Marker in his documentary *Sans Soleil* (1983), forces us to "wonder if those dreams are really mine, or if they are part of a totality, of a gigantic collective dream of which the entire city may be the projection." But, as noted above, instead of Karatani's "inversion of consciousness" that once created historical and psychological depth, what we are left with in *The Host* is a perverse landscape containing a computer-generated monster. Within this depthless surface, *The Host* attempts to create a drama about crossing boundaries, "causing deterritorialized flows of desire to circulate."[31] The popular convenience store run in a trailer by Kang-du and his father, which is located in the park on the bank of the river, thus becomes a focal point of deterritorialization. This transformation redetermines the conditions of capitalism: Kang-du's snack shack, where beer and sundries were traded for cash, now assumes the position of critical war-zone frontier post—with sentries like those in John Ford's Westerns. Not only does the convenience store function as a half-way station stocked with food and providing a place for fatigued hunters to rest, but it also allegorizes a vital defensive bulwark against the attack of viruses and monsters. The store, emptied of its commercial traffic, is a place where Kang-du, who is misidentified by the state as the host of the virus, sits, sleeps, and fights in order to prove that he has been wrongly accused. Ironically, this post that supposedly contains the host assumes a role essential to the survival of healthy bodies.

12.1 When the government's hysteria in *The Host* forces the city to empty its riverfront . . .

12.2 . . . the only safe passage is inside the sewer tunnels, where the submerged "line of flight" runs.

Only when the city has been reimagined as a barren landscape does the presence of *flâneurs* and nomads become conspicuous. In *The Host*, just as the monster is decisively evil, there is something menacing, inhuman, and barbaric about the masses of people who, not unlike those in Fritz Lang's 1927 classic *Metropolis*, are hypnotized by corporate-controlled agencies. The speed with which people rush past one another is not only very great, but it also reveals the selfishness of each member of the mass. Once the discipline that had tamed their bodies dissipates and is replaced by savagery that matches the vigor of the monster, mayhem and chaos erupt.

13 In *Sopyonje*, humans are pitted against nature.

When order fails and the city can no longer effectively be patrolled by the state apparatus, instead of the amorphous masses or the useless authorities, individual city dwellers on the margins such as vagabonds and urchins emerge as heroes, helping Kang-du's family defeat the monster. If the contact with a middle manager in the high-tech industry (Fat Guevara, played by Im P'il-sŏng), for instance, proves in the narrative that no one within the corporate structure remains uninfected by the atmosphere of vice and corruption, vagabonds whose "dwelling is subordinated to the journey"[32] and who occupy the striated spaces of sewers, tunnels, and concrete holes under the bridge, become critical in aiding the family's quest to rescue Hyeon-seo and concoct the final punishment for the monster.

If, in *Sopyonje*, deterritorialization culminates visually in the aimless wandering of the itinerant musicians past Korea's rice paddies and undeveloped mountainsides, in *The Host*, Kang-du's family's futile search for their lost relative cannot go beyond man-made walls, concrete labyrinths, and polluted water. In *The Host*, spaces of everyday urban life such as convenience stores, high-rise corporate headquarters, hospitals, gigantic parking garages, and sewers turn into what Deleuze and Guattari call the "operation of the line of flight,"[33] delineating a movement along which both deterritorializations and reterritorializations must take place. Instead of housing state apparatuses, private enterprises, workplaces, and sites of financial transactions, these territories (office buildings, hospitals, and concrete holes) are constantly invoked as "lines of flight" where

14   Korean Rapunzel—with a line of clothing rather than the hair? *The Host*.

Kang-du and his family must run for their lives. The world of offices, reg-
istries, and hospitals reminds us of the musty, shabby, and dark rooms
where Kafka's somnolent and unkempt monsters vegetate. The list of dirty
parasites include not only the half-fish, half-dinosaur creature, but also
the corrupt city bureaucrats, who demand payoffs from the grandfather,
and Fat Guevara, a former student activist, who has sold his soul to the
national security agents and the mobile phone company to make a quick
buck. As the family makes their escape, they confront the tension in the
cityscape between "smooth space" and "striated space," which achieves
a meaning that is both concrete and abstract. It is made concrete when
Kang-du and his family, now homeless and identified as "contaminated,"
are chased not only by the monster, but also by American medical person-
nel and their Korean conspirators—all of whom are symptomatic of the irrational hysteria that can develop under the pressures of neoliberal globalization, ecological disasters, and essentialist nationalisms. Yet the family's
escape is also abstract: captured on speedy cameras on tracks, it expresses
a kind of movement that virtually exceeds all of the aforementioned allegories. The line of flight that Hyeon-seo invents through the concrete hole
that has served as a pantry for the monster is the most abstract of all. Not
only does this escape invoke mythological identity by requiring a line of
clothes to be strung together for escape (reminiscent of *Rapunzel*), but
it also requires leaping over the sleepy monster, a feat whose athleticism

reminds viewers of the young Korean gymnasts and figure skaters who achieved Olympic glory shortly before *The Host*'s release, thus mollifying the national anger stemming from South Korea's ignominious national status vis-à-vis the United States, Japan, Soviet Union-cum-Russia, and now increasingly China. The escapes of Kang-du and his family thus deterritorialize the traditional power dynamics that have humiliated Korea, but in failing to transcend the borders of national allegory, the escapes also reterritorialize these power dynamics.

Conclusion

늘어진 계수나목 *끄끝터리에다*	On the edge of a laurel tree,
대랑 매달아 놓고	I will clip my meaningless, passive life.
국곡투식 허는 놈과 부모불효허는 놈과	Then I will catch and throw into hell
형제화목 못허는 놈 차례로 잡어다가	Those bastards who abuse
저 세상으로 먼저 보내버리고	their national resources, parents, and siblings.
나머지 벗님네들 서로 모아	I will host a killer party, play,
앉어서 한잔 더 먹소 덜먹게 허면서	Offer and not offer drinks
거드렁거리고 놀아 보세	With the rest of my remaining buddies.
	—Song of Four Seasons (Sach'ŏlga)

The last stanza of the "Song of Four Seasons," with which I began this chapter, calls for a radical transformation of consciousness and specifically manifests an action that brings it closer to the revolutionary interiorization that lies at the paradoxical heart of modernist discourse. The first line of this stanza begins with the laurel tree (계수나무 *kyesu namu*), which sets the tone for the fantastic nature of this celebration because laurel trees are often paired in Korea's folk tradition with the galaxy (은하수 *ŭnhasu*), far beyond the realities of the earth. The element of the fantastic is already conditioned not only in this folk song, but also in other literary traditions such as *Tale of Chŏn U-ch'i*, from the early Chosun Dynasty (sixteenth to seventeenth centuries). U-ch'i, having learned the trick of disappearing from an ascetic trained in martial arts, descends from a mountain to punish corrupt officials. His story was revived in 2009 in Choi Dong-hun's sci-fi adventure film called *Jeon Woo-chi: The Taoist Wizard* (*Chŏn U-ch'i*). The commercial success of *Jeon Woo-chi* was unprecedented because the Korean film industry has not done well in the fantasy genres of science fiction and adventure. Touted as Korea's answer to James Cameron's *Avatar*,

15.1 After taunting the corrupt king, Woo-chi . . .

15.2 . . . disappears into the landscape painting . . .

15.3 . . . which could be more real than the actual mountain. *Jeon Woo-chi.*

Jeon Woo-chi employed sophisticated computer-generated graphics. The film unpacks the potential of the virtual landscape — foreshadowed by Im Kwon-Taek as an essential component of the postmodern game — through its deployment of the traditional landscape painting as the magic portal through which Woo-chi moves between reality and fantasy, and between past, present, and future.

Thus, the fantastic celebration yearned for in a "killer party" — "let us play" (놀아보세 *nolabose*) — the crucial subversive trope in the folk literary and art tradition in Korea, is appropriated as both an admission and a denial that there is an inner self that gives us room to seek justice against the corrupt system.[34]

Distasteful as the idea may be, governments are going to continue to dump waste into natural environments and throw out traditional culture, resulting in terrible monsters and suicidal creatures like Yu-bong. In *Sopyonje*, melancholia and the alienated man's impotent resistance against the tide of Westernization produce tear-jerking melodrama; for he lacks the martial arts power to actually move between fantasy and reality, Yu-bong is only remembered after his death by his son. In *The Host*, humans are not the only ones being threatened. The viewer feels horror because nature, which had fascinated Bong Joon-ho's modernist predecessors, is also endangered.[35] In between these two box office hits lies Sang-gwon's commentary on his encounter with the naked mountain in *The Power of Kangwon Province*, again serving as both a warning of the impending destruction of the mountains and a frightening example of an antihero's impotent rage against the inevitable: the loss of nature and, subsequently, his or her own interiority. He or she has consented to the disintegration of nature but has come to feel that the price for this may have been too high. In *Sopyonje*, which mourns the disappearance of pristine landscape, the absence of the crowd is crucial, for the itinerant musicians' perfection of their art can occur only when they become one with nature. The absence of the crowd in *The Power of Kangwon Province*, on the other hand, projects something uncanny and abhorrent about the very nature of both barren landscapes and their potential destruction. Consequently, a postmodern text such as *The Host* recognizes that no one is left to spare even a glance at nature unless a monster is threatening to devour every one of us. By recognizing this, however, Bong Joon-ho's film reaffirms the irony of entertainment cinema: although the monster and the virus have been vanquished by the film's end, the monster's potential for reproduction and thus the possibility of the virus's recurrence are never properly addressed. Environmental disasters, focusing on a single incident of formaldehyde spillage and the defeat of the monster, are there to be both acknowledged and denied, raising the question: will the earth be saved by slaying the half-fish, half-dinosaur? And will Korea be saved by its magic ride through the landscape painting?

Spring of Korean Peninsula and *Epitaph*

Toward the end of *Spring of Korean Peninsula* (*Pando ŭi pom*, 1941), Young-il (played by Kim Il-hae), a Korean music producer who has been charged with embezzling company funds to finance a movie adaptation of a national folk tale, falls ill. The characteristics that made this film so ground-breaking in its day can be found in several elements. First, Young-il's crime is immediately forgiven by the audience and the characters around him, since it had been committed to serve a cause above and beyond his self-interest. Second, the reason Young-il has stolen one thousand won (today's equivalent of ten thousand US dollars) is to cinematically restage *Ch'unh-yangjŏn*, perhaps Korea's best-known traditional tale, in a version that—as far as can be ascertained from the "film within the film," remains faithful to the original, subversive p'ansori (traditional peasant opera).[1] Last, and perhaps most important, Young-il, the film's protagonist, is a pale-faced, gaunt fellow whose slow and often lifeless Korean is the result of his ill-ness.[2] Such characteristics are surprising given that the film was produced three years after the war with China forced the Japanese government to accept Korean "volunteers" in 1938.[3] Because of the intensification of the war, on January 1, 1940, the office of the Japanese governor general of Korea issued the Chosun Film Decree, which effectively placed the Korean film industry under its complete political control. Within three years, the Chosun Film Production Corporation, which incorporated all other pro-duction companies, was launched. In other words, *Spring of Korean Penin-sula*, which highlights decadent and sick Koreans defending its national folk tale *Ch'unhyangjŏn*, was made during the period of all-out war that had little room for films other than blatant propaganda efforts.

Sick and hospitalized, Young-il needs the constant care of a nurtur-ing woman; he's been eviscerated of his independent manhood. Young-il's tuberculosis-riddled body, as represented in a film made in 1941, is an amalgamation of several contradictory discourses that concern the colo-nized male body: the practical necessity of mobilizing Korean men into the Japanese war effort and therefore into the masculine corporate body; the

16 In *Spring*, Young-il, afflicted with tuberculosis, is in need of a nurturing woman's care.

popular image of Korean masculinity in the literary and cinematic canon of colonial Korea (1910–45), which swung wildly from muscular mad men to feeble, bedridden men; and, perhaps most significant, the heterogeneous linguistic space of the colony, in which colonized subjects spoke both Japanese and Korean, and names themselves were no longer markers of nationality or ethnicity.

In terms of the first discourse, *Spring*, which was rediscovered in 2006 after many years in obscurity, stands out from other recently discovered propaganda films of its period that all insist upon healthy, masculine bodies. As proven by other Korean films from the period of all-out war— such as An Sŏk-yŏng's *Volunteer* (*Chiwŏnbyŏng*, 1941) and Pak Ki-ch'ae's *Straits of Chosun* (*Chosŏn haehyŏp*, 1943), which feature lengthy sequences of healthy male Korean protagonists enduring the rigors of military training—a sickly body adds no value to the war effort. Thus, *Spring* forces us to consider whether or not its foregrounding of a sickly, bedridden Korean body is able to articulate interests that undercut the insistence on healthy, corporate bodies demanded by the Japanese Empire's hegemonic ideologies.[4] Japan at the time had insisted that the maintenance and expansion of the empire depended on the cleanliness and healthy bodies of its colonized subjects.[5] In addition, Takashi Fujitani, who has studied propaganda films made between 1940 and 1945 about Koreans serving in the Japanese military, writes: "For [Korean] men, becoming Japanese and achieving adult manhood were mutually constitutive. In other words, in order for a Korean male to become Japanese, he had to achieve adult manhood."[6] This chapter argues that Young-il's sick body featured in *Spring* is subversive, as it potentially disrupts the discourses of "healthy body" and "adult manhood" demanded by Japan of its colonial subjects during the war.

Considering the second discourse, though Young-il's sickness is prominent in the narrative of *Spring*, it cannot be placed in the same category as the plethora of characters with disabilities (*pulguja*) that comprised the colonial period's most popular literary icons. The invisibility of the tubercle bacilli that afflicts Young-il departs from what Kyeong-Hee Choi has argued is Korean colonial literature's "trope of disability," metaphors of the colonized nation figured through the literary representation of mutes, blind people, and hunchbacks.[7] This literary imagining of physically disabled, filthy bodies, so pervasive in colonial literature, can be seen as one subversive maneuver of colonized Koreans who deliberately turn away from the hygienic obsessions of Japanese military doctors and the governor general.[8] But while blindness, muteness, and fractured spines are normally congenital conditions of physical deformation that frequently become sites of thinly veiled metaphors of colonial resistance, tuberculosis was often regarded as a degenerate symptom of modern Romantic intellectuals. What I am interested in exploring in this chapter is how the tuberculosis-ridden body of Young-il could be both hailed as an allegory of anticolonial struggle (for it resists the Japanese nationalist insistence of healthy bodies [*kokutai*] at a time of war) and condemned as a complicit, feeble, and demasculinized undertone (for no physical resistance can be tolerated at this point of the colonial era).

In terms of the third discourse, Korean is the primary language through which *Spring*'s characters communicate, though the sporadic use of Japanese is an accepted mode of exchanging pleasantries and jokes. In his reading of Shimazaki Toson's *Broken Commandments*, a novel that centers on *burakumin*—outcaste—characters, Michael Bourdaghs describes the dialogic process of reading sick bodies as "plural utterances."[9] What this chapter proposes is that the frail body of Young-il, which is both quarantined from and welcomed by others, redefines the boundaries between pure and impure, between healthy and infectious, and between a community and its exterior. In other words, *Spring of Korean Peninsula*, made during the height of *naisen ittai* (squashing of two nations—Korea and Japan—into one), proposes—unlike its colonial-era nationalist cinema predecessors, such as Na Un-gyu's *Arirang* (1926) or An Chong-hwa's *Crossroads of Youth* (*Chŏngch'un ŭi sipjaro*, 1934)—that there are no more pure Korean male bodies left to salvage the nationalist spirit. As I will show below, this demasculinized, colonized body overextends itself while protecting the national folk tale production (*Ch'unhyangjŏn*) and ends up itself needing care. After a long bout with tuberculosis, Young-il triumphantly returns for the crucial opening night gala of *Chunhyang*, staged as the climax of the film, before departing for Tokyo at Keijo Train Station at the film's end. But even this compromised ending falls short of striking a celebratory note. During this scene, Young-il does not seem to have fully recovered, and his friends, particularly Director Yi, seem worried as they bid him farewell.

Though some of the films discussed in this chapter were made prior to the hallyu period this book focuses on, it is worth noting that throughout the first decade of the 2000s, "colonial modernity" was not only a hot intellectual item, but also a subject of broad public interest. After the 1999 publication of Kim Chin-song's *Sŏul e ttansŭhol ŭl hŏhara* (Grant Dance Hall a Permit in Seoul), which was based on his research of popular culture and everyday life in colonial Korea, many books dealing with social life including dating and popular cultural consumption during that era—such as Kwŏn Podŭrae's *Yŏnae ŭi sidae: 1920-yŏndae ch'oban ŭi munhwa wa yuhaeng* (Age of Dating: Culture and Trends of the Early 1920s) and Chon Pong-gwan's *Kyŏngsŏng kidam: kŭndae Chosŏn ŭl twihŭndŭn sarin sakŏn kwa sŭk'aendŭl* (Horror Stories of Keijo: Murders and Scandals That Shook Modern Korea)—became hot items in bookstores and made study of colonial era less didactic and essential nationalist. Recovered films from the colonial period long considered lost also helped increase modern Koreans' exposure to the visual popular culture of the era. *Crossroads of Youth*, for instance, miraculously turned up in one of the old warehouses of a theater projectionist in Seoul in 2007. This was originally a full-length feature consisting of nine reels of film; seven, all in pristine condition, were recovered. Since neither a script nor a recorded *pyŏnsa* (*benshi*) to accompany this silent film were to be found, the Korean Film Archive commissioned young filmmakers to update the film for modern viewers, with a small orchestra and a live *pyŏnsa*.[10] Also, the retrospective screenings of some of these newly rediscovered films—for instance, *Spring of Korean Peninsula* at the Pusan International Film Festival—helped make postcolonial engagement with colonial-era films an exciting reality, as Pak Hyŏn-hŭi notes in her study on two Korean actresses of the colonial era, Kim Sin-jae and Mun Ye-bong.[11]

In response to popular demand for stories and historical accounts set during the colonial period, the South Korean film industry spewed out several high-profile films. One of these is Yun Chong-ch'an's *Blue Swallow* (*Ch'ŏngyŏn*, 2005), a biopic drama about the first Korean woman aviator, Pak Kyŏng-won, who was one of the heroes of Korea when it was a Japanese colony. Though this expensive venture failed to make a profit for the industry, several more notable films that exploited the colonial setting followed. One was Jeong Ji-woo's big-budget *Modern Boy* (2008), a spy drama about a young Korean libertine who works in the urban planning section at the Japanese General Government Building (Chosun ch'ongdokpu kŏnmul). This apolitical modern boy's romance with a *Moulin Rouge*–style dancer turns out to be a dangerous affair when the dancer is revealed to be a Korean independence fighter. Also released in 2008 were *Radio Days* (directed by Ha Ki-ho), a comedy about a radio drama producer set in the 1930s, and *Once Upon a Time* (directed by Jeong Yong-gi), an action comedy thriller set during August 12–15, 1945, several days before Emperor Hirohito announced Japan's surrender, in which two of Korea's best swindlers crash the Japanese colonial governor's farewell ball in order to secure the biggest diamond in Korea. Perhaps the most prominent colonial-era film to be released during this decade was Kim Jee-woon's *The Good, the Bad, the Weird* (*Choŭn nom, nappŭn nom, isanghan nom*, 2008). As discussed above, this is a Manchurian Western set during the colonial period that broke the record for the most expensive Korean movie ($20 million) and was 2008's highest grossing film in Korea.

This chapter proposes to introduce three ways in which impaired Korean colonial-era bodies have been used: first, during the 1920s and 1930s, as unambiguous colonial allegory (in Na Un-gyu's *Arirang*); second, during the late colonial period, as decadence that resists militarization through the figure of deteriorating bodies contaminated by consumption (*Spring of Korean Peninsula*); and third, as genre film tropes (for example, one-armed gunmen in Manchurian Westerns or abject, animal-like female ghosts in horror films) in contemporary Korean films. For this reason, I pay attention to postcolonial horror films such as Kwon Cheol-hwi's *The Public Cemetery of Wolha* (*Wolha ŭi kongdong myoji*, 1967) and Jeong Beom-sik and Jeong Sik's *Epitaph* (*Kidam*, 2007), and examine how they redeploy these figurations of national *ressentiment* as haunting images and abject sick bodies that constitute a shock for contemporary viewers, whose rampant collective amnesia is a symptom of late capitalism.[12] *Epitaph*, which will be discussed below, is a horror film set during the colonial period that has been an essential part of the recent explosion of colonial-era films. Set quite deliberately in February 1942, just two months after Japan's attack on Pearl Harbor, *Epitaph* takes place for the most part at a modern hospital in Keijo (the Japanese name for Seoul in the colonial period) that houses a morgue, a research laboratory, and a learning space for medical students and interns. With its depiction of various kinds of contact between the dead and the living and between the sick and the healthy, *Epitaph* follows a trend in Korean popular culture: that of thinking virtually about Korea's colonial past, a feat that encompasses the twin impulses of modernism and the cultural appropriation of history by mass media.[13] As I will explain below, schizophrenia, a modern disease, lies at the heart of the mysteries of *Epitaph*, a genre film that exploits the haunting truth of mass collaboration with the Japanese on the part of Koreans during the war.

The Triangulated Archetype, *Arirang*, and *Crossroads of Youth*

Unlike railroads, buildings, and human casualties, cinema from the colonial period—though essential to colonial rule and its development throughout the first half of the twentieth century—has been largely forgotten in Korea. That is mostly because no prints from that era were known to have survived—until former Communist nations opened their film archives to South Korean film scholars. Since 2004, several feature-length Korean films from the late 1930s and the early 1940s have been found at the China Film Archives, in Beijing, and Gosfilmofond, in Moscow. *Angels on the Streets* (*Chip opnŭn ch'ŏnsa*, 1941) and *Volunteer* (*Chiwŏnbyŏng*, 1941), Korean-language talkies that had been believed to have been lost, were the first to be discovered in the China Film Archives. Several more titles were found at the same archive in 2006, including *Sweet Dream* (*Mimong*, 1936) and *Spring of Korean Peninsula* (1941). Along with explicit war propaganda films from 1943–45) found in Russia, these titles constitute an expanding catalogue of what So-young Kim has described as Korea's "hollow archive."[14] Because these films quickly became known as the oldest extant Korean films, and because they were the first films to feature Korean-language dialogue, they have garnered enthusiastic response from many scholars in Korea and Japan who work on questions of nationalism, national identity, war, literature, and cinema from 1937 to 1945.

During this period, Japan was fighting an all-out war against China and the other Allies. As a result, the Japanese realized they had to devise a more effective way of managing their Korean colonial subjects. That led to a policy of assimilation called *naisen ittai* (Japan and Korea collapsed into one body). Michael Baskett writes: "Imperial Japan understood the ideological value of modern technology and quickly took steps towards controlling its own imperial image."[15] Concurring with Korean film historians such as Yi Yŏng-il, Baskett continues: "Japanese films legitimized Japanese imperial expansionism, sometimes even before the fact; newsreels such as *The Korean Crown Prince at Oiso Beach* (*Oiso kaqigan no kankoku kotaishi*, 1908) or travelogues like *A Trip around Korea* (*Kankoku isshu*, 1908) naturalized the presence of Korean royalty traveling to Japan or future Japanese Resident-General Ito Hirobumi's tour of Korea a full two years before Japanese annexation of Korea."[16] Throughout its period of operation, the Korean colonial government sought to create a pro-Japanese film culture through its Korean Colonial Cinema Unit (Chosen sotokufu kinema). Despite Japan's efforts, between the 1910s and the 1930s, film theaters in Seoul had been sites of fierce contestation where popular forms of nationalism often ran into trouble with the Japanese colonial government.[17] The film industry was finally consolidated into one company in 1941, after the war had entered its final stages, and censorship of all film production and distribution began to be strictly enforced, resulting in blatantly pro-Japanese films.

The most popular movie icon of the early colonial period was the star actor and director Na Un-gyu, who undeniably represented Korea's rebellious underdog spirit to Korean workers and peasants. Na cinematically represented the colonial subject's unpredictability, wrath, and madness, conjoining what Kyeong-Hee Choi has called the "impaired body as colonial trope" in colonial-era Korean literature and anticolonial unrest among Koreans.[18] Na Un-gyu not only directed Na Tohyang's celebrated short story "Samnyong the Mute" (1925)—starring in the title role as an abject

17 In one of the few stills that have survived from *Arirang*, Na Un-gyu raises his sickle against the collaborator.

body that transforms itself into a violently resistant one by the end of the film—but he was also the driving force behind *Arirang* (1926), perhaps the most conspicuous example of Korean nationalist cinema.

Arirang's plot involves a philosophy student, Yŏng-jin, who goes mad in the middle of his studies. Every effort is made to treat him, but to no avail. Only when his sister, Yŏng-hŭi, is on the verge of being raped by Ki-ho—a *marum*, the Korean supervisor of a tenant farm, who bows and scrapes before the Japanese landlord—does Yŏng-jin regain his senses. He grabs a sickle to strike the collaborator. Yet his reawakening—not unlike Korea's Enlightenment project, which was initiated only after the country had been gobbled up by Japan's colonial machine—takes place too late: he has already murdered the collaborator. Yŏng-jin is taken away by the authorities. He passes over the Arirang hill, beyond the point of no return. Na was only twenty-four when he directed *Arirang*, which went on to become an overwhelming colonial-era favorite that spawned no less than two sequels before Na died of tuberculosis in 1937, two months shy of his thirty-fifth birthday.

The film presents the archetypal formula of the colonial relationship between the colonized male (A), who despite insanity or other agony, re-

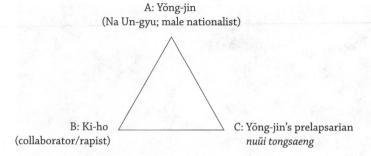

A: Yŏng-jin
(Na Un-gyu; male nationalist)

B: Ki-ho
(collaborator/rapist)

C: Yŏng-jin's prelapsarian
nuŭi tongsaeng

18   Graph of Na Un-gyu's *Arirang*.

gains his consciousness and recovers his masculinity toward the end of the film when he physically overwhelms his lecherous opponent (B), who has either raped or has attempted to rape the *nuŭi tongsaeng* (younger sister) from home (C) (see fig. 18).

Though no print of *Arirang* survives, judging from its script and pyŏnsa recordings, as well as the example of *Crossroads of Youth*—the oldest Korean film and the only silent-era film to have survived to the present—we can see that the most popular form of colonized masculinity from that period is one steeped in health and deeply rooted in rural, physical labor. It is a kind of masculinity capable of inciting protest against loan sharks and against modern male libertines. In *Crossroads of Youth*, Yŏng-bok, the movie's main protagonist, is a farmer who lives in rural Korea. He migrates to Seoul and works as a porter at a train station, but he suffers from poverty and others' condescension. When he finds out that both his sister and a female friend from home have been taken advantage of by his landlord, a loan shark, he takes revenge with his fists. In a dramatic, climactic scene, the loan shark suffers several blows from the masculinist hero, Yŏng-bok; each blow underscores the fury and frustration of a nation whose sovereignty has been usurped. Only violence can mend a spirit whose voice has been silenced and whose body has been castrated.

By resorting to violence, Yŏng-bok repeats the archetypal formula described above (see fig. 20) This triangle shows the relationship of the remasculinized colonial subject of the peasant class (A) who has risen to power to protect prelapsarian Korea, represented by the beautiful, yet endangered young woman (C), and to combat the degenerate figure of the

19 *The Crossroads of Youth*'s Yŏng-bok with his younger sister. Photo by Kyung Hung Kim.

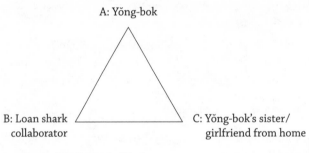

A: Yŏng-bok

B: Loan shark / collaborator

C: Yŏng-bok's sister/ girlfriend from home

20 Graph of *The Crossroads of Youth*.

corrupt official or the declined *yangban* genealogy (also of Korean origin) (B) who threatens what is metaphorically equivalent to the natural pristine body of Korea.

Spring of the Korean Peninsula: Give the Man a Sickle and Let's See What He Does

Spring of the Korean Peninsula, released several years later, proffers a radically altered version of colonized masculinity. Its central character, Young-il, is an executive at a record company; his passions are books and music. When he meets a friend who studies in Tokyo, he asks: "Would you be able to send a few good books that you find there?" His scrawny physique suggests that he would not be capable of any labor other than intellectual. He wears Western attire and is played by Kim Hae-il, an actor known at the time for his delicate looks and for never being photographed without wearing a soft felt hat, tie, and jacket. There is an almost feminine delicacy of Young-il's emasculated, intellectual body, and at one point even his appliance of makeup on the lead actress Jung-hee seems natural. Young-il's emasculated subject threatens his position as the virile colonized man on the top of the archetypal triangle who must exploit by every means necessary in order to protect the woman from the lecherous figure of the collaborator. The trouble brewing in the film is this: give Young-il a sickle, and he wouldn't know what to do with it. Kim Hae-il had been trained in a Japanese film studio in Tokyo. An accomplished actor, he had at least seven years of experience acting in Japanese movies.[19] Needless to say, he spoke Japanese without an accent—his soft-spoken delivery of lines moves fluidly between Korean and Japanese. Kim was in many ways the perfect choice for the role of Young-il—a character with a knack for literature and music, who eventually falls sick and ends up needing the constant care of others.

From the opening of the film, it is clear that *Spring of Korean Peninsula* is a masterfully crafted film. The audience is led at first to believe that they are watching a version of the national folk tale *Chunhyang*, only to realize a minute later, as the camera pulls out to reveal the crew and the camera shooting the scene in the film, that the story will be about people making *Chunhyang*. The real principal actors are the ones behind the screen, not the ones on the screen. Such self-reflexivity, which blurs the boundary between art and the process of making art, and between fiction and reality, is of course one of the devices used in modernist creative expression. Like Stanley Donen's American classic *Singin' in the Rain* (1952), *Spring of Korean Peninsula* demonstrates how difficult it is to make a work of art—in this case, a film version of a classic Korean folk tale.

As it turns out, Yi Pyŏng-il (1910–78), the director of the film—like Young-il, its protagonist—had also been a record company executive before changing to a career in film. One of the main narrative thrusts of the film is, of course, the completion of a talkie, *Chunhyang*, and the technical and financial difficulties that this entails. *Chunhyang* (1935) was in fact the first-ever Korean talkie to become an instant success, catapulting the actress Mun Ye-bong into stardom. Though another star of the era, Kim So-yŏng, replaced Mun Ye-bong in *Spring* and plays Jung-hee, the actress who is given the lead role in *Spring*'s version of *Chunhyang*, all of the situations that surround the making of the movie within the movie remind the viewers of actual events that had happened six years earlier.

Despite various difficulties, the crew is able to complete production on the movie within the movie because of the sacrifices made by Young-il, who had made an unauthorized decision to spend company funds, which he managed under the miserly Mr. Han. It is important to note that Young-il first thought that he could repay the company funds he misappropriated, since he had just won a literary prize from a newspaper. But because Korean-language newspapers at that time were forced to close—a fact not made explicit in the film due to censorship—the prize money never arrives. This places Young-il under extreme duress. Meanwhile, Mr. Han, who is both Young-il's boss at the record company and an investor in *Chunhyang*, is not really interested in helping Young-il or in completing the film; he's only interested in seducing Young-il's surrogate *nuŭi tongsaeng* (younger sister) Jung-hee, who has replaced Anna—a bargirl in *Spring* who plays an actress playing a bargirl, in the movie within the movie—as the lead character Chunhyang. Anna, unable to afford to work in the production of *Ch'unhyangjŏn* with neither food nor pay, had run away from the company and returned to her old job as a bargirl. Jung-hee might have replaced Anna in the title role of Chunhyang, but Anna is the one who ultimately replaces Jung-hee as Young-il's girlfriend. This is because Anna voluntarily uses her body to help Young-il make bail. When Jung-hee, who refuses Mr. Han's advances, is unable to save Young-il from incarceration, Anna goes to the police station to make a special plea to the police and to provide the bail money needed to free Young-il—money she had to earn by sleeping with other men. In this sequence, Japanese policemen display a humane face by accepting her plea for Young-il's release. Anna is thus able to become (albeit temporarily) Young-il's girlfriend while Jung-hee, who refuses to sleep with other men, loses her place as Young-il's primary romantic interest. By nursing Young-il without any trace of her early delinquency, Anna later is able to complete her redemption.

Yi Pyŏng-il, *Spring*'s director, was an accomplished filmmaker, who was trained in the Japanese Nikkatsu Studio system under Yutaka Abe.[20] His use of a modern jazz score; his daring selection of high-angle shots; the fluid transition between shots, which clearly displays familiarity with classical film language; the film's economical and lyrical use of tracking shots; its elegant and crisp lighting;, and the bold and felicitous interspersing of cinéma vérité shots throughout the film all point to why *Spring of Korean*

21 In *Spring of the Korean Peninsula*, Jung-hee, in hanbok, refuses the sexual advances of
Mr. Han, the capitalist.

Peninsula is one of the greatest achievements in cinema—not only among Korean films, but among all films made during that period. However, unlike earlier films such as *Arirang*—which to this day stirs debates about whether or not it is a Korean film (the producer and cinematographer, among other key participants, were Japanese)[21]—*Spring* was definitely Korean. It was produced by a Korean company, the Myŏng-bo Film Company, and its main credits include no Japanese names.

In *Spring*, Japanese are also not given prominent speaking roles beyond those of colonial government officials at penitentiaries and police stations. In *Spring*, everyone speaks Korean except for Anna, the actress who quits her role as Chunhyang and returns to her work at a bar, and Mr. Han, probably the most despicable character in the film. (He refuses to grant financial support to the starving film crew, then proceeds to turn Young-il over to the law for embezzling company funds.) It is perhaps not coincidental that Anna and Mr. Han, the two people most responsible for threatening the completion of the production of *Chunhyang*, speak only in Japanese. But it is surprising that such an indelible linguistic mark of difference could be inscribed onto a film that was produced and released in 1941. (Nearly twenty years later, Stanley Kubrick's *Spartacus* [1960] would exploit the different accents of English and American actors to distinguish that film's evil Romans from the good slaves.) *Spring's* insistence that morally reprehensible characters (though Anna reforms at the end of the film by nursing Young-il) speak only in Japanese must not have been lost on audiences back then. Language becomes extremely important not only in distinguishing between good (Korean) and evil (Japanese), but it also helps to restore the subjectivity of Young-il, and by extension that of all Koreans at a time when they had begun to recognize that they were supposed to become modern subjects and even soldiers in service of the Japanese Empire, and that they were to learn to become Japanese.

It is important to note that the naisen ittai policy mandated not only the abandonment of the Korean language, but also the acquisition of the Japanese language. Learning Japanese and using it for the regimentation of the modern body were fundamental to the primacy of order, especially of fascist principles. One must understand, interpret, and redeploy language so as to adjust the movements of the body and its health, critical in maintaining both social and military order. The ubiquitous, pale face of Young-il in *Spring of Korean Peninsula*—made at the critical juncture in Korean history when Koreans were forced to abandon their own language and faced conscription into the Japanese army—is therefore a metaphor of pain that requires no interpretation. Young-il is unfit to serve. His transition between two languages (Korean and Japanese), between the two domains of art and commerce (as a producer of *Chunhyang*), and between two women (one pure and the other impure) is seemingly fluid, but as time progresses, it breaks him down.

Young-il's tuberculosis, acquired during his incarceration, is a direct result of having occupied an impossible position between his friend Lee, the director of *Ch'unhyangjŏn*—the movie within the movie—and the evil capitalist, Mr. Han, who speaks only Japanese, which denies any kind of mediation. Young-il's position is already fraught with impossibility; he can maintain neither a healthy mind nor a clean conscience. Like an independence fighter forced to commit an act of terror in order to achieve a higher goal, Young-il has no choice but to steal to save the film company and its production. (Koreans during this period, like Palestinians today, were stereotyped as loathed terrorists.) By overextending himself, he soon falls sick and also earns his place in prison.

His multinational identity, straddling both Japan and Korea, is delicately articulated, but at the end of the day, his reward for having achieved bilingual and binational subjecthood arrives in the form of tuberculosis, which undoes both his body and his faculty of language. Though no specific reason for his illness is ever clearly articulated, Young-il's pale face, thin body, chronic cough, fever, and lifestyle in the urban entertainment business all suggest that he is afflicted with consumption. Young-il's tuberculosis-infected body has had removed from it all traces of his bucolic and underdeveloped origins — signified by resistant masculine bodies in previous films by Na Un-gyu and others. As Susan Sontag claims in "Illness as Metaphor," tuberculosis was a "disease in the service of a romantic view"[22] and endowed the self with narcissistic self-pity and reliance on others. Also, while speeding up life, it "was thought to produce . . . exacerbated sexual desire."[23] Karatani Kojin has also described the tuberculosis-infected body as representing "gentility, delicacy, and sensitivity among snobs and social climbers."[24] Through Young-il's decadent, Romantic body, *Spring* demonstrates the central role that cinema played in both propagating and ruffling the hegemonic ideologies of Japanese and Korean nationalism. Tuberculosis, once contracted, cannot easily be treated; only long periods of nursing, clean air, and antibiotics can overcome it. The colonized body becomes severely frail and thin, requiring constant attention and the care of others. The sick colonized body becomes unfit to serve in the emperor's army, and it is also unable to raise a sickle against the colonizer and his sympathizers.

The idea of the pale, intellectual patient who conforms to the Romantic idealism of the 1920s and the 1930s had been fully exploited in the literature from that period that, as has been pointed out numerous times, attempted to overcome the horror of colonialism and the tumultuous chaos inflicted on Korea by modernization and war. For instance, the poetry of Yi Sang (1910–37) sardonically depicted the progressive wasting of his own body. In the process, the progression of illness became a sort of index of his superior sensibility as a writer, rather than an account of the kind of debased physical deformation typically depicted in literature featuring disabled subjects. Yi Sang died from tuberculosis at the age of twenty-seven, and most of his stories and poems—including his seminal *Wings* (*Nalgae*) —depict protagonists with consumption. After Yi's death in 1937, however, the modernist and decadent literature in Korea was declared dead and, by the late 1930s, the number of characters suffering from tuberculosis became much smaller.

The last literary instance of tuberculosis, as far as I can tell, is in Ch'ae Man-shik's "My Innocent Uncle" ("Ch'isuk," 1938). One of Korea's finest literary satirists, Ch'ae writes in this short story about a relationship between a young, opportunistic Korean narrator whose dream is to marry a Japanese woman and collaborate with the colonizers for his own economic gain, and his socialist uncle, who has been in and out of jail and is, from the narrator's perspective, wasting his time. The story opens with this statement by the narrator: "My uncle? You mean that fine gentleman who married my father's cousin, the man they put in jail when he was younger on account of that darned socialism or scotchalism, or whatever you call it, the one who's laid up with tuberculosis?"[25] Such depictions were unusual in the late 1930s and disappear completely in the early 1940s. At that point, the standard depiction of Koreans becomes something like the one in *Straits of Chosun* (1943), which begins when a rogue Korean son, returned home after the death of his brother, seeks his own redemption by joining the army. Though his family members continue to discuss his past, the son has turned his life around. The film cautiously sidesteps the issue of his past; he is now healthy and mentally and physically prepared to face the enemy on the Pacific front. (The decadent past of the son is framed outside the film's temporal narrative arc, denying the audience the pleasures of that past.)

The sick protagonist of *Spring of Korean Peninsula*, on the other hand, foregrounds the notion of a body that can no longer engage in the nationalist fantasy of the previous decade—in which provincial, masculine bodies were mobilized to wreak revenge against miserly capitalists who charged high interest rates and raped younger sisters. Young-il, bedridden and too feeble even to raise his voice against the Japanese-speaking capitalist, Mr. Han, would be incapable of raising a pencil, let alone a sickle. The patriots of the late 1930s and early 1940s have now settled in the city. They read books, have acquired a binational identity, and plot cultural enlightenment projects through the staging of a subversive folk tale in the indigenous language. But because of his sickness, Young-il must relegate his role as the primary defender (A) of the prelapsarian Korea (C) from the evil advances made by the collaborator (B; see fig. 22), and ironically Anna becomes the primary caretaker of the national spirit that is struggling against the tide of naisen ittai. In this revised form of the triangle, the emasculated Young-il settles into the position normally occupied by the woman (see fig. 23).

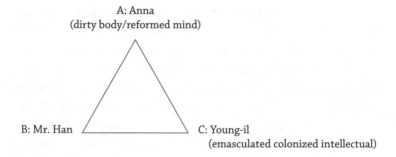

A: Young-il
(sick body/pure mind)

B: Mr. Han
(corrupt capitalist)

C: Jung-hee
(nuŭi tongsaeng)

22　Graph of *Spring of the Korean Peninsula*.

A: Anna
(dirty body/reformed mind)

B: Mr. Han

C: Young-il
(emasculated colonized intellectual)

23　Revised graph of *Spring of the Korean Peninsula*.

Despite the success of *Chunhyang*, Young-il has become complicit in order to conform to the rule of the day, naisen ittai. Once he regains his health, Young-il must depart for Japan to serve as a subject of the emperor, instead of going back to jail or to Manchuria, the only two havens for a nationalist at that time of war. Young-il's body is too weak for him to either mount an organized charge against his opponent, Mr. Han, or sever himself completely from the campaign for *kokutai*. During the last segment of the film, Mr. Han conveniently disappears from the narrative. He has been replaced by the "good capitalist," who toward the end of the film delivers an impassioned speech endorsing naisen ittai and the role of Korea's filmmakers in upholding its values. Under these confusing circumstances—in which neither capitalists, police, or women can any longer retain either a purely virtuous or a solely evil marker, and that complement the time's hybrid half-Korea, half-Japan policy—the salvation of the colonized native's soul can be met only halfway. Using his intellectual faculties, Young-il has successfully saved the national folk tale, but his frail body ultimately cannot guard either a woman or the nation.

Postcolonial Films: The Public Cemetery of Wolha and Epitaph

As noted in the previous chapter, the Korean film industry has traditionally been weak in the area of fantasy genres, including science fiction, musicals, animation, and fantasy adventure. Not only have Korean filmmakers lacked the astronomical budgets required to realize the images and sounds of fantasy in this digitized age of special effects, but also the national literary roots from which such fantasy genres might grow have for the most part been neglected. Blockbuster action-comedy-melodrama adaptations of classic Chosun-era tales—like *Jeon Woo-chi: The Taoist Wizard* and *The Servant (Pangjajŏn)*—which are subjects of chapter 8, did not appear until the latter part of the first decade of the twenty-first century. However, the one genre that has successfully integrated many of the formulaic, box-office conventions required for the establishment of a unique Korean film aesthetic is horror. Throughout Korean film history, horror films have occupied a central place in the popular discourse. Kim Ki-young's classic *The Housemaid (Hanyo*, 1960) features a housemaid-cum-vamp who plots revenge against her employers for having violated her body and forcing her to abort her unborn child.[26] *The Public Cemetery of Wolha* (1967) became one of the first Korean horror films to reach mainstream audiences, and it spawned many copycat films and sequels during the latter days of the golden age of Korean cinema (1955–72). During the New Korean Cinema period, from the late 1990s to the early 2000s, the *Yŏgo koedam* (*Girl's High School Horror Story*) series, set at a girls' high school, became stock horror blockbusters. The original 1998 film (*Whispering Corridors*) has thus far spawned four sequels—*Memento Mori* (1999), *Wishing Stairs* (*Yŏu koedam*, 2003), *Voice* (*Moksori*, 2005), and *A Bloody Pledge* (*Tongban chasal*, 2009)—all of which have remained in the public subconscious, having introduced an entire generation of television and movie stars including Ch'oe Kang-hŭi, Kong Hyo-jin, Pak Chin-hŭi, Kim Min-sŏn, Pak Han-byŏl, and Kim Ok-bin.

As the Korean literary critic Paek Mun-im has argued in her discussion of *The Public Cemetery of Wolha*, Korean female ghosts have long been intimately tied to both recollection and amnesia regarding Korea's colonial past.[27] The fear and anxiety associated with the trauma and complicity ex-

24.1 Wolhyang, once a courtesan . . .

24.2 . . . has no choice but to return as a ghost. *The Public Cemetery of Wolha.*

perienced during the colonial period have enabled Korean horror films to show them dramatically with a poised and almost uncanny reality. Though there is no direct relationship between Na Un-gyu's *Arirang* and *The Public Cemetery of Wolha*, which was made forty years later, an attentive viewer can immediately discern similarities between the two. In *Wolha*, set during the later colonial period, a female ghost, Wolhyang, haunts a rural village, defending innocent victims from the greedy hands of crooks such as the maid whose evil doctor prescribes poisonous medicine for her. Unjustly treated when alive, Wolhyang refuses to stay put in the cemetery. When the origins of Wolhyang's resentment are finally revealed, we realize that in many ways, she is the shadow image of the imperiled nuŭi tongsaeng (younger sister) in a white hanbok, who is almost always threatened with rape by collaborator capitalists in films from the colonial period. Examples of nuŭi tongsaeng just from the films covered in this chapter are Yŏng-

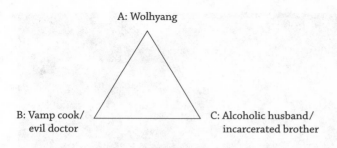

A: Wolhyang

B: Vamp cook/
   evil doctor

C: Alcoholic husband/
   incarcerated brother

25   Graph of *The Public Cemetery of Wolha*.

hŭi from Na Un-gyu's *Arirang*, whose narrow escape from rape prompts her older brother, Yŏng-jin, to retaliate with a sickle; Yŏng-bok's sister in *Crossroads of Youth*, who is seduced by a playboy loan shark with a Kaiser mustache; and Jung-hee in *Spring of Korean Peninsula*, who resists the advances of Mr. Han, an evil capitalist who threatens to halt the production of *Chunhyang* and to prosecute her brother's friend Young-il for embezzling his money. Unlike these three films from the colonial period, in which the women are either saved by outraged local men (*Arirang* and *Crossroads of Youth*) or narrowly escape the advances of a male predator (*Spring*), *Wolha* is told from the perspective of an imperiled and resentful woman. In other words, she is not confined to the role of fantasy object for a male hero and instead emerges as a subject at the top of the triangle, which traditionally has been occupied by the rejuvenated nationalist (see fig. 25).

Instead, and not unlike the reality of Korea's rape and ravaging by foreign colonizers, the nuŭi tongsaeng—who will return later to haunt the countryside village—has had to give up her body in order to save her would-be husband from jail. She saves her husband from dying in prison by becoming a kisaeng (courtesan) and adapting a new name, Wolhyang, but she is still prevented from achieving happiness: first, she has to live with the stigma of having sold her body for money; second, her older brother, Chun-sik, an impulsive student activist not unlike earlier male heroes, is serving a life sentence in a Japanese prison; and third, Hansu, her husband, for whom she has traded away her chastity, turns out to be a typically effeminate colonized man who spends all his time drinking and even takes another wife, a vamp-like seductress who plots to eliminate Wolhyang. With no one left to protect her, she has no choice but to die and then return only as a ghost.

In probing 2007's *Epitaph*, a horror film that takes place almost entirely in a hospital, I will focus on how the return of the repressed is also marked by both mental and physical sickness. By doing so, I hope to come to a better understanding of how the body in colonial and postcolonial cinema becomes an essential terrain for the cultural contestation of both Korea's nationhood and identity formation. In colonial-era films such as *Arirang* and *Crossroads of Youth*, the rural-based male hero is shown as possessing a sick mind in a healthy body, and in the self-reflexive modernist film *Spring*, the reverse (a sick body with a healthy mind) is presented. But, in postcolonial films, no one—not even doctors—is spared from being both mentally and physically sick.

Epitaph is set in Keijo around 1942, in a modern hospital run by a Japanese female director. A group of young, bright Korean doctors based there are engaged in medical experiments, as well as in treating patients and performing autopsies on dead bodies. The number of dead bodies is on the rise. In addition to suicides and car accidents, both common forms of death at the time, it appears that a serial killer eager to murder Japanese and Korean soldiers is on the loose. "Why did the killer mutilate the soldier's body and leave the document he was carrying?" asks Lieutenant Akiyama of the Japanese Imperial Army, who has assumed control of the local police function. The presence of the document leads him to rule out Korean terrorists or freedom fighters as suspects. Instead of analyzing viruses and germs in order to find cures for diseases, the medical students and doctors spend most of their time in morgues identifying dead bodies and helping with the military investigation of the elusive serial killer.

Structured with a Robert Altman-like three-part, interwoven part, the film features three parallel stories. In the first, Chin-gu, a young intern, is ordered by his hospital director to work the night shift at the basement morgue for one week. That very night, a young female teenager's body, found underneath a frozen pond, is brought in. Chin-gu ends up befriending the dead woman, whose face is as pale as snow. The girl, whose identity remains mysterious, had apparently committed suicide because her parents had not approved of her boyfriend. The ring placed on the girl's ring finger slips off, only to be picked up by Chin-gu. Unable to put the ring back on the girl's finger, Chin-gu keeps it and, out of curiosity, puts it on. Stranger things happen deeper into the night. The female hospital director, who is almost always dressed in a kimono, pays Chin-gu a visit and, without explanation, asks him the date and time of his birth. Chin-gu hears the sound of a wooden gong, a woman's cry, and Buddhist chants from the corridor. He realizes that a Buddhist monk is attending a wake with his hospital director.

During his shift, Chin-gu has a nightmare. He is sucked into the crematory hole by the ghost of the dead girl and, in the subsequent fantasy montage sequence, an occult wedding is performed between the dead Japanese girl and the live Korean boy with a promising career in the profession of curing others. In this dream—as in the landmark dream sequence in Mizoguchi Kenji's *Ugetsu monogatari* (1953), to which the directors are paying homage—seasons endlessly change in the background while the couple, the living boy and the dead girl, produce a family together and live happily ever after. We are later told that unbeknownst to Chin-gu, the Buddhist monk and the hospital director had not been performing a preburial ceremony for the dead, but rather a wedding between the dead girl, who is revealed to be none other than the director's daughter, Aoyi, and Chin-gu, the boy the director had intended her daughter to marry. In other words, Chin-gu is possessed by the spirit of a dead girl from Japan who committed suicide in the colony of Korea, and as a result he will never be able to consummate a meaningful romantic relationship with another woman. When he is found dead of natural causes thirty-seven years later, in 1979—which also happens to be the year Park Chung Hee (known as Lieutenant Takaki Masao in the Kwantung Army during the war) is shot to death—we realize that all of his marriages were short-lived.[28]

In the colonial-era Korean hospital, doctors trade their places with their patients as they, in actuality, are the ones who need psychiatric help and intervention of the law. It turns out that of the four Korean doctors featured in *Epitaph*, Chin-gu is the only one whose life is spared. In the second story in the film, Dong-gyu, the most accomplished doctor working at the hospital but a person with disabilities, is assigned to treat a ten-year-old Korean girl named Asako, who has survived a freak car accident. Asako suffers from aphasia resulting from post-traumatic shock. Not only were both her Korean mother and her Japanese stepfather killed in the accident she has just survived, but Asako was also directly responsible for the accident: she had been hysterically protesting her mother's marriage to the Japanese businessman when the accident occurred (see fig. 26).

Asako's faculty for language evaporates after the accident. As Kyeong-Hee Choi argues: "For the colonized, the ability to speak is not inherently better than the inability to speak. Under a regime of censorship, speech

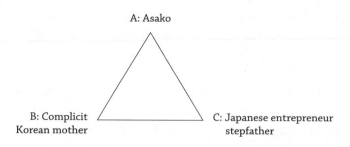

26 Graph of *Epitaph*.

is shaped by the lack of freedom to speak 'undesirable truths.'"[29] Asako's postcolonial inability to produce language, however, is different from the kind of speech impairment suffered by characters found in the colonial era's literature of disability. For instance, the muteness of Samnyong, the colonial-era icon described above, is represented as a congenital condition derived from Korea's backwardness. In contrast, Asako's aphasia is derived from her guilt at having spoken against her mother's complicity with Japanese capital.[30] Before the accident, she spoke too much; afterward, she has to remain silent for she has spoken an "undesirable truth." Indeed, the "ability to speak," Asako has learned, is no better than the "inability to speak." Asako cannot be cured even by Dong-gyu, the best doctor in the ward, and she falls into an even deeper abyss of madness and guilt before dying. Dong-gyu, having failed, is also hit by a car on his way home and later dies in the very hospital where he worked. This failure as a doctor brings out Dong-gyu's own secret. Right before Asako dies, Dong-gyu tells her that his disability was the direct result of a childhood accident; he had fallen into a well and been miraculously saved by his brother. Dong-gyu's life had been spared, but only because his brother had died while saving him. Like Asako, he has lived in guilt, and his disability, unlike Samnyong's congenital muteness, is a metonymy of his guilt for the death of his sacrificed brother. *Epitaph* insists that every Korean was not a victim of colonial domination and instead proposes that Koreans were capable of becoming complicit with the colonizers and joining the guilty party.

The theme of the guilt-ridden doctor surfaces again in *Epitaph*'s third story. Kim Dong-won (also addressed as Dr. Kaneda) and his wife Kim In-young are both elite brain surgeons in their thirties who were trained in Japan. They have returned to Seoul and are responsible for teaching medical students at the hospital. At one point, In-young, the beautiful wife, tells Dong-won: "You should be watching your tail. There are many smart *hubae* [junior associates] seeking a chance to take you over." Meanwhile, the serial murders have extended beyond soldiers. A young nurse is also found dead in the nearby road, right next to the mountain. Like the soldiers, she has been severely stabbed and mutilated. The morning after the murder, Dong-won finds his shirt smeared and blood still gushing from a sharp cut on his arm. It is the same kind of cut as one his wife had suffered when killing the nurse the night before. Dong-won/Kaneda calls the investigator, Lieutenant Akiyama, intending to turn himself in as the serial murderer. In a letter addressed to the lieutenant, Dong-won/Kaneda claims: "It may be hard for you to fathom this, but, two people reside in my wife's body, one who is the murderer and the one who isn't. I am the one responsible for the murder."

During the investigation, the lieutenant realizes that neither Dong-won nor Kaneda is alive, and therefore neither can be considered a suspect. Dong-won/Kaneda had been killed while performing surgery on a Japanese soldier who had been suffering from a brain tumor. Who, then, is behind all of the serial murders? Akiyama yells at In-young, who persists in believing that she is Dong-won. "There is no Kim Dong-won! He died over a year ago in Japan. He is only an illusion you have created in your head. You are Kim In-young!" he insists. In-young/Dong-won, dressed in kimono, is holding up a knife, ready to commit seppuku. Before the lieutenant or his subordinates can react, s/he lowers his/her arm and thrusts the knife deep inside his/her belly.

We have thus come to a full circle. Like tuberculosis, insanity is a kind of exile. *Ressentiment* is also still with us, but unlike in *The Public Cemetery of Wolha*, both the source and the target of revenge in *Epitaph* remain a riddle. Distinctions between man (Kim Dong-won) and woman (Kim In-young) and between Korean (Kim) and Japanese (Kaneda) have disappeared. This erasure quotes Hitchcock's classic case of schizophrenia in which Norman Bates (like In-young) in *Psycho* commits murders all the while believing that it is his mother (like Dong-won/Kaneda) who, jealous of him (In-young), is responsible. So the boundary between the colonizer perpetrator (serial killer) and the colonized victim (innocent)[31] is also eroded. After all, no one is free from guilt when colonial policies have successfully elicited both complicit collaboration and acquiescence.

The list of the guilty and the sick in *Epitaph* includes the hospital director and her doctors, as well as the hospital patients—including the little girl who had spoken out against her mother's marriage to a success- ful Japanese businessman. In an ironic twist, the only character spared from guilt and resentment, and who also exudes both physical and men- tal health, is Lieutenant Akiyama, whose ethnic identity is never clearly defined. Though not a main character, this Korean/Japanese army officer remains a dedicated professional whose mission is to find the killer and, consequently, to stop the spread of madness. At a time of war, however, this may be an unrealizable goal.

This harboring of resentment and subsequent plotting of revenge, one of the main themes of the colonial period, can no longer serve as a leitmotif once the line that separates colonizer and colonized—and, consequently, good and evil—ceases to exist. How can female ghosts like Wolhyang from *The Public Cemetery of Wolha* be resuscitated from her grave when there are no native vamps or opportunistic loan sharks left to avenge? *Epitaph* asks what can be considered good or evil for a Korean during the later stages of colonialism and assimilation—a period when a young widow might seek a comfortable life for herself and her child by marrying a successful Japa- nese businessman, and when a young, promising doctor might, without his consent, end up falling into a prearranged marriage with a girl from Japan.

The German novelist Theodor Fontane, who has been quoted many times by prominent literary critics such as Georg Lukács and Fredric Jameson, argues that "you can situate your novel in a period no more re- mote than that of the life experience of your own grandparents."[32] The zone of literary time, he claims, is negotiated between the author, who has to mediate between reality and fantasy, and the site of historicity that has already been constituted as a living experience for his or her grand- parents. Both films discussed here no doubt manage to open up uncanny spaces that are both familiar and unfamiliar: for example, the wooden fur- niture and art deco windows of early modern architecture, the double- buttoned white doctor's uniforms from the 1940s; the 78-rpm RCA record players with protruding, horn-shaped speakers; the round, horn-rimmed spectacles; and the neoclassical buildings reminiscent of Keijo's colonial governor's building, which was demolished in 1995. These densely layered images are both colonial and postcolonial, like historical palimpsests and subterfuges. They make us shudder like a bad dream. Late capitalism and suburbanization (with the accompanying atomization of families) have successfully deleted the memories—and even the physical presence—of our grandparents from our collective consciousness. Memories of grandparents are sometimes frightening: they remind us of the irretrievable, of the irreversible fragility of life and time. A history of collaboration and complicity also denies us the possibility of clean conscience. We are left with only what stories are still left to tell.

THREE

Virtual Dictatorship

The President's Barber and *The President's Last Bang*

Early in Im Chan-sang's *The President's Barber* (*Hyojadong ibalsa*, 2004),[1] Sŏng Han-mo, whose barbershop is located in Hyoja-dong, the same district that holds the Blue House (the main executive administrative building where the president also lives), receives a call from the president's office.[2] Han-mo is about to become the president's personal barber, a new honor for him. Though the president's name is never mentioned, there is no doubt that the person depicted in this film—which covers the period from the late 1950s to 1979—is meant to be Park Chung Hee, the military dictator who ruled Korea from 1961 to 1979. Before meeting the president, Han-mo receives instructions from Chang Hyŏk-su (loosely based on a historical figure, Ch'a Chi-ch'ŏl), the head of the presidential security guard: "You should always seek permission from the *k'akha* [great leader] first before you lay your blade on him . . . The cut should be finished within fifteen minutes. Should any scar be left on the great leader's *yongan*, you know what would happen to you, right?" Han-mo fails to understand the question because he does not know the meaning of *yongan*, which is derived from two Chinese characters (龍顔: dragon and countenance) and refers to the leader's face. He asks Chang, "What does *yongan* refer to?" Irritated, Chang replies, "Yongan! The honorable countenance of the great leader!" Han-mo responds indifferently, "Ah, yes."

Such an indifferent response is not to be tolerated; whenever anyone says k'akha, it is supposed to be met with a dazzled and spectacularized bodily response. The dreadful security man lashes out: "What the hell? You have failed to respond to me properly. Lie face down."[3] Han-mo, an ordinary citizen in his thirties, is punished where he drops. When Chang says "one," Han-mo is forced to bend his arms; with "two," he straightens them. Han-mo is also forced to recite the phrases "repetition" when going down and "improper manners" when coming up. The barber is in great shape, and soon his face turns red. As he shows signs of fatigue, the chants quickly lose their verbal accuracy. "Reee-pee-tee-shion." "Impro-o-opeer maaaneers." These blurred words are soon replaced by other phrases. In-

27 The barber gets his instructions: "You should always seek permission from the great leader first before laying a blade on him." *The President's Barber.*

stead of "repetition and improper manners," he is now to say "great leader" and "nation-state" (*kugga*). As his body continues to move up and down, Han-mo is forced to chant "The great leader is the nation."

"Pokch'ang 復唱 pulryang 不良" (Repetition! Improper manners), like "chŏngsin t'ongil" (reunifying body and mind), are disciplinary verbal chants that must be accompanied by difficult bodily movements. Han-mo instantaneously has to acquire "the air of a soldier" rather than that of a peasant.[4] Only through the repetition of painful bodily movements such as push-ups would these words retain their authoritative functions. The film here lays bare the intersection of language, bodily pain, and power. The more regulated the body becomes, the film seems to assert, the more inflated the agency of the sign becomes. The regulation of the body and the dissolution of language's rational function, in other words, are intimately tied to authoritarian power. As Michel Foucault has argued, body is often the central target of power, where it is "manipulated, shaped, [and] trained, . . . at the centre of which reigns the notion of docility."[5] The reducibility of the body to its "docility" requires language to become technical and dismantled to its bare form through a precise system of command. Learning through corporal punishment (bodily pain) that the sounds (signifier) of k'akha are equivalent to those of kugga, means that the rational utility of language, which seeks a balance between the signifier and the signified, has to be both unlearned and destroyed.

In a fascist regime, which has highly advanced techniques of submitting forces and bodies to calculated verbal commands, language is often stripped to its presymbolic sounds, cries, and chants (despite their meticulously precise utterances of signifiers) accompanied by regulated bodily movement.[6] For instance, words like k'akha and pokch'ang underscore authority, not because of their actual meanings (great leader and repetition, respectively), but because they automatically trigger memories of corporal discipline and punishment. In other words, what a film like *The President's Barber* stresses is that these words resist interpretation beyond their phonetic symbols. Ironically, through this resistance, a common terrain between fascist tactics and postmodern humor can be found. Slavoj Žižek's most interesting contribution to academia, for instance, has been to point out that there has always been an interesting meeting point between totalitarianism and postmodernism.[7]

Many political theorists and critical thinkers—ranging from Ernesto Laclau and Wilhelm Reich to Gilles Deleuze and Michel Foucault—have refused to acknowledge that fascism is a specific attribute tied only to a certain epoch or nationality.[8] Though the presence of some characteristics such as anti-intellectual populism, authoritarian ethics of self-sacrifice, valorized dictatorship of a small reactionary clique, frenzied nationalism, economic corporatism, and mandatory calisthenics in schools does not prove that a given society is fascist, the presence of all of them—as in Korean society during Park Chung Hee's regime—could make the society's associations with "fascist investments" undeniably strong.[9] Marilyn Ivy concurs with Žižek: "Fascism describes an attempt to have capitalism without capitalism."[10] Perhaps nowhere was this more evident during Park Chung Hee's regime, when rigid anticommunist and anti-union policies shaped South Korea's economy, driven by exports and US aid.[11] The necessary capitalist mechanisms of free-market competition and signs of class antagonism were virtually rooted out during this period by Park Chung Hee's appeals to Korean workers, saying that sacrifices were necessary for the greater cause of national economic progress. Though some historians such as Michael E. Robinson argue that the loyalty and duty shown by the hard-working labor force during this period of intense economic push was a response to Park Chung Hee's appeal to Confucianism, I hasten to add that the vestiges of the fascist culture of the Second World War also played a large part in keeping class warfare largely dormant during the two decades of Park Chung Hee's rule. The remarkable suppression of labor unrest and the laissez-faire market was possible only because Park Chung Hee's appeal to the traumatic, war-ridden South Korea as an organic community did succeed in achieving a sort of fascist fantasy that transcended the inevitable capitalist contradictions and conflicts. Park—who graduated from the Manchukuo Military Academy in 1942 and served as a lieutenant in the notorious Kwantung Army under his Japanese name, Takaki Masao—was familiar with the power of corporatist nationalism that negated liberal, capitalist democracy. The principles of his presidential leadership derived from his personal hatred of free debates, intellectual snobbery, and decadence. As Cho Kap-je, a conservative Korean political commentator notes, the seeds of those principles were sown during Park's youth, when he witnessed dilettante and self-indulgent attitudes among his Korean seniors from wealthy backgrounds in his hometown of Daegu that prompted him to pursue a military career at the height of Japanese fascism.[12]

The President's Barber and Im Sang-soo's *The President's Last Bang (Kuttae kŭ saramdŭl*, 2005) both depict a dark period in modern Korean history by amplifying the moment when words are stripped of their meanings, signaling both a reminder of fascist terror and the contemporaneous postmodern condition. These two films are virtually committed in their resistance against gentrification and globalization, remaining unpalatable for audiences outside Korea because they specifically address what Fredric Jameson terms the "return of repressed historicity," his key postmodern phrase.[13] Recent Korean cinema has been able to virtually reconstitute subjects as different as the Chosun Dynasty (the subject of my final chapter), the Korean War, and—as I will argue in the next chapter—the Chinese diaspora in South Korea and North Korea for foreign consumption, helping to expand the hallyu market. But the repackaging of Park Chung Hee stands out as an item strictly slated for domestic consumption for mature audiences. This "repressed historicity," I must stress, dislodged the realist style, which quickly became unfashionable after the 1980s, when Korea's intense political period faded out.[14] It is nothing new to suggest that these dark memories from modern history have returned in contemporary cultural variants twenty or thirty years later, as a compensation for the political failure of a generation of filmmakers who spent their left-leaning youth protesting against military dictatorship during the 1980s (Im Sang-soo was born in 1962, Im Chan-sang in 1969). What I intend to investigate instead is, first, how these films that depict the period of military dictatorship characterize it as already having been impregnated with postmodern characteristics; second, how the Deleuzian "virtual-actual" could help the reading of these historical films; and third, whether it's possible for cinema to provide ethical guidelines by resisting enslavement by a single hegemonic image, sign, or cliché and by not falling into the trap of transcendental yearnings.

The President's Barber and *The President's Last Bang* were both inspired by historical events (*The President's Barber* depicts a military coup, fraudulent elections, anti-Communist witch-hunts, and other human rights abuses; while *The President's Last Bang* depicts the day—October 26, 1979—when Park Chung Hee was shot to death), but each is also arguably a "simulation" (to use a Baudrillardian term) that is "the generation by models of a real without origin or reality."[15] In other words, the gestures, words, and face of Park Chung Hee sever themselves from their historical origins and are processed as a simulation or a hyperreality. These two films are not motivated by a desire to faithfully reproduce historical landscapes and figures, but rather by a desire to deliberately release cinema from them through the tension proposed between the audience's memory of history and the cinematic image projected before their eyes. So far, however, there is nothing extraordinary about this postmodern maneuver. Isn't this a working principle for any cinema available nowadays in most First World countries? Along with my interest in how these films render virtual the very mechanism of fascism—for example, the continual metonymic sliding of signifiers accessed by the interchangeability between, for instance, k'akha and kugga—and make that mechanism into something that postmodern audiences can consume, I am interested in identifying how these two films primitivize or infantilize Park Chung Hee, to end up challenging the orthodox image of him that has persisted as a hypermasculine and military corporate man.

As Rey Chow argues in her groundbreaking study of Chinese films, "primitivizing 'China'" was one way sought by the writers of the May Fourth Movement and the post-Mao Fifth Generation filmmakers to engage with the modern masses. She writes that in the "medium of film, Chinese intellectuals find a wonderful means of elaborating these dialectical meanings of primitivism . . . The peculiar affinity between film and primitivism is, I think, one reason why Chinese cinema, together with Indian

28 The president as a child in need of mother's milk? *The President's Last Bang.*

and Japanese cinemas, has been perceived as a major place for the nego-tiation of cultural identity."[16] While the cinematic figures of women and rural nature prominently featured in the Fifth Generation Chinese Cinema support Chow's claim that China is "primitivized," her analysis of Chen Kai-ge's *King of Children* (*Haizi wang,* 1987) shows that children also "con-tinue to fascinate modern Chinese intellectuals."[17] In the second half of *The President's Barber,* not only does Nak-an, the infant son of the president's barber, emerge as the principal character, but also there is an attempt to place the domestic affairs of Park Chung Hee in a presymbolic, infantile state. Because the main relationship is between the president and his bar-ber, Park often acts like a child by sleeping in his barber's chair, trying on new sunglasses, and paying excessive attention to his hairstyle. Such attempts to primitivize the president and his private domain also rever-berate in *The President's Last Bang,* where Park is pictured not as a feared tyrant, but as a petulant baby in need of a mother's milk.

The President's Barber

In one of the most disturbing and humorous scenes of *The President's Barber,* the barber's thirteen-year-old son, Nak-an, is taken to Korean CIA (KCIA) headquarters. He is suspected as being a potential host of the "Marŭgusŭ" virus. The etymology of "Marŭgusŭ," a made-up name, is derived from the transliteration into hangŭl of Marx (as in the Karl Marx of the *Commu-nist Manifesto*). In an act consistent with all totalitarian or fascist policies that attempt to extract meaning from something that is fundamentally a

29 "What is a young boy like you doing in here?" *The President's Barber.*

lack, the South Korean government has officially declared Marŭgusŭ to be a subversive threat to the nation—when, as a matter of fact, it is nothing but an easily treatable bacterial disease. Therefore, anyone who defecates *mul-ddong* (semiliquid shit) including Nak-an, is immediately suspected of being a *ppalgaengi* (red).

When the boy enters a torture chamber, a Korean intelligence agent asks him: "What is a young boy like you doing in here?" The agent badly slurs his words—not unlike the way that Marx has metamorphosed phonetically into Marŭgusŭ—a word that also resembles the Korean word *"maryŏpta*, a verb that designates a need to defecate. Laughingly, Nak-an responds: "Because I've been having diarrhea." The agent then wires Nak-an to a high-voltage electric box. From then on, every question the agent asks, and every increase in wattage, elicits an irrational response from Nak-an. Nak-an laughs and later breathes into a harmonica, which has suddenly appeared along with Christmas lights. Nak-an's failure to respond with any logic is, of course, not inappropriate; before he had even arrived, the intelligence agency had prepared a statement for him to sign: "It was because of my father I had contracted the Marŭgusŭ disease." Once Nak-an's defecation is identified as diarrhea, a sign that is positioned somewhere between two desires—to defecate and to be liberated from class oppression (both deemed subversive acts)—all the authorities would be required to do would be to match the name Marŭgusŭ with a face or person (another signifier), not even bothering to determine exactly what it signified. The authorities are unwilling to provide evidence proving a precise correlation between diarrhea as a signifier and Marxism as its signified; all they want is a statement from the accused that retroactively affirms that he has contracted not Marŭgusŭ (which doesn't exist in any case), but something else.

Torture—used as dark comedy throughout *The President's Barber*—is a means of getting a confession for a crime that has yet to be committed. But torture produces real pain, and that is why fascism is feared, whereas postmodernism is jeered. Instead of acknowledging the postmodern irony behind the signs of "bodily sacrifices," "patriotism," or "national allegiances," fascism continues to insist that there is a surplus of meaning behind them. The way in which ppalgaengi, for instance, like Marŭgusŭ or *Chosenjin* (Korean) or "the Jew" or "the Negro," is an enunciation of a purely dazzling slant where its surplus meaning is held together by a "self-referential, tautological, [and] performative operation."[18] The properties clustered around these signifiers (stinky, dangerous, slurring, intriguing spirit, and so on) are important, but none is more significant than the performative function that serves to distinguish the speaker who is uttering them from the person being addressed. The surplus property of "X" produced by these references is more than what a simple tautology could offer: ppalgaengi do these things because they are ppalgaengi. This X is what Žižek calls an "irreducible gap that remains between the Real and the modes of its symbolization."[19]

In chapters 6 and 7, on Lee Chang-dong and Park Chan-wook, I will argue that the voice is the Lacanian *objet petit a* that is both idealized and fetishized in films like *Oasis* (where the epileptic Kong-ju cannot talk very well) and *Oldboy* (where Oh Dae-su speaks in strange grammatical tones who after his release from a private penitentiary and, during the film's climax, loses his tongue altogether), but that in *The President's Barber*, the relationship between the slurring torturer and the inarticulate child also exposes how language or the lack of linguistic facility is one way for fascism to maintain its order and tyranny. The slurring of the words and its solicitation of a laughing response from the tied-up, yet amused, child who has no idea what has prompted his arrest not only diffuses the relationship between the interrogator and the accused, but also exposes the working logic behind fascist politics. Verbal infelicities, the arbitrary nature of language, and the subordination of the signified, as evidenced by the impossibility of locating a substance (X) behind Marŭgusŭ (is it shitting or spying?)—precisely because it is invented and exists in its name only—fit the profile of what Žižek points out as the functioning of the Lacanian "radical contingency of naming," where both the jouissance of late capitalism and fascism could be experienced. Refusing to adhere to either antidescriptivism, which fastidiously insists that every name has a logical a priori genesis (sometimes called a primal baptism), or descriptivism, which declares that there is no external causal link between a word and its meaning, Žižek attaches himself to the Lacanian paradigm where names are retroactively acquired only after the surplus meanings behind names such as "Jew," "Commie," or "Chosenjin" are pre-assigned by the Big Other and then function as an unobtainable and unidentifiable *objet petit a*.

The relationship between the slurring agent and the laughing boy progresses to the point where words vanish and music takes their place. At this point, we remember that language in a fascist regime is often stripped to presymbolic sounds, cries, and chants. Instead of words and screams, we hear a harmonica melody while the agent and the boy perform a song and dance—producing an effect somewhere between horror (fascism) and comedy (postmodernism). Since the authorities have already prepared the boy's statement, what is there left to confess anyway? After endless pleas to the authorities (even to the naïve president himself) by the barber, Nak-an is eventually released from the torture chamber. But the torture applied to his body has had an indelible effect on him. His weakened legs cause him to be disabled from the waist down. The entire second half of the film focuses on how Nak-an's barber father, a simpleton who has acquiesced in all the corrupt government's actions throughout his life, proceeds to betray the interests of the kugga (nation) in order to save his son.

So militantly protean a form as *The President's Barber* raises serious problems for those who seek to confine it to a linear shape of historical representation. The tension between human corporeality (symbolized by these bodily sounds) and the official ideology of the Park Chung Hee regime (symbolized by the chants of "great leader is the nation") inspired me to think about what Mikhail Bakhtin famously termed "grotesque fantasy" in his analysis of Rabelais's fiction, where temporal and spatial dimensions have a way of expanding—not by exaggerating a transcendental view of the world such as "the false scholaristic thought, by a false theological and legalistic casuistry and ultimately by language itself,"[20] but by purging such transcendentalism. Bakhtin argues that, in his effort to rebuild a world that eliminates symbolic and hierarchical interpretations, Rabelais grabs some of the crudest and most vulgar connections forged between things and people from folklore before the rise of social classes. Copulation and defecation, for instance, are the two tropes emphasized by Bakhtin that restore the relationship between the word and the body, which had previously been marked by an immeasurable abyss. Politicized use of language has ordained and subordinated the body, but *The President's Barber* lays out a cynical and almost clownish form of life that centers on the fundamental functions of the body: fucking, shitting, farting, and burping.

Defecation in the film is so important a discourse that it could almost be considered the film's theme. Though mul-ddong almost always invokes a horrified response, it often appears in jokes across many cultures because it is tied to a natural response of the body after a feast of excessive eating and cheerful drinking. After all, it is a symptom of pleasure and satisfied body (albeit perhaps not a healthy one). We notice that the first time that Marŭgusŭ disease is detected in Hyoja-dong, the district where the barber and other characters live, is when the "village chief" detects that the owner of the dumpling restaurant spends far too much time in the bathroom stall. While laughing, the village chief claims: "I kept warning you that you were eating too much today." Soon, however, remembering that the government has sent down a decree to immediately report anyone who spends excessive amounts of time in the bathroom, the village chief turns the restaurant owner over to the authorities. And the restaurant owner soon finds himself in a torture chamber.

Defecation plays a grotesquely pivotal role as a chronotope that weaves together all of the film's three temporal moods: the historical, the mythological, and the present. Marŭgusŭ, of course, is a diarrheal disease that is a metaphor for a brutal historical climate where the excessive proliferation of the word *kanch'ŏp* (spy) ultimately necessitates the actual mass production of kanch'ŏp. Because *The President's Barber* allows its audience to be "in" on the fact that Marŭgusŭ is part of a KCIA scheme to start a "red scare" as a way to sustain the legitimacy of military dictatorship, the Marŭgŭsu veers away from the McGuffin often used by Alfred Hitchcock—like the microfilm putatively hidden in the statue in *North by Northwest*. And yet Marŭgusŭ serves the socially symbolic function of empty signifier, for it must lay bare the gap between the real (Communist spy) and its fictive representation (ordinary citizen) that the government has forged during

Park's regime. Just as the "Jew" or "Negro" must bear the surplus derogatory signifiers such as "stinky" and "slurring" in order to distinguish the essence of a fascist nation, the "ppalgaengi" or the "ones infected by Marŭgusŭ" must be identified and labeled for Park's regime to stay in power.

The President's Barber is therefore a film that pays attention to this double articulation between language and its representation, farcically lumping the two together, and using various chronotopes as well as temporal and spatial tropes such as mysticism and the postauthoritarian present from which the film is shot and projected. The present is often self-referentially registered by the viewer through the voice-over of the young Nak-an, who serves as the primary narrator of the film. The use of the past tense to tell the story about the barber-father first of all enables an undeniable recognition of the "present" from which the past is framed; second, it makes clear that the dominant form of the film is resistance against realism. In addition to the historical plane, which encompasses stories of fraudulent elections, the state-sanctioned "red scare," and human rights abuses, the film also makes use of a folkloric setting: when Han-mo travels with Nak-an to seek a cure for the ailing boy, they go deep into mystic mountains, where any sense of real historical time has been lost. There, Han-mo meets a *tosa* (a sage), who predicts their future by analyzing Nak-an's past. By traveling into a mystical landscape and following the guidance of this supernatural being, Han-mo transcends the constraints of time and space, and of historical facts, and himself achieves a folkloric quality. He later becomes a hero by resisting corporal trouble when faced with the horrible task of removing the eyes of the ex-president from the portrait of the deceased to make the medicine that the tosa has prescribed for Nak-an. The film's most climactic scene of the film ironically takes place in an outhouse, where Han-mo sits to defecate the container he swallowed the night before, after putting the black paint scraped from the president's "eyes" inside it. As Han-mo undergoes deep pain to retrieve the cure for his son, the funeral car wrapped in chrysanthemums slowly proceeds with the body of the dead president to its burial site. It is here where the mystical element (the tosa's mysterious medicine contained in the eyes and chrysanthemums) not only meets the historical (the dead president's funeral), but also the present after Park Chung Hee (the voice-over by the now cured Nak-an serves as a marker of the present). All of these are ironically balled up inside the feces causing Han-mo great pain.

Both films discussed in this chapter depict the era of military dictatorship and the immediate culture surrounding President Park Chung Hee, but instead of focusing on the president himself, their protagonists are auxiliary characters in history. The central character in *The President's Barber* is, of course, Han-mo, the great leader's haircutter. In *The President's Last Bang*, a section chief of the Korean CIA, Chu, is the lead character.[21] Chu's official title is manager of the presidential palace used as a weekend house (Kungjŏngdong). This gives him the ultimate responsibility for all the arrangements made for the occasional soirees held there for the president. Chu's duties consequently include supplying female singers and escorts. Though both Han-mo and Chu are semifictional characters who appear only as anecdotes in the official historiography of the Park Chung Hee era, they end up anchoring the two films' narratives. Between the minor history (the president's barber and the president's pimp) and the official historiography (the various historical episodes that involve the president) lie the mythological undercurrents that serve as the virtual tropes of history.

The President's Last Bang is another film that closely scrutinizes the relationship between the body and history. The film opens by introducing Chief Joo, who handles the president's personal affairs, including providing young female escorts for the drinking parties hosted at the presidential palace. It also introduces the film's other main character: Kim Chae-gyu, one of the most powerful men in Korea during the Yushin dictatorship, and the person who ended up killing the president. He is receiving treatment in a doctor's office. The function of his liver, declares the doctor, has been reduced to only a fifth of that of a normal one, resulting in afternoon fatigues, bloating, gas, and most important for the film, a stinking odor from his mouth. This stinking smell emitted from a body that cannot function well means that he constantly reaches for a piece of gum at critical moments in the film. (Kim Chae-gyu offers a piece of gum to the army's chief of joint security after murdering the president.) But a piece of gum can only mask the bad smell in Kim's mouth; it provides no relief for his malfunctioning liver. His inability to properly process food and waste leaves him constipated and fatigued.

The film is fascinating in many respects because it captures the essence of what amounts to a failed coup d'état against a military strongman who

30 Chief Joo, chewing gum, picks up an escort for the president's party on October 26, 1979.
The President's Last Bang.

came into power through an earlier coup, but the film's success does not come through the depiction of the conventional historical agents of insurgency. October 26, 1979, was an unusual date in the history of Park's regime, as the film accurately reports that no civil unrest was registered on that date in Korea. Instead, the film meticulously depicts the principal characters of history engaging in small talk about historical figures' obsession with sexual virility, taking bathroom breaks, and chewing and spitting out gum through a lyrically moving camera that often uses wide-angle zoom and steady-cam techniques. As if these weren't enough, *The President's Last Bang* also blasphemously distorts the truth about the fateful night that changed Korean history. Instead of casting actors whose faces match some of the most recognizable faces in that history, the film deliberately uses actors who look nothing like the real figures they are asked to play. All of the secret agents on screen wear fancy postmodern Georgio Armani suits that hardly recall the tasteless fashion of government employees in the 1970s. The backdrop to these events have also undergone a radical face-lift; none of the furniture and props used in the film's presidential palace match the ones shown in the countless photographs of Park Chung Hee's murder site that were printed in newspapers and broadcast on television. Despite the fact that the images of the events of October 26 have been imprinted in many people's memory, these newly reproduced images of the date elevate *The President's Last Bang* to a truly rare film that refuses to assign history a nostalgic marker. The deliberate gap between the

31 History breaks down into images: the real Kim Chae-gyu poses for journalists in one of the most famous photos of twentieth-century Korea. The *Chosun Ilbo* Collection.

32 The fake Kim Chae-gyu aims his gun at the president in *The President's Last Bang*.

fictional figures, settings, costumes, and art in the film and their historical referents naturally underscores the fact that the film's cinematic simulations are nothing more than that: simulations.

History does not break down into stories but into images. Stories, by definition, insist on some form of coherent unity between events, characters, and language that motivates a plotline. Images, on the contrary, are much less likely to produce that kind of coherent unity. *The President's Last Bang* almost withdraws from the need to tell a story and instead interrogates the potential of the image to dissolve history through the episodic arrangements of one glossy, self-reflexive image after another. *Tout Va Bien* (1972), a Jean-Luc Godard classic from his radical experimental days in the Dziga Vertov Group of the late 1960s and early 1970s, is an exemplary text where saturated reds, blues, and greens continue to break down the barrier between fiction and reality, as if to suggest that stories can only refictionalize history. In this way, the film forces its viewers to better understand the blurriness between truth and fiction. Unlike *The President's Barber*, *Tout Va Bien* turns away from a narrative, making it impossible initially for us to determine exactly where the locus of its ideological reflection might be, and thus, subsequently, its mapping within a system of allegorical interpretation. Fascism or totalitarianism relies on the principle of absolute power that normally demands a heavy emphasis on form rather than on content. As Slavoj Žižek points out: "For Fascist ideology, the point is not the instrumental value of the sacrifice, it is the very form of sacrifice itself."[22] In other words, fascism says: "Obey, because you must! Sacrifice yourself, but do not ask what you are sacrificing yourself for." Through its spotlight on the form of sacrifice, fascism successfully erases the meaning and value of sacrifice. Perhaps no other filmmaker captures this essence better than Pier Paolo Pasolini, and it may not be a coincidence that Im Sang-soo is the Korean director whose work most closely resembles that of Pasolini.

Though *The President's Last Bang* chronicles one of the most memorable events in modern Korean history, it is extremely difficult to find another docudrama quite like it. The film contains no trace of a conspiracy theory, unlike postmodern docudramas such as Oliver Stone's *JFK* (1991), nor does it possess the kind of antisubject subject that reflects history from an ahistorical perspective, as in Robert Zemeckis's *Forrest Gump* (1994). Instead, *The President's Last Bang* self-referentially recognizes that any time an image is recreated for the purpose of placing the viewers in a specific time and place from the past, a tension between fiction and history is going to be unavoidable. If *Forrest Gump* "confuses the fictional with the historically 'real' in an absolutely seamless representation,"[23] *The President's Last Bang* confuses them in a way that contests the suturing relationship between the signifier and the signified. David E. James has ironically remarked: "The interruption between signifier and signified that is the condition of signification separates signs, not only externally from their referents but also internally from themselves. Constituted in difference, all images are thus inhabited by an otherness that erodes the affirmation of their apparent presence."[24] This description of the anti-allegorical condition of images in experimental films is nowhere more relevant in Korean cinema than it is to *The President's Last Bang*, where images of men in expensive suits and women in fancy dresses brush against each other, but hardly against historical referents. Like China's current exploitation of Mao mostly as a Warhol-ian sign rather than as a harbinger of real Communism, at this point in history Park Chung Hee's simulation is a sign that rarely pushes above the surface.

Furthermore, *The President's Last Bang* muffles historical truth and makes it unidentifiable by, for instance, deliberately substituting actors who hardly resemble them for the visually familiar faces from history. This prompts the question: was there ever any substance beyond the signifier of the dictator? This provocative relationship between the signifier and the signified continues to penetrate into the historical core—even in an era dominated by entertainment value in Korean cinema. An overdetermined utterance of history is produced, where the form and the content—or the imaginary and the symbolic—continue to exchange meanings and values until the distinction between the two becomes nullified. The point of fascism or totalitarianism is to overcode the signifier, (salutations) render the signified (sacrifice) irrelevant, and then simply produce a spectacle out of signs in order to manipulate the masses. The point of a postmodern art is, well, to do the same. But if executed right (without abandoning the modernist agenda), postmodern art counters the spectacle with a self-referential cynicism that ultimately denies that there ever was a transcendental origin behind these signs and seeks instead for the erasures of traces. I believe that this ultimately does away with the need for bodily sacrifice, or any form of allegiance toward signs, producing a denial that reduces the likelihood of finding allegories within a sign and instead engages in a jouissance of the metonymic sliding of signifiers.

Virtual History?

Both *The President's Barber* and *The President's Last Bang* attempt to interrogate a historical cliché that has been regulated and maintained by several representative photos that have endlessly looped through the mass media and the Internet. In so doing, they utilize black-and-white archival news footage to first shore up the historical veracity of the settings that they depicted, before desecrating those settings and manipulating them to fit actors onto the screen. The superimposition of action of actors over the actual newsreel footage background not only obfuscates the boundary between reality and fiction, but also challenges the popular perception of history that has resonated in Korean cultural memory as an incontestable truth. About halfway through *The President's Last Bang*, Ch'a Chi-ch'ŏl (in this film he is called by his real name, though in the barber movie he was called Chang Hyŏk-su) requests that the television be turned on for people to watch the 9:00 p.m. news. The president's attendance at the completion ceremony for the Sea Wall at Sapgyo Plain, Park Chung Hee's last public appearance on camera, is being featured. The restored footage for the film replaces Park Chung Hee with the veteran actor Song Chae-ho, who looks nothing like the real-life president. Since Park's assassination was not accompanied by a Zapruderesque eyewitness film, these images are as close to the dying moments of the dictator as we are going to get. When the historical characters gather around the TV set and watch the black-and-white footage of themselves cutting the ceremonial tape earlier that day, the film bifurcates between two different times—one that is based on virtualized actual image on the TV screen, and one based on the actualized virtual image outside of the screen. This shifts the viewers from chronological time and possibly into a Proustian chronotope, much like Combray (here, the Kungjongdong; the presidential palace), where we are inside time—a time, as Deleuze notes, that constantly divides itself in two, "a present that passes and a past that is preserved."[25] *The President's Last Bang* thus recreates history as something that no longer dwells on the difference between the way things appear and the way things really are, placing it instead in the opaque category where viewers simultaneously experience both the preserved past and the fleeting present.

Rather than reconstructing the set as a replica of the genuine thing, Im Chan-sang and Im Sang-soo, the makers of these two films, have deliberately done everything wrong according to the standards of realism. They

33 President Park Chung Hee's final televised ceremony, with Song Chae-ho playing the president. *The President's Last Bang.*

have visually altered historical settings and costumes to obfuscate the present and the past. An affective relationship that challenges the "power of cliché" that had formatted our sensory motor scheme thus emerges out of the relationship between viewer and image. The creation of purely new visual landscapes transforms signs that had previously been familiar to all Koreans, such as the image of Park Chung Hee, his voice, and his everyday activities. (What interests me in these two films, as well as a number of other recent Korean films, is not how the system of language becomes relegated to a secondary role, but what actually becomes retroactively expressed in images and signs that call attention to their disassociations from their historical referents.) We recall the famous black-and-white photographs of Kim Chae-gyu pointing his gun at Park Chung Hee in the presidential palace, photographs that still circulate endlessly in textbooks and on television and the Internet. (These are hegemonic clichés despite the fact that they were staged by military investigators for the media.) Supposedly Kim Chae-gyu yelled, "You worthless piece of shit!" to Park Chung Hee right as the final shots were fired into his skull. But is this accurate? Or is it inaccurate? Does it matter? By featuring the butler of the presidential palace having a feast as an inconclusive ending, *The President's Last Bang* refuses to answer the questions that many historians have asked over and over: What was the motivation behind the assassination? To advance democracy? To settle a personal vendetta, resulting from a presidential snub? How relevant is it that Kim Chae-gyu's dramatic line was changed from "You worthless piece of shit!" (putatively accurate) to "When you die, a stinking body is all that you are" (the film's reinterpretation)? Are the events too recent to tweak even the slightest detail, for a dramatic effect? Moreover, is it relevant whether or not Park Chung Hee responded angrily when the entertainer sang the Japanese enka "Kanashi-i sake" (sad wine) on the night he died? Without seeing Park's reaction to the song, could audiences today accept listening to a Japanese song sung in the Korean presidential palace as just sound and image without attaching any values or memories of the colonial past to it?

This is not to suggest that cinema ought to be completely free of clichés, but like historical reality, they too must undergo virtual-actual swaps. Unlike novels, in cinema the creative realm is defined by a system of signs that makes the best use of the relationship between a star's persona and the public, and of music, props, art, costumes, and cinematography that often places cinema outside normal narrative conventions. For instance, the semiotic content of "Han Sŏk-gyu" (then one of the biggest stars in the Korean film industry, he was cast against type as the president's pimp) congeals as a significant element in the film's aim to reclaim history from the plane of truth and falsehood. Such maneuvering gets us closer to pure sight and sound, demanding the reconfiguration of a memory-scape that has already been fully saturated by the iconography of Park Chung Hee as a key figure in Korea's modern success. After all, in the late-capitalist, image-driven environment that we live in, power is automatically guided by a preprogrammed system where only certified images and rhetoric can circulate in the media, despite the fact that individual blogs sometimes intermittently usurp the mechanism of this system. A simple tweaking of this cliché automatically jams the sensorimotor schema that regulates the hegemonic notion of power and self-reflexively raises the question of whether the relationship between historical reality and its representation was ever stable.

Films such as *The President's Last Bang* and *The President's Barber* suggest that the best strategy for resisting fascism—under which the meanings of leader, nation, and human values are putatively substantiated—is not to submit alternative meanings for them, but simply to expose the fact that the image, the symbol, and the signifier cannot always be guaranteed entry into the system of language. Fascism has always had a way of reducing language into ritualistic forms or mechanical slogans that bypass mental processes and register directly onto the body. As an art form that is dependent on the image, cinema is often at odds with the intellectual medium and thereby possesses, as Rey Chow argues while describing the underlying reason behind Lu Xun's career change from a medical student to a writer, the potential to serve fascism.[26] But, ironically, it is also a medium that can effectively lay bare the processes of any sign's double articulation, where we can naturally have a discourse about the relationship between the signifier and the signified. Furthermore, it may be the only medium where affect (emotions) can be achieved through the combined use of pure sight and sound. After decades of military dictatorship in South Korea, not to mention the totalitarianism that remains in North Korea, have Koreans finally learned that effective resistance against fascism requires tactics other than substituting for k'akha or kugga other signifiers such as "the people" or "justice"? I am reminded here of the scene I described at the opening of this chapter, when Chang gets upset at the question Han-mo asks because there is no satisfying, nontautological answer to the question of what "an honorable countenance" might be. *The President's Last Bang* and *The President's Barber* undercut the movement to symbolize Park Chung Hee's face by asking us whether we could imagine an image that is beyond words, beyond interpretation, and beyond allegory. The word "yongan" remains just that; a word—two characters—a dragon's face that is just as fictitious and elusive as the k'akha or the kugga.

Reading the North Korean as an Ethnic Other

It only took a couple of minutes. The bus operated by Hyundai Asan swiftly crossed the DMZ, the 2.5-mile-wide demilitarized zone separating North and South Korea.[1] There was hardly any traffic, and the only other vehicle I could spot on the road—other than the row of tourist buses making the crossing—was a North Korean military truck. I was in North Korea for the first time. Though it was the first day of March, the weather forecast had predicted heavy snow. The day remained overcast, as the weather between Seoul, which I had left only four hours earlier, and the Geumgangsan (Diamond Mountain) Special Tour Region was the same. But weather was probably the only thing that remained the same between the two Koreas. The usual noise of cellphone chatter, heard on almost every corner in South Korea, had disappeared. As we boarded the special bus that makes the run between the North and South, our phones were placed in plastic bags and taken away by the tour agents. Also gone were the traffic noises that you hear almost everywhere you go in the vast Seoul metropolitan area.[2] The North was unbelievably quiet—on and off the bus. The absence of cellphones and cars, along with the ubiquity of guards and agents wearing Kim Il-Sung badges, had suddenly transformed the usually raucous and temperamental South Korean tourists into remarkably laconic and obsequious creatures.

Virtual Tour

At the border checkpoint, I took out my navy blue US passport, expecting hostile questions from the dark-skinned, lanky fellow in the ill-fitting North Korean uniform. However, despite the fact that I was the only one in my group of about twenty tourists who did not have a South Korean passport, I was spared any special treatment. All I got was a brief stare—no longer than the one the person ahead of me in line had received. The North Korean representative took only several seconds to review my passport, stamp a special visa on the entry card that the Hyundai Asan agent had

34 A view from my hotel room in North Korea in 2008. Photo by Kyung Hyun Kim.

given each of us earlier, and call for the tourist waiting behind me to come forward. No words, no smile, and no questions. For me, the agent was the first person from the Communist North that I ever had come into physical contact with; for him, I was just one of the many Korean Americans passing through, meriting no more than a split-second review during his mundane routines of browsing through documents, stamping entry visas, and matching passport photos with real faces.

Close to two million South Koreans have visited the Geumgangsan Special Tour Region since the tour officially began in 1998, and since this entire zone is separated from the real North Korea with green fences, it is tempting to call this region a part of the South. In order to allow this region to be a South Korean tour resort, Onjeong Maeul of the North had to be rezoned and its residents evacuated from the site. And as the fatal shooting of the South Korean tourist Park Wang-ja in this mountain resort proved, anyone who wandered only a few yards into the restricted area was likely to be met with North Korean guards equipped with AK-47s and ready to fire.[3] Only specially trained North Koreans, Hyundai Asan employees from the South, and migrant workers from Yanbian (China's Korean Autonomous Prefecture) work in the region—ironically, North Korean civilians also have only limited access to it.

Though at the moment of writing, this tour symbolizing the reconciliation between the two Koreas remains suspended and a South Korean company (Hyundai Asan) manages most of the jointly run restaurants, hotels, shops, theaters, and other facilities, it is difficult not to acknowledge that a form of crossing had taken place during the three days I was in North Korea. For the first time in my life, I had struck up casual conversations with North Koreans who had neither defected nor intended to defect: tour guides, restaurant workers, and even a North Korean party cadre. Though they were hardly evidence of transgressions and disorders, I could expand them mentally into a reproducible relation of forces that I could reimagine as what amounted to a virtual site.

During a couple of four-hour hikes along the Geumgangsan ridge, you encounter North Korean guides and party cadres who greet you at every stop and are willing to engage you in conversation. On a cold spring day in March 2008, the topics ranged from casual everyday matters ("What did you have for breakfast today before coming to work?") to serious politics ("Do you really think the United States would abandon its hostile policies toward North Korea if it successfully developed nuclear weapons?"), which might as well be a dream—filled with potentialities and truthfulness—in which the secretive Communist North partially and briefly reveals itself to be the capitalist South's alter ego. Every question and answer posed threats (somewhere between real and unreal) to the other side's legitimacy that one could hardly imagine taking place in either the United States or South Korea, countries that have moved far beyond the era of intense ideological struggle. Even the slightest admission that Americans are capable of producing musical sounds (as evidenced by the New York Philharmonic's visit to Pyongyang a couple of weeks before my trip to the North), exercise tolerance toward minorities (as Barack Obama's political career was demonstrating), and share their wealth with Koreans (as South Korea's ascendancy, first with US aid and assistance, to the rank of world leaders in many economic fields had proved) probably took more than a small amount of courage on the part of the young North Koreans I met. And my cynical questions—such as "How often do you travel to Pyongyang?"—had been motivated by the stereotype of Communist countries' restrictions on travel. "There is no social system that does not leak from all directions, even if it makes its segments increasingly rigid in order to seal the *lines of flight* [my emphasis]," write Gilles Deleuze and Félix Guattari.[4] Though it would be a great exaggeration to state that ordinary conversations between North Korean officials and visitors from capitalist countries represent perilous, subversive acts, these virtual passages and exchanges would, I had come to believe, continue to expand and extend such lines of flight. However, perhaps even these small openings were too risky for both Koreas. Geumgangsan Tours once a symbol of cooperation between North Korea and South Korea remains shut more than three years after the fatal shooting of the South Korean tourist.[5]

South Korea's Popular Images of the North

Just as many North Koreans have only one-dimensional ideas about the United States, most Americans believe the stereotypes about North Korea, including the image of Kim Jong-il as a ruthless, mad ruler who dreams of firing nuclear weapons at the United States. Therefore, it may surprise American readers to learn that in South Korea, a sworn ally of the United States over the past six decades and a country where approximately 30,000 US troops remain, the cinematic representation of North Korea has radically changed in recent times. In the popular media of South Korea, North Koreans have been transformed from despicable enemies into characters worthy of redemption. Long gone are the days when images of North Koreans as unredeemable villains dominated all of South Korea's cinema, television, radio, and even pulp fiction.[6]

Most of the North Korean characters in recent films veer away from the reprehensibly violent figures that were stock characters in all Korean War films and spy action dramas in the Cold War period. During most of the military dictatorship that stretched over the three decades of 1960s, 1970s, and 1980s, the vigilant South Korean censorship board, then known as the Public Performance Ethics Committee, discouraged any depiction of war that failed to include anti-Communist messages. For instance, Yi Man-hŭi's *Seven Female Prisoners* (*7 in ŭi yŏp'oro*, 1965), a Korean War film that for the first time attempted to depict soldiers of the North Korean People's Army humanely, was found to be violating the then-terrifying Anti-Communist Law.[7] The dominant images of the Korean War then were the arms of a soldier reaching desperately out of a trench to rescue his wounded comrade, handsome faces of South Korean pilots in red scarves who risked their lives to carry out dangerous missions over enemy territory, and vicious expressions of North Korean soldiers motivated by nothing more than killer instincts. In the 1990s, however, as the political mood in South Korea began to shift toward liberalization, dichotomous depictions of the war that simplistically characterized every North Korean Communist as a villain and every South Korean nationalist as a virtuous victor became unfashionable. Chŏng Chi-yŏng's *The Southern Army* (*Nambugun*, 1990) was the first of a flood of films that questioned the validity of depicting wartime Communists as one-dimensional enemies. Because of subsequent films such as Park Kwang-su's *To the Starry Island* (*Kŭ sŏm e kagosip'ta*, 1993), Im Kwon-Taek's *The Taebaek Mountains* (*T'aebaek sanmaek*, 1994), and Yi Kwang-mo's *Spring in My Hometown* (*Arŭmdaun sijŏl*, 1995), which attempted to represent the complexities of the Korean War by focusing on characters' internal psychological conflicts, the stereotypes of the villainous North Korean and the heroic South Korean became largely invalidated.

By 1999 the South Korean government had adopted a position of peaceful coexistence and cooperation with North Korea, known as the Sunshine Policy. Concocted by Kim Dae-jung—who emerged as South Korea's most prominent dissident leader during the decades of military dictatorship and became South Korea's president in 1998—the Sunshine Policy abandoned South Korea's previous staunch anti-Communist approach, including the refusal to recognize North Korea's legitimacy. Instead, the new policy sought to induce change and economic reform in North Korea through economic and other incentives. The liberal Roh Moo-hyun administration, which followed Kim Dae-jung's presidency, continued the policy. The two Koreas further warmed up to each other when Kim Dae-jung and Kim Jong-il met in 2000—the first meeting ever between the heads of North and South Korea. However, with the conservatives voted into office during the 2007 election for the first time since 1998, South Korea's liberal policy toward North Korea has all but ended.[8]

If Kang Che-gyu's *Shiri* (1999) was the last film to rely on a Cold War dichotomy to produce a ruthless North Korean villain and to attempt to reclaim South Korean male agency through the destruction of a North Korean *femme fatale*, Park Chan-wook's *JSA: Joint Security Area* (2000) was the first film to defuse the stereotype of North Koreans as South Korea's less-than-friendly Other.[9] In *JSA*, a defiant North Korean soldier, Sergeant Oh (played by Song Kang-ho) is depicted as a kind of hero. Sergeant Oh is wittier, ideologically more loyal to his country, and psychologically stronger than his South Korean counterpart, Yi Su-hyŏk (Lee Byung-hun).

While Yi Su-hyŏk remains traumatized—first by his fraternization with the enemy (Sergeant Oh) and then by having been forced to kill his friends when his nocturnal visits across the DMZ are detected by a North Korean commander—Sergeant Oh appears capable of pulling both himself and Su-hyŏk out of the "fine mess" that Su-hyŏk has created. But despite Sergeant Oh's efforts, Su-hyŏk is unable to push himself beyond his trauma and commits suicide. In contrast, Sergeant Oh appears to have fully recovered from his crisis by the end of the film, implying that his excellent composure is the prerequisite of a capable soldier. What is remarkable about the Sergeant Oh character is that he neither compromises his patriotic allegiance to his country nor is he uncompromising, as all North Koreans who have chosen not to defect to the South are presumed to be. Still, such a confident and positive North Korean character in South Korean films has been extremely rare. After all, t'albukjas (North Korean defectors) who seek to get into South Korea for work—and who are more frequently portrayed in more recent South Korean films—require both the tolerance of South Koreans and the crucial knee-jerk response to South Koreans of mea culpa (an acknowledgment of personal guilt or error) in order to be eligible for an entry visa and work permit.

No fewer than twenty feature-length films were made about North Koreans by the South Korean film industry between 2000 and 2007, the so-called Sunshine Policy period. Like a Puritan finally breaking through the deepest of sexual inhibitions, South Korea churned out film after film during this period using North Korean characters. From big-budget blockbuster productions such as JSA and Welcome to Dongmakgol (2005) to forgettable B-movie duds such as Whistling Princess (Hwip'aram kongju, 2002), Love of North and South (Nam nam buk nyo, 2003), and North Korean Guys (Tonghaemul kwa baektusan i, 2003),[10] North Korean characters created by the South Korean film industry no longer adhered to the stereotypical image of the North still widely seen in American films (Die Another Day) and video games (Rogue Warrior). Ranging from accidental defectors (North Korean Guys) to the humane North Korean platoon leader during the Korean War (Welcome to Dongmakgol) and the effervescent teenaged daughter of the Dear Leader, Kim Jong-il (Whistling Princess), these films revealed that South Korea has already parted ways with the United States on how to approach and represent the North. Even the most despicable North Korean character of recent times, Sin (played by Jang Dong-gun) in Kwak Kyŏng-t'aek's Typhoon (T'aep'ung, 2005), was given a tragic childhood on which his malice can be blamed. Once fervently anti-Communist, South Korean films helped to demonstrate after 2000 that the country had removed North Koreans from its list of fictional villains.[11]

A few of the films featuring North Koreans were quite successful, but most of them were not. Though *Shiri* and *JSA*, two blockbusters made in 1999 and 2000, pivoted around North Korean characters, North Korea as subject matter had become stale a few years later. Driven in part by the liberal views of South Korean directors and producers, and inspired by the global appetite for hallyu, which demanded easily digestible plotlines incorporating Cold War ingredients, screens in South Korea had for a while featured a stream of stories centered on North Korea or North Koreans. However, much as the commercial fad for North Korean dialects and retro-style bars and restaurants that served dishes named after North Korean cities passed after peaking in 2003, these kinds of films stopped appealing to the South Korean public. By the end of the Sunshine Policy era, it became clear that neither reunification comedies such as Kim Jong-jin's *Underground Rendez-Vous* (*Mannam ŭi kwangjang*, 2007) nor serious t'albukja dramas such as Kim T'ae-gyun's *Crossing* (*K'ŭrosing*, 2008) could revive the public's interest in North Korea as the subject matter of films.

Despite the plummeting popularity of such films, a number of common tendencies and patterns among them emerge on closer examination. First, the plotlines tend to be about border crossings that take on transnational dimensions beyond just North and South Korea. Many of them focus on t'albukjas, whose numbers are growing each year. (Though reliable data is unavailable, some estimate that more than 100,000 talbukjas are scattered all over Asia, only a fraction of whom have been allowed into the South.) Because so few North Koreans have been let into South Korea, most South Korean films featuring t'albukjas take place in locales outside of Korea, such as China, Russia, Uzbekhistan, and Mongolia. Second, when the films exploit conventions of melodrama between a South Korean and his or her unfortunate Northern counterpart, they frequently do so according to the formula that tends to make the North Korea Other a naive newcomer who must learn to adapt to capitalist values in order to avoid tragic death. Third, in these romantic tales about relationships between North and South Koreans, Northerners are usually females.[12]

One of the main objectives of this chapter is to argue that just as the Sunshine Policy is in essence a liberal policy that perceives the North as the Other (undemocratic, resistant to a capitalist marketplace, and impenetrably real nation in a postmodern universe that cannot be either absorbed or absolved by the West and therefore earns a place in George W. Bush's notorious Axis of Evil) and that ultimately seeks to change North Korea through reform, the tendency of South Korean films to liberalize their depictions of North Koreans reflects South Korea's desire to make North Korea a different kind of Other. This liberal form of otherization is critical in the mode of knowledge production, albeit somewhere between factual and fictional, by which South Korea comes to understand its Northern counterpart. It is a cultural mission—matching the political tenor of the Sunshine Policy—that departs from the Cold War precepts that simplistically sought to vilify and annihilate the North, and instead tries to inculcate the beauty of market reform and globalization in the North. This process of liberal otherizing aims to transform North Korea (in due time, and at least in the popular imagination) into a subject willing to embrace reforms that remain in the best interest of a South Korea hoping to provide peace and stability in the region, rather than having to engage the real North Korea in another nightmarish war.

Perhaps the best way to track this argument is by following the depiction of Korean diasporic women from either North Korea or Yanbian Prefecture in China in recent popular South Korean films. Such characters play significant roles in the blockbuster thriller *Typhoon*, comedy *Wedding Campaign* (*Na ŭi kyŏlhon wonjŏnggi*, Hwang Pyŏng-guk, 2005), and *Innocent Steps* (*Taensŏ ŭi sunjŏng*, Pak Yŏng-hun, 2005), which features a Korean Yanbian woman. All three films enjoyed wide theatrical releases in South Korea. *Typhoon* tells a story that stretches over five countries (China, Thailand, North Korea, South Korea, and Russia) and twenty years (1985–2005). Though the film focuses on a male character Sin (though the more widely used romanization of this common Korean surname is Shin, the film deliberately dropped the "h" to accentuate his degenerate profile), a renegade North Korean who has sworn to destroy both South and North Korea since the countries had betrayed him and his family when they tried to cross the border from China, also highlighted is his long-lost sister, Ch'oe Myong-ju. Myong-ju, when found by the South Korean authorities—who want to use her to help them capture Sin—is a prostitute from North Korea who is dying of a terminal disease in Vladivostok. The plot of *Wedding Campaign* follows a young North Korean woman in Uzbekistan, Kim Lara, who longs to move to South Korea. In the third film, *Innocent Steps*, a South Korean dancer revives his career as a trainer of other dancers when he marries Chae-rin, a Yanbian woman, to allow her to become a legal immigrant.

All three films depict North Korean or Yanbian women as characters who are both unwavering in their goals and capable of redemption, in the process establishing new stereotypical characterizations of North Korean women. The moments of exculpation for these North Korean female characters, who had been forced to endure long periods of suffering (Myong-ju dies in the middle of the narrative, Lara has to spectacularly jump over the gate of the German Embassy in Tashkent to seek amnesty in the free world, and Chae-rin has to escape from a seedy nightclub where she was sold as a young prostitute), can be said to reflect an acknowledgment of North Korean and Yanbian suffering. In other words, they function as a kind of cultural *mea culpa* by South Koreans who have long neglected the plight of North Korean and illegal migrant workers. This *mea culpa* found in popular narratives has much in common with the melodramatic "race card" that has been widely exploited in the United States through novels and films such as Harriet Beecher Stowe's *Uncle Tom's Cabin*.[13] More specifically, for the first time since the colonial period (1910–45) — when *min-jok* (nationalism based on homogeneous ethnicity) had first entered the public consciousness because of the Japanese insistence on making Koreans second-class citizens — these films about North Korea and other diasporic groups demonstrate that new versions of ethnic victimization have emerged in South Korean popular culture. North Koreans undoubtedly are the leading subjects in these "race card" melodramas, but also frequently depicted are members of the Korean diasporic group from Yanbian, the Korean autonomous prefecture located in the northeastern part of China.

This chapter argues that, though they initially promote *minjok-juŭi* (nationalist) and humanist agendas, the films made during the Sunshine Policy era ultimately inspired and helped create one-dimensional stereotypes about North Koreans in the South that rarely moved beyond the creation of a pathetic Other. A closer examination of films like *Typhoon*, *Wedding Campaign*, and *Innocent Steps* further clarifies how the South Korean production of North Korean subjects continues to serve the interests of a South Korea that is trying to come to terms with an internal psychic and economic crisis of the anxious male subject. That anxiety is itself a displaced symptom that engages the neighboring nation's women without being either conscientious or reflective about them. This in turn affirms a self-deluding otherization that could be described by Edward Said's notion of the "metropolitan transfiguration of the colonial dilemma,"[14] a condition that could be said to be no different from a hegemonic nation's racialized construction of the colonized. Here I insist that the relationship between North and South Korea is no different from that between Occident and Orient characterized by Said as "a relationship of power, of domination, and of varying degrees of a complex hegemony."[15] Just as much as Flaubert's depiction of an Egyptian courtesan represented a woman who could never speak for herself, in these films, South Korea is presented as a "metropolitan male subject" who is suffering from psychological angst while noncapitalist North Korea and Yanbian are the pristine, gendered Other that helps alleviate his malaise of excessive urbanization, messy modernization, and the inevitably collusive relationships among business, politics, and capitalist expansion.

Typhoon

Touted as the most expensive South Korean film made at the time of its release ($15 million),[16] *Typhoon* is loaded with action sequences. When someone steals a nuclear weapon receiver kit from an American naval ship that has been attacked near the Taiwan Straits, it turns out that Sin—initially identified as a stateless pirate captain—is the mastermind behind the theft. The South Korean intelligence team, headed by the naval officer Kang Se-jong, soon realizes that Sin intends to spray nuclear waste over both South and North Korea using the energy of a typhoon that is approaching the peninsula. Sin, who speaks in a thick North Korean accent, wants revenge. Both North and South Korea had betrayed him and were responsible for his family's massacre twenty years earlier when they attempted to defect to South Korea. Needless to say, Sin is destroyed at the end of *Typhoon* by the South Korean officer, but not before leaving behind a bad taste of sentimental guilt in South Korean audiences for having created a monstrous "racialized victim" (though he shares their Korean heritage) caused by South Korea's intolerant sociopolitical policy toward North Korea, North Korean defectors, and anyone who helps them.

The most powerful role in this action-packed but substanceless film is that of Sin's sister, Myong-ju. Past South Korean films involving North Korean women, such as *Shiri*, relied on a Cold War formula in which women were feminist monsters and violent double-agent terrorists. Myong-ju's

35 Sin, the feared North Korean terrorist, sheds his tears upon finding his sister, but to no avail. *Typhoon*.

character is more realistic than a one-dimensional terrorist, but she is still a fatalistic woman who can never emerge from a fatalistic victimhood. Having been separated from her brother twenty years before and addicted to opium, Myong-ju has barely been surviving as a prostitute in Usurisk, a Russian town near Vladivostok, where a sizable population of Koreans has settled since the beginning of the twentieth century. Though only in her thirties, Myong-ju has the body of a septuagenarian. She suffers from a brain tumor, she can barely see, and her frail arms are covered with bruises. Shots of penicillin are all that keep her terminally ill body alive. Taken to a cottage by Kang, who has misled her into thinking he is an investigator hired by her brother Sin, she soon finds herself surrounded by Korean CIA agents. She refuses at first to be used as bait to capture her brother and manages to steal a gun from Kang. But her resistance ultimately collapses after Kang tells her that her brother has done unforgivable things to inno-cent people.

This revelation prompts Myong-ju to reminisce in a thick North Korean dialect about how their entire family had crossed the Tumen River in 1983 to escape from the totalitarian terror of North Korea, only to be fooled into believing that the Chinese government had struck a deal with the South Korean government to send them back to North Korea. Facing tor-ture, an indefinite period of incarceration, and even decapitation on their return, Myong-ju's family tries to escape, only to be shot down by Chi-nese guards. The two surviving members of the slaughtered North Korean family, Myong-ju and her brother Sin, vowed as a result never to trust either South or North Korea and, indeed, to seek revenge against both.

Kang's father, a South Korean officer, had also been gunned down by North Koreans in the early 1980s while commanding troops in an action against a North Korean spy submarine, so he remains sympathetic to Myong-ju. She has unfairly suffered the nomadic life of a t'albukja with neither citizenship nor a home, forced to wander the plains of Manchuria.

The film's most painful scene takes place when the South Korean intelligence agents who have surrounded Sin and are close to capturing him gun Myong-ju down. By throwing herself between the agents' guns and her brother, she sacrifices her dirtied, beaten-up body, producing the pathos of a film that seeks to dramatize the tragedy of the people (t'albukjas) who have been left outside the protection of either the Communist North or the Capitalist South. However, her death, which takes place halfway through the film, never moves beyond mere pathos: Myong-ju is never given the chance to say that her rights as a Korean citizen had been infringed, even though she could have been better off if she were to say these words: "I was a Korean and hate Communism, my rights to enter anti-Communist South Korea were denied. I have suffered, and therefore I deserve retribution." Myong-ju's resentment is buried as little more than one thread of the film's pathos, one that is moreover ultimately usurped by the film's far more prominent action sequences. Myong-ju is never allowed the agency that could actually allow her proper repatriation and recognition of her citizenship.

Wedding Campaign

The story of *Wedding Campaign* revolves around the real-life crisis facing men in South Korea's countryside who have been forced to remain bachelors because the eligible women keep moving to the cities. The film's premise thus combines two of South Korea's largest social issues: the rising number of male farmers who are unable to find brides; and the growing influx of migrant workers and t'albukjas who provide cheap labor in South Korea. The decreasing number of women in South Korea's countryside and the increasing number of female North Korean defectors and migrants in the South has led the South Korean film industry to develop dramas that exploit the old Korean proverb *nam nam buk nyo* (南男北女), which roughly translates as "the best men are found in the South and the best women in the North."

Man-taek is a thirty-eight-year-old farmer who has yet to find a suit-

36   Lara is a t'albukja, a North Korean defector. *Wedding Campaign.*

able mate. This failure is not just Man-taek's personal problem but also an issue that affects his entire family: Man-taek is his family's first-born son and needs to produce a male heir who can continue to perform the family's annual ancestral rites. His father is long gone, but his grandfather worries about Man-taek's wedding prospects, and his sixty-three-year-old mother still needs to "work her butt off" without seeing any help from a daughter-in-law in the future. His best friend, Hee-chul, a taxi driver, encourages Man-taek to explore the possibility of finding a wife in Uzbekistan, where a sizable Korean settlement has existed since the Stalinist era.

Man-taek and Hee-chul pay $2,000 each to a Korean-Uzbek match-making company and land in Tashkent after a seven-hour plane ride. Coming from rural homes, both men are impressed by the charming urban milieu of Uzbekistan's capital, Tashkent, and by the ample number of tall single women there. However, finding a bride turns out to be far from a smooth ride for either man. Hee-chul thinks that he deserves better than the affable and modestly attractive woman who has been assigned to him. Man-taek's problem is even more pronounced. He has a congenital tremor when he is in the presence of women, and unsurprisingly he fails at each and every date that his translator Lara arranges for him. After all opportunities for Man-taek have been exhausted, he realizes in a Jane Austen-esque plot twist that it is Lara with whom he has fallen in love.

Lara is a t'albukja who has been eagerly awaiting her chance to begin a new life in South Korea. She has arranged for a counterfeit South Korean passport to be prepared for her by her boss, but he insists that she pay the full amount she owes. She is $2,000 short, an amount she'll be able to earn as a bonus once Man-taek successfully finds a mate. It turns out, however, that the Korean-Uzbek matchmaking agency has been deemed illegal by the Uzbek government. After the Uzbek police raid the office, the boss is nowhere to be found, and without him, Lara cannot get her passport. Both Man-taek and Hee-chul face deportation with neither a refund nor a wife. Lara, now an illegal resident in Uzbekistan, would also face expulsion to North Korea if caught by the authorities. However, unlike Myong-ju, who remains a persona non grata in both North and South Korea, Lara earns the respect of Man-taek, who promises her that he will return to Uzbekistan to fetch her.

Neither pity nor guilt motivates Man-taek to fall in love with Lara. Though a t'albukja, she exemplifies both the professional competence (as indicated by her linguistic skills in both Korean and Russian) and career motivation (she needs to earn $2,000 to buy her passport to South Korea) that are desirable traits, according to South Korean men. Lara is both healthy and resourceful, and in many ways, bears no stigma of the famine-stricken and backward Communist North. While this causes her character to differ from past characterizations of North Koreans, neither can she be described as a realistic portrayal of a t'albukja. The healthy t'albukja Lara is more capable of attaining agency for herself than the sickly Myong-ju in *Typhoon*, but she ultimately needs help from Man-taek for she is still unable to cross the border on her own. This places her in the framework of South Koreans' *mea culpa*, which shows guilt over their government's inability to provide proper and timely political citizenship and economic asylum for these subjects who share their ethnicity. If it is indeed a *mea culpa* that is being invoked in these films, this demonstrates that the predominant ideology in South Korea has yet to move beyond the hegemonic American interest in separating ruthless North Korean leaders from the innocent hungry masses who are seeking refuge elsewhere.

In *Wedding Campaign*, the notion of rural South Korean men rejuvenating themselves results, ironically, in a fantastical depiction of a North Korean woman who is in many ways more business-minded and transnational than the South Korean male. The film ends with Korean intelligence men visiting Man-taek in his hometown to ask him whether he knows Lara, a t'albukja, who identified him as her guardian in South Korea when she entered the country. In this respect, *Wedding Campaign* also moves into the *mea culpa* discourse that dominates many South Korean films about North Korea. By helping the North Korean woman, the inept South Korean man, who literally shudders at even a whiff of the scent of a woman, has become revitalized. It is only a matter of time before the unattractive and clumsy South Korean Man-taek reunites with the savvy and resourceful North Korean Lara, who needs a fresh new start in South Korea. Realistic or not, the film allows the insufficient South Korean man to find a North Korean woman to help restore his masculinity.

Innocent Steps

If over fifty years of post–Korean War films in South Korea have produced powerful American characters—both white and black—as the most dominant form of the ethnic Other and the unsullied signifier that precipitated Korean men's devirilization,[17] recent years of economic prosperity have brought about a renewed Korean interest in finding its inferior ethnic Other in its Asian neighbors. That interest has helped to remasculinize South Korea. While the nation's economic recovery and the restored democracy of recent years have helped to weaken the popular image of demasculinized Korean men held up against the powerful image of American occupiers, the South Korean film industry continues to make narratives of phallic revitalization. These remasculinization plots exploit not only North Korean women but also the bodies of Korean diasporic women from Yanbian, through whom the impotent men can be nourished and reinvigorated. The use of what is familiar to us as typically colonial and racialized dynamics supports this chapter's contention that contemporary Korea no longer qualifies as simply a victimized subject reeling under foreign military occupation. Both migrant female bodies from Yanbian and North Korea extend the genderized vicitimization discourse of modern Korean women that began with the early colonial figures of the endangered nuŭi tongsaeng (younger sister) who is the half-courtesan half-schoolgirl discussed in chapter 2, and that has continued with the postcolonial GI bride prototype into the twenty-first century.[18] In other words, embedded in the virtual deck of *mea culpa* are the old race, nation, and gender cards that continue to be reshuffled in order to address the new crisis of urban decay experienced in postmodern Korea today.

If Albert Camus's depiction of Arabs punctured French imperialism's exhaustion, the melancholia and anxiety of Korean men could be said to have sprung from a paradigm that belongs to both the First and the Third Worlds. Thus the otherness of the immigrant worker is both defamiliarized and made familiar. After all, to use the term "colonized" to refer to the North Korean immigrant workers in South Korea is no small irony—not only because the North has never been colonized by South Korea, but also because it is often impossible to distinguish between South Koreans and many immigrant workers from North Korea, Yanbian, and other Chinese territories just by looking at their faces. Many of these immigrant workers (especially those from Yanbian and North Korea) are capable of speaking with a standard Seoul accent after a few months in South Korea. Yet the recently heightened awareness of their position as disenfranchised Other within their own ethnic group continues to reinforce the all-too-familiar bifurcated notion of South Korea as an impotent, desecrated fatherland and the immigrant women as a locus of maternal imagination.

Innocent Steps foregrounds aging male protagonists whose dreams of making it big in the city have been shattered by both injury and ineptitude. The film—a star vehicle that sought to appeal to teenage girls and that performed strongly in the box office, selling more than two million tickets in South Korea[19]—features several themes and elements. First, it extends the theme explored in the films discussed above, the transformation of the aimless and unprincipled lives of the male protagonists who occupy remote corners of urbanized Korea: Na Young-sae undergoes a process of revitalization through the love he develops for Chae-rin (played by Moon Geun-young), a woman from outside South Korea who unexpectedly enters his life. Second, Chae-rin—who is from Yanbian, China's Korean Autonomous Prefecture in northeastern China, and who seeks a better future in South Korea—embodies the fantasy of the male protagonist by providing a bottomless well from which purity, innocence, and loyalty pour out. Third, because Chae-rin had been randomly matched with Young-sae in a classic fake marriage scheme to provide legal residence in South Korea in exchange for cash, *Innocent Steps* naturally deconstructs marriage as an accouterment of love and at the same time reaffirms the possibility of love only in fantasy, not reality.

I have previously argued that the most prevalent trend in Korean cinema during the past two or three decades has been its turn toward remasculinization.[20] Identifying the desire for dominant men as the chief trope of the New Korean Cinema of the 1980s and the 1990s, I have analyzed Korean film texts anchored in characters' transformation from pathetic, masochistic, and aimless youth to responsible men destined to acquire political agency. Even though the politicized, post-traumatic recovery of the Korean male subject is no longer the dominant narrative leitmotif of the new millennium, I have claimed that images of the wretched men who have had their dreams and ideals taken away in the city still linger as a vestige of an almost-formulaic recipe for South Korea's commercial cinema. I have cited Pae Ch'ang-ho's *Whale Hunting* (1984) as a representative film in which the mission of a young college student, Pyŏng-t'ae (played by Kim Su-ch'ŏl) is carried out in a rural space where families and pastoral values still provide identification—both collective and putatively individual—that temporarily alleviates the anxiety and libidinal effects of urban exposure.

Young-sae in *Innocent Steps* faces a predicament exactly like those of Pyŏng-tae or Ch'il-su, the male protagonist of *Chilsu and Mansu*, created more than twenty years earlier. All of these South Korean male characters, in other words, have been exiles in their own homes. In *Innocent Steps*, Young-sae, a professional dancer, has been defeated by his rival, Hyun-se, in a national dancesport competition and has lost his lover as a result. He is no longer concerned about keeping himself in shape and has become a slacker, idly waiting for time to pass. When Young-sae is introduced after the opening titles, he is seen stretched out on a sofa surrounded by empty bottles, an ashtray filled to the brim, cups of instant noodles, and other items that show both his deterioration and unkemptness. Nothing in his immediate neighborhood can reinvigorate Young-sae, who is already past his prime. It is only the purity of outside women who can reawaken the passion and the dreams of men like him, whose hopes had long vanished in the city ruled by greed and money.

Innocent Steps points briefly to the prominent Chinatown in the Karibong-dong administrative section of Seoul, where urban spaces suffer from deindustrialization and decay. Karibong-dong (in Yeongdungpo District) was a vibrant industrial center with hundreds of factories during the Park Chung Hee era (1961–79), but most of them have shut down since then. Not even the spectacle of a dance competition can lighten up the film's urban ambience. Young-sae, whose performing career had ended prematurely because of a leg injury, is reborn as a dance trainer when he is matched with Chae-rin, the woman from Yanbian, who knows neither standard Korean nor professional dance moves. No longer accompanied by a competent partner, Young-sae must first train the girl who has landed on his lap after swapping identity with her sister, a professional dancer.

Innocent Steps continues to exploit markers of the provincial that are no longer drawn from local women but rather from women outside of Korea. Chae-rin has been saved by a fabricated marriage with Young-sae. Her hard-working ethics combined with her loyalty toward her fake husband contrast sharply with the qualities of Young-sae's previous Korean girlfriend, who abandoned him for greener pastures within the film's first ten minutes. Playing Chae-rin is perhaps the biggest young star in Korea today: Moon Geun-young, who at the age of only sixteen catapulted into the ranks of A-list Korean actresses. With her naturally flat nose, uneven teeth, and tiny physique, Moon is an anomaly among Korean actresses today who are vastly aided by plastic surgery and disassociates herself from the desires and yearnings for the West and the libidinal economy of the city generated by the emission of sexual lust and consumerism. Moon's popularity is partly derived from her unspoiled provincial background: she was born and raised in Kwang-ju, a city in the southwestern part of the Korean Peninsula, a bedrock of Korean democracy. Her character therefore cannot easily be incorporated into the sexualized labor marketplace, despite the fact that the she is sold to a pimp the minute she sets foot on Korean soil. The binary between the desecrated and corrupt Korea that sprawls endlessly into ugly urbanization and the nurturing provinciality embodied by the Yanbian woman can be maintained only after she is denied entry into South Korea as a migrant sex worker.

Fearing that secret immigration inspectors are on their trail, Chae-rin and Young-sae decide to pose for wedding pictures that they plan to pin to their apartment wall. This precipitates a moment in *Innocent Steps* where Chae-rin and Young-sae slip into a fantasy landscape, as they both attempt to construct a story of how they first met and fell in love. While training for their dance competition, they start jabbing at each other about their fictitious love story—one that will be both possible and plausible to the authorities. In this fictional story, Chae-rin is a female guide from Yanbian and Young-sae is a Korean bus driver. In dreams, they tour the sites of Seoul and its vicinities together—Suwon Castle, the World Cup Soccer Stadium, and the Korean Folk Village—until love ignites between the two. Since their marriage is only a pretense, this too is an imagined memory. Yet this fantasy tour of famous sites reveals an ironically subversive attempt to undermine Korean history, both traditional and modern. All three sites—a ruin of a fortress destroyed during the Korean War that had to be reconstructed in the 1970s, the venue where the Korean national soccer team won matches in the 2002 World Cup in controversially refereed games against technically superior European teams, and the folk village erected during the tyrannical Park Chung Hee regime in order to attract foreign tourists—historicize an identity of Korea that is neither natural nor genuine. Like this self-referential acknowledgment of the sites' superficial, postmodern foundations, the love that develops between Chae-rin and Young-sae is stuck somewhere between genuine and invented feelings. If indeed their forced marriage escapes the grim qualities of everyday realities—economic misery for the Korean man and deportation for the Yanbian woman—who is to say that their love, with its melodramatic ending, is more real than the fake wedding photos pinned up on the wall of their apartment? Which is more real—the "I love yous" exchanged between Chae-rin and Young-sae through e-mail and seen in the fantasy sequence, or the dance between the two that is part of their training for a competition that does not exist outside the film's diegesis?

As is expected in every melodrama that features fake marriage schemes,[21] *Innocent Steps* flirts with a tragic plotline. Though revitalized and all set to compete in the national dancesports championship, Young-sae breaks his legs right before the important finals. Chae-rin has matured into a professional dancer and desperately seeks a partner. Since Young-sae is unavailable, Chae-rin has no choice but to accept his rival, Hyun-se, as her partner in the competition. She of course wins the national title, but only because Young-sae has accepted his role as a trainer rather than an active dancer, which completes his journey to responsible manhood. Though Chae-rin's predicament initially is rooted in artificially constructed otherness, she is still ethnically Korean. Therefore, the moment she adopts the survival tactics of capitalism (Internet skills and agile dance moves) and the ideological discourse of phallocentrism (curing the male hysteria and impotence), she is fully integrated into a nation that habitually claims one of the highest percentages of ethnic homogeneity in the world. *Innocent Step*'s melodramatic ending satisfies both the male fantasy and the nationalist discourse that seeks to exploit victimization and pity based on gendered ethnic differences.

Conclusion

For a very long time, Korea has prided itself on its ethnic homogeneity. Despite the fact that the number of non-Korean residents and migrant workers in South Korea has rapidly been increasing over the past two decades, it is inarguable that all of the documented uprisings of the recent past have been rooted in strife over region, class, dictatorship, and colonial policy—not ethnicity. The representation of North Korean and immigrant female workers in recent South Korean films registers the emergence of a new variety of melodrama that exploits victimization and pity based on ethnic differences. In other words, despite the fact that North Koreans do not constitute an entirely new ethnic group, I would argue that the sixty-five years of division into North and South Koreas—spanning more than three generations—combined with the influx of recent immigration make it impossible to continue to subscribe to the "one people" theory. Even a small exchange between the two Koreas such as the Geumgangsan Tour, which potentially constitutes a line of flight, unfortunately has proven to be costly for both countries. Too many years have elapsed for anyone to insist that all Koreans are bound by the same cultural, behavioral, linguistic, and physical commonalities. After more than six decades of economic, political, and military ties with the United States, wouldn't a South Korean share more common ground with an American than with a North Korean? The segregated status between the North and South for almost three generations that has never even officially sanctioned marriages between people from the two countries has prompted *Joongang Ilbo*, one of the leading dailies, to print a front-page article in 2006 that questioned the ethnic sameness between the two Koreas.[22] This article claims that beyond the ideological differences, there is a serious gap now between North and South in several areas—such as body shape, because of the differences in nutrition and medical care.

Though such reports are surely exaggerated—they do not fully consider comprehensive scientific and cultural data—there is a general agreement among both North and South Koreans that the differences between the two in language, cultural behavior, and physical appearance have been growing. Unless the severe segregation ends, these growing differences will eventually divide Koreans into separate ethnic groups. Exploiting such differences as a melodramatic ingredient of pathetic victimhood, South Korean popular discourse constructs North Koreans and immigrant women as racialized subjects. The poor, victimized female bodies of Myong-ju, Lara, and Chae-rin, all of whom risk their lives to escape from the totalitarian regime of North Korea or an underdeveloped region of China, only to be shunned by the prosperous South Koreans, render meaningful the visible signs of difference. The sick and bruised North Korean women in these films create a *virtual-actual* space in the South Korean popular discourse, much as the beaten body of Uncle Tom evoked a specific white liberal guilt reaction in the United States in the nineteenth century. These characterizations are in some ways a throwback to a distant era that predates the postmodern and industrialized South Korea—an era when families were uprooted from rural communal spaces and women carried with them *bojakis* (bundles of clothing) to escape from high rents charged by evil landlords or Japanese colonialists.

"Nationalism," remarks an African character in Raymond Williams's 1964 novel *Second Generation*, "is in this sense like class. To have it, and to feel it, is the only way to end it. If you fail to claim it, or give it up too soon, you will merely be cheated, by other classes and other nations."[23] For many South Koreans during the first decade of the twenty-first century, when they were forced to grapple with a coherent, independent national identity after undergoing the country's colonization by Japan and the military occupation and wartime operational control by the United States over a region that technically is still at war, North Korea and the Yanbian women were an additional postideological entity that they needed to engage: one that might be more complicated than the fight against Communism itself. Contemporary South Korean melodramas that feature pathetic women from outside the country insist on both the sameness that is derived from ethnic homogeneity and the difference precipitated by the undeniable chasm between affluent South Korea and starving North Korea. The plight of t'albukjas and Yanbian women in the present is real, but the one added to the melodramatic plotlines of these entertainment films reiterates an artificial *mea culpa* whose primary intent is to produce tears from the affluent South Koreans.

The renewed interest in identifying China or North Korea as South Korea's ethnic Other helps to shore up national identity in the South rather than diminishing it. Despite the climate of economic free trade and the promotion of a supposedly borderless world, this revitalized nationalism has proven to be more durable in Korea than any other ideological mantras that have swept over the country in the past decades. Instead of defamiliarizing Koreans' stable national citizenship, all of these films that foreground victimized women as racialized Other reaffirm the notion that the most salient site of citizenship is established through the imaginary singular mode of nationhood, where the artificial flag of homogeneous ethnicity still waves. By joining the list of personae non gratae made up largely of Southeast Asian and African migrant workers in Korea, t'albu-jas awkwardly complicate Korea's myth of homogeneity and diversify its national space. But by largely depicting them as refugees, squatters, and prostitutes, even the films from the liberal Sunshine Policy era largely fail to interrogate the conservative Cold War–era political discourse that vili-fied the North Korean Communist leadership and instead ends up exploit-ing the t'albujas as subjects that meekly provoke a *mea culpa*.

FIVE

Hong Sang-soo's Death, Eroticism,
and Virtual Nationalism

I went down to the river bank and joined the crowd. The dead woman was facing the river, so I couldn't see her face but I could see her permed hair and plump white limbs. She was wearing a thin red sweater and a white skirt. It must have been rather cold early in the morning. Or maybe she had a liking for that outfit. Her head was resting on rubber shoes with flowery patterns and lying on the ground in the rain and a few feet away from her limp lifeless hand was a white handkerchief, which, as it did not blow about in the wind, seemed to be wrapped around something. To get a glimpse of her face, the children stood in the stream facing my way. Their blue school uniforms were reflected upside down on the water and were like blue flags surrounding the corpse. *Strangely, I felt rising within me a great surge of physical desire for the dead woman.* I hurriedly left the scene. [my emphasis]

—Kim Sŭng-ok, "A Journey to Mujin"

The passage above is the story that established Kim Sŭng-ok as one of the most celebrated Korean writers of the period after the Korean War. He belongs to the first generation of writers to be educated in Korean after Korea's liberation from Japan.[1] The story is written from the perspective of a young man, Yun, whose frustration at returning to his western seashore home is highlighted in this passage when he encounters a young woman's corpse. In Seoul, Yun has established a successful career as a young executive at a pharmaceutical company through his marriage with the daughter of the company's president. The encounter with the dead body takes place during his annual trip home in order to visit his mother's grave. His old friends no longer amuse him, however, and a brief love affair with a local music teacher sours when she resists separation from her husband. Yun's sudden encounter with the body of an apparent prostitute who has committed suicide signals an almost existential shift in the story: it reveals not only the vast wasteland that Korea's countryside has become, but also the death that exists in life.

"Death as the absolute point of view over life and opening on its truth," writes Michel Foucault, "is also that against which life, in daily practice comes up against."[2] What Foucault is suggesting here is that the perspective offered by death is essential to cracking open the truth of life, and also that death's meaning is so absolute and inescapable that it is not easily perceived in everyday existence. Does Yun become embarrassed about the philistinism of his own erotic response because the young woman's dead body signifies an absolute purity? Also, does his necrophilia have something to do with the uneasy relationship between his life as a successful, urban, corporate executive and the dilapidated countryside in which he was born and raised? Fulfilling his desire is impossible, and Yun runs away, but the close affinity between death and sex in this scene unconsciously disengages sexual desire from procreation, since necrophilia is ultimately a nonproductive discharge of semen.

Written nearly fifty years ago when the draining of Korea's young labor force and the denuding of Korea's hills were both at their peaks, this description of a young woman's body emerges as a shocking allegory of Korea's ravaged landscape. The corpse, in other words, is a sign both of the plundered countryside that is echoed in the infertile land and barren women and of the tamed revolutionary spirit of the early 1960s that was characterized by repressed political agency as well as wasted eroticism. The woman's body—already lifeless, immaterial, and insubstantial—is not unlike Korea's national body, which had displayed a momentary democratic cultural renaissance that would be killed off by a single blow, a military coup, less than a year later. Eroticism and death are central to this passage, but they are also a disturbingly sensual reminder of a nation's history.

I begin this chapter on the filmmaker Hong Sang-soo with this literary excerpt from 1963 because there is a sense in which the postwar Korean literature of the 1960s, which featured writers such as Kim Sŭng-ok, Yi Ch'ŏng-jun, and O Chŏng-hŭi, forms a continuum of sorts with Hong's films. Kim Sŭng-ok's narrator's pointless outburst of eroticism, his obsession with death, and the unattractive landscapes in which his tale is set together signal a withdrawal into interiority that partially reflects the political crisis that occurred after the short-lived April 19th Student Revolution. This modern awareness of interiority is accompanied by both an intense form of narcissism and a realization of the futility of conscious exteriority. This triumvirate that makes up modernist subjectivity— narcissistic interiority, the de-linking of the individual and the social, and an obsession with death and mourning—is also especially relevant to Hong Sang-soo's films, which have been favorites of the critics since his debut in 1996.[3]

I am also interested in how an unlikely dialectical relationship is forged between cosmopolitanism and eroticism in the texts of both Kim Sŭng-ok and Hong Sang-soo. Korea's two postideological fervors (after the 1960s for Kim and after the 1980s for Hong) both generated a strong movement toward massive interiorization, reflected in the two men's work. The demand for space for narcissistic, libertine sexuality competes with a desire for universality and cultural pluralism. Both Kim and Hong have been attacked by some critics who think their work is too pessimistic (*yŏmse-juŭijŏk*), inculcating in their audience a disgust with life and even with democratic principles. Though Kim's and Hong's characters appear to be nihilistic, I argue in this chapter that they obey the universal law of effervescence: sustaining life as active as it is passionate. The drive toward pleasure is ultimately tied not only to the depoliticized environment in which both artists were active—immediately after the intense politicization of the 1960s and 1980s, respectively—but also to the need to expose the lousiness of human existence, which reveals, for them, very little difference between "man and beast."

Every intense political movement in twentieth-century Korea has been followed by a cultural renaissance. The gap between the individual and the social was erased during these periods of heightened politicization, and an aesthetic movement that sought to defend the space of the individual ego followed. After the anti-Japanese nationalist movement of the 1920s, symbolized by the Kwangju Student Uprising (1929), had lost steam, the poetry of Yi Sang startled literary circles and became the bedrock of Korea's modernism. Once the democratic regime established through a student-led revolution in 1960 had come to an end, modernist writers like Kim Sŭng-ok and Kim Su-yŏng became the stars of the literary world that anchored postwar Korea's intellectual discourse. During the most recent postpolitical phase, Hong Sang-soo has emerged not only as a favorite of film critics, but also as the prodigal son of literary critics. These critics have seen in Hong's work a profound crisis of meaning in language that is intimately tied to the withering of political agency, a symptom of any postpolitical model.

Terms like "gender," "class," "ethnicity," and "national identity" appear to have little connection with Hong Sang-soo's thematic concerns about everyday life in such a postpolitical paradigm. Indeed, Hong's films, notorious for overstressing the difficulties of communication, can be said to awaken the potential destabilization of already fragile relationships: friendships, family, or national communities. He strips away the thin veneer of reason and decency that covers every social network and shows, through his indignant, socially inept characters, that miscommunication is not the exception but the norm in everyday interactions between people. In this cultural formation, any type of ideology—including national subjectivity, which ought to function as the glue between the individual and the social—becomes highly suspect and even irrelevant. In Hong's *Night and Day* (*Pam kwa nat*, 2008), shot almost entirely in Paris, Kim Sŏng-nam, a South Korean painter living in exile in France because he violated the marijuana possession laws in his home country, tries to atone for an offensive comment he once made about Kim Il-sung to a North Korean student in Paris. Realizing that they have nothing more to say to one another, the two Koreans—one from the South and the other from the North—decide to settle accounts by arm wrestling. As Louis Althusser has suggested, language is a key ideological access point to an individual's dominant framework.[4] Here is a key Hong Sang-soo moment: since the two can no longer speak to each other, the only way they can communicate is by going outside the domain of language. Refusing to enter the social (symbolic) sphere, they become silly kids, wrestling each other in a playground.

Such a childish portrayal of the most fractious nation-state in the world today, still split into Communist North and Capitalist South, both dislodges the traditional austere representation of Cold War Korea and engages a new line of historical confabulation. If portraying the banality of everyday life is a way of sublimating the social totality of this particular epoch, then even the slight annoyance of failing to understand each other (or of walking around aimlessly, both typical occurrences in Hong Sang-soo films) expresses what Akira M. Lippit describes as being "at the end of the political lines that traverse and constitute Korean history, *at the other end of politics*."[5] Therein lies also the virtual engagement with Korean history implicit in Hong Sang-soo's films. This real and unreal engagement delves deeply into the interiority and past of the nation, which is itself undergoing a painful process of decolonization that is still far from complete.

Before the US military occupation (1945 to the present) and Japan's colonization (1910–45), Korea had a long and arguably unremarkable history under the Chosun Dynasty (1392–1910). This extended period was marked by an abiding fear of foreigners, especially after the devastating invasions by the Japanese and Manchus in the late sixteenth and early seventeenth centuries. In order to sustain sociopolitical stability and cultural autonomy, the Korean kings of the Chosun Dynasty submitted to the

Chinese policies of so-called unity and peace, and to Chinese suzerainty. Though Hong Sang-soo's films are neither epic dramas nor folk traditions that can help to manufacture a sense of nation, they propose everyday temporalities of both cosmopolitanism and narcissism—however contradictory the two may seem—that are sought out by Korean intellectuals. That is to say, the antiheroes of Hong Sang-soo's films are those who confer value on the city and the egotistical intellectuals who live in them—and, by extension, on the nation and society that are repellent to them.

Most people might squirm at the idea of an association between Hong Sang-soo's films and nationalist (minjok) discourse. The presumption is that being engaged in a Korean nationalist cinema means seeking to re-inscribe the conventional bonds between the nation's symbols (such as the flag, the thirty-eighth parallel, and memorabilia from the Korean War) and their historical signification. Kang Che-gyu managed to do this with his box-office hit *Tae Guk Gi: The Brotherhood of War* (2004), as did Kang Woo-suk in *Silmido* (2003). In other words, landscapes, objects, and people must serve as allegories or metaphors. However, both these options are unacceptable as creative praxis for Hong Sang-soo. Through his films, he asserts that language and systems of signification are inherently arbitrary, sometimes even forcing the erosion of the bonds between a signifier (a word or cinematic image) and its corresponding signified (the meaning or concept represented).

For example, whether or not Su-jeong is really a *ch'ŏnyŏ* (virgin) in *Virgin Stripped Bare by Her Bachelors* is still a matter of intense conjecture in discussions after screenings of the film at Hong Sang-soo retrospectives at various film festivals around the world. This debate eventually leads to questioning the very meaning behind the idea of "virgin." Common sense might suggest that this is unnecessarily complex for a film running 90 to 120 minutes and meant to be shown in commercial multiplexes. Questions such as "What is the meaning behind ch'ŏnyŏ?" resist the mind's inclination to neatly slot all complicated philosophical issues into categories of race, gender, class, and national identity. Of course, it is difficult to deny that those categories constitute important aspects of the social discourse and affect how we interpret culture.

All thinking requires interpretation. But, as Susan Sontag reminds us, "that does not mean there aren't some metaphors we might well abstain from or try to retire."[6] Hong Sang-soo's films attempt to save many objects from the tyranny of metaphors. In the process, they achieve a virtual refiguration of objects and space, including the nation. In this Internet age, where cinéma vérité style as rendered by reality TV like Korea's *Na kasu* (*I Am a Singer*) and hit sitcoms like *The Office* and *Curb Your Enthusiasm* have become the most dominant commercial visual medium, how could we ever trust that an image issuing from late capitalist culture could belong to the terrain of truth? The attempt to achieve this degree of trustworthiness is, as I have argued throughout this book, different from the objective of realism, which desperately seeks to break down the boundaries between an object or a thing and its representative filter, thereby replacing—even if only metaphorically—the truth behind the object or thing that has been filmed. The kind of self-reflexivity that admits only the essence of subjectivity is a doubly layered one, in which the past coexists with the present. Such self-reflexivity lies at the foundation of Hong Sang-soo's modernist take on cinema, which can itself be seen as a last-ditch effort to reclaim the truth of human fallibility from the visual medium saturated by metaphors that tend to allegorize every representation.

This arrival at a truth that is ungraspable and unrepresentable is the point from which we can begin to understand Hong's tenacious desire to flirt with his own eroticism, death, and national identity. This tendency, evident in all of his films since *The Day a Pig Fell into the Well* (1996), has become even more pronounced in those he has written and directed in the twenty-first century: *Turning Gate* (*Saenghwal ŭi palgyŏn*, 2002), *Woman Is the Future of Man* (*Yŏja nŭn namja ŭi miraeda*, 2004), *Tale of Cinema* (*Kŭkjangjŏn*, 2005), *Woman on the Beach* (*Haebyŏn ŭi yŏin*, 2006), *Night and Day*, *Like You Know It All* (*Chal aljido mokhamyŏnsŏ*, 2009), *Ha Ha Ha* (2010), and *Oki's Movie* (*Okhi ŭi yŏnghwa*, 2010).[7] This chapter considers how these films reconstitute the fallacies of erotic desires, fear of death, and nationalist values. Reversing the pattern of Yasujiro Ozu, whose films "pick[ed] out the intolerable from the insignificant itself,"[8] Hong Sang-soo is at ease picking out the insignificant from the intolerable.[9] All of the impulses listed above—sex, death, and minjok identity—are either matters of grave importance or taboo subjects for most Koreans.

However, for Hong Sang-soo, they are just depictions of everyday life and thus fraught with mundane insignificance, especially since they are typically deployed to heighten personal jealousies and narcissism. The premise of *Night and Day* is a case in point. The painter protagonist, wanted by the Korean authorities for having puffed just one marijuana joint, bemoans the fact that his crime resulted from a momentary lapse caused by a capricious desire to try a new experience just once. Jail is like death to him. His fear of the penitentiary is so great that he seeks refuge in a city—Paris—where he knows no one. However, as revealed later in the film, his crime is actually only a misdemeanor, which means he could have taken care of it by paying a small fine. Here again, what Hong has managed to do is unscramble the intolerable from the insignificant for the purpose of scrambling the two back together. Curiosity about an unknown substance (insignificant) escalates into a serious violation of the nation's drug laws (intolerable). Later, the fear of prosecution (intolerable) is translated into paranoia and hypochondria (insignificant).

Two other films featured here, *Woman Is the Future of Man* and *Woman on the Beach*, focus on yuhaksaeng characters who have just returned from studies abroad. Because these characters are in Korea for the first time after a long absence, they tend to complain about the difficulty of adjusting to life there, as well as the irrational values they now detect among Koreans and the deep-seated prejudices the community has against outsiders. Hong is often unforgiving in his analysis of Koreans—both those who have never left home and those who have returned from studying abroad—who continue to suffer from fear of freedom, fear of cosmopolitanism, and fear of complexity stemming from their own lack of experience (the result being that they end up borrowing the customs, values, and economic structures of both Japan and the United States). Neither the remarkable economic renaissance enjoyed by Koreans after long years of destitution nor the democratic transformation that Koreans have experienced are to be celebrated, according to Hong; they are, to put it crudely, fake. Self-denial and intellectual bickering among Hong's characters indicate an exquisite sense of loss and mourning for the valorized Korean spirit, which can perhaps never be restored, and for the possibility that various inauspicious characteristics acquired during the colonial and postcolonial periods may never be erased.

Turning Gate

In *Turning Gate*, Kyung-soo, an actor in the midst of a career change from stage to film, finds himself between jobs. As the film opens, he receives a phone call from his director friend, who notifies him that he's been fired. Kyung-soo is told that he is being blamed for the box-office failure of the last film in which he had appeared. When he visits the production office, he receives a million won (about $1,000) as pay for the film. But since the movie has flopped so badly, the director insists that it would be unethical for Kyung-soo to take the money. He is entitled to it according to a clause in his contract, but Kyung-soo's friendship with the director is jeopardized the moment he accepts it. The director warns Kyung-soo: "It is difficult to be human, but let's try not to become monsters." This satirical statement stands out as one of the story's central themes, as Kyung-soo struggles between being human and a monster throughout the film.

Ironically, because he has been fired, Kyung-soo has earned some free time. He travels to Ch'un-ch'ŏn, a three-hour train ride from Seoul, to see an old friend, a writer, before visiting his family in Pusan. Kyung-soo's nomadic identity allows the story to find some space in a modern existence split between routine drudgery at work, family responsibilities, and sleep. In other words, the narrative space of *Turning Gate* escapes conventional causality because Kyung-soo is temporarily relieved from having to work. The film follows the aimless trajectory of its idealistic protagonist as he pursues the meaning of life on the road. (The direct translation of the film's Korean title is "discovery of life.") By being released from work and the maddening city of Seoul, Kyung-soo has time to indulge in a capriciousness and idealism that is amusing to viewers, who are themselves constantly being battered and baffled by the dense human traffic of urban centers.

The main characters of all Hong Sang-soo's films to date are humiliated at some point, and Kyung-soo is no exception. His idealism and obstinacy may be noble, but, in practical reality, he is a person who—as a fortuneteller tells him—"cannot easily blend with the others." He resists love when it is offered to him, yet he clamors for it when it is denied. Kyung-soo meets Myung-sook, a dancer, in Ch'un-ch'ŏn, the first city he visits. Despite the fact that Sung-woo, the novelist friend he is visiting, already fancies Myung-sook, Kyung-soo sleeps with her without guilt or love. Myung-sook has already seen Kyung-soo several times in the movies and has fallen helplessly in love with him. Her attempt to win his love is to no avail, however. Kyung-soo leaves town by train, abandoning Myung-sook, whose eyes are swollen from crying. However, Kyung-soo will also soon feel unrequited love. On his way to Pusan, he happens to meet Sun-young, an attractive woman who is traveling home to Kyŏng-ju. Helplessly drawn to her, Kyung-soo gets off at her stop and surreptitiously trails her to find out where she lives.

This unscheduled stop releases Kyung-soo from the linear plotline and

37 Kyung-soo is caught sneaking a peek. *Turning Gate.*

also from his final destination, Pusan. Since he has no plans, and only a vague idea of seduction, which may or may not happen, he has effectively freed himself from the chain of dramatic causality. Kyung-soo is not just a lonely traveler; he is also an outsider from the metropolis in a small town where he is not particularly welcome. He finds himself in Kyŏng-ju, an ancient capital of Korea and a city where the only person he knows is Sun-young—who, it will soon be revealed, is a married woman. Although he has found out where she lives and will soon visit her, surprising her and the rest of her family, he has yet to make up his mind about what to do next. He checks into a cheap boardinghouse. Alone, he takes a walk to a part of the city that tourists rarely visit and nonchalantly enters a restaurant. In this flimsy yet crowded barbeque place, he orders some *kopch'ang* (beef intestines) to grill at the table and a bottle of *soju* (cheap Korean liquor), thanks to which he will slowly become intoxicated.

"In a day made up of twenty-four hours, couldn't you possibly spare ten minutes to make one simple phone call?" asks a male diner with a thick accent who is sitting at a table next to Kyung-soo. The woman with him— who has the same accent—replies, "I was too busy . . . I'm sure that you understand." The tension between the couple reflects the all-too-common situation of a country boy who has been anxiously left behind while his girlfriend pursues her dreams in the metropolis. It does not take long for the already irritated young local man to catch sight of a stranger from Seoul sneaking a peek at his girlfriend.

"What were you looking at?" the young man asks Kyung-soo, rudely jolting him from the reverie he had fallen into while eating and staring at the woman's slender, exposed legs. The male diner's thick, provincial accent is even more pronounced now, marking him as someone rooted in this traditional, conservative town. Kyung-soo immediately denies the charge, replying meekly: "What . . . me? Nothing. I wasn't looking at anything." Despite Kyung-soo's denial—he protests that he had been checking out a poster pinned right above the woman's head—the audience already senses Kyung-soo's guilt. His feeble lie—the denial that he was looking—exasperates the other man. Irritation soon turns to rage, producing obscenities and insults directed at Kyung-soo, a stranger who has violated a code of ethics. "*Ssakaji ka bakajine* [you ain't got no fucking manners]!" the angry diner, who himself seems to have lost any semblance of decency, blurts out in his regional slang. The woman pleads for her boyfriend to calm down, and fortunately, the quarrel does not explode into physical violence.

Though deeply textured with action and drama, this scene—shot in a single take—creates a sense of emptiness by detaching itself from the rest of the narrative. Instead of suturing the drama together, it almost punts the audience right out of the plotline. Ironically, because the scene gives viewers a reprieve from the narrative's structural tyranny, it forces them to explore the details of the space, the community in which Kyung-soo finds himself, and intricate dramas beyond the primary one.

The use of provincial accents—though common in postwar Korean literature; comedy films such as *My Wife Is a Gangster* and two other sequels it has spawned; and, as I will show in the next chapter, Lee Chang-dong's films featuring central characters who speak in thick regional dialects—is rare in Hong Sang-soo's films. In the ten feature-length films and one short he has made thus far during his career (1996–2010), he has never featured a major character whose accent comes from outside Seoul. As in his other films (*Woman on the Beach*, with the irate motorcyclist restaurant worker from the Shindori Beach Resort; *Tale of Cinema*, with Dongsoo's friend who tells the outrageous story of Young-sil's scar; and *Night and Day*, with the irritated North Korean student in Paris), in the scene in the barbeque restaurant, the shifting of accents from the standard Seoul variety of Korean to more regional ones poses an often somewhat humorous threat to a main character. If in the works of Lee Chang-dong or Im Kwon-Taek, the use of the provincial accent of either Kyŏngsang-do or Chŏlla-do demonstrate the historical and geopolitical depth of Korea, Hong Sang-soo's reliance on standard Seoul speech for almost all of his characters—even those who live in the provinces—conveys the flatness that South Korea has achieved in the postmodern age, when regional accents have all but vanished in the sprawling metropolis and other urban areas. The intervention of regional accents moves the focal point from the protagonist to the minor characters, but not at the expense of diverting attention away from the main narrative arc.

The restaurant scene's long take not only leaps over the constraints of the narrative and proposes to divert the audience's gaze to different aspects of the mise-en-scène, it also serves as a temporal guide through the process of Kyung-soo's awkwardness: first, the stage of initial desire (looking at a woman's legs), then guilt (for having peeped), and finally, obsessive denial (insisting that he was just looking at a poster on the wall). The entire scene—taking place in real time, in a simple, long shot with very little camera movement—is critical for diversifying the audience's gaze. What is also remarkable about this emotive quick shifting of gears between desire, guilt, and denial is its very condensation of the discursive assembly of eroticism (realizing his voyeuristic pleasure), hypochondria (which I use to mean the cowardly gesture of peeking in order to avoid direct contact or confrontation), and the fear of death (insisting that he was looking at something else).

Public and private are constantly crashing into and eroding one another. This also happens between the metropolis and the province, and between English and Korean, which serve, respectively, as synecdoches for elitist snobbery and local traditions. Kyung-soo blurts out, "Can you speak English?" in English at a critical juncture in the film, when he runs away from Sun-young's house after having been caught by her husband, who has just returned home. Kyung-soo's awkward use of English here is humorous not for its explicitness, but for its recporditeness. "Can you speak English?" is one of the first English sentences Koreans learn in school, yet such a question is hardly appropriate to the situation of two Koreans meeting for the first time in a provincial town. It is also a question—at least, so Koreans are taught—usually posed when you want to start a conversation with a stranger, not something you blurt out when trying to avoid meeting someone.

Up until the point when Sun-young's husband approaches him, there's nothing about Kyung-soo that suggests he has done anything unusual or unethical. However, Kyung-soo finds himself caught not only in an interstitial space between public and private (the alley he is in leads only to Sun-young's house, so there could be no other purpose for his presence than to see her), but also in an awkward bit of timing, since he had sex with the man's wife the night before. Therefore, he is trying to beat a hasty retreat from the scene of his crime so as to avoid a potential eruption of hostility or violence from a jealous husband. This "Can you speak English?" scene is a repetition of what has taken place earlier in the barbeque restaurant, where Kyung-soo's awkwardness can be summed up as the result of an initial stage of desire (in the latter scene, looking over the gate to see if Sun-young was there), guilt (for having peeped), and finally, obsessive denial (insisting that he does not even speak Korean). Again, we find that the rotating wheel of desire, guilt, and denial sustains a tripartite structure of eroticism, hypochondria, and fear of death. In both scenes, the exaggerated fear of pain or death also registers as a deep-seated fear of cosmopolitanism, sexual freedom, and the complexity inherent in being a nomad in an unfamiliar space between private and public.

All of these repetitions take place in a kind of double articulation of past and present integral to the temporal rhythms of Hong Sang-soo's films. In earlier films such as *Virgin Stripped Bare by Her Bachelors*, Hong experimented with time taking two different paths, staging the same event twice. *Turning Gate*'s time remains linear, but it constantly weaves the past as well as the future into the present.

Repetition also plays a critical role here. For instance, during a bit of pillow talk between the two toward the end of the film, Kyung-soo confesses to Sun-young that he remembers seeing her husband on a date with another woman. This questioning of her husband's moral integrity—despite her protest—is the result of an accidental encounter between Kyung-soo and Sun-young's husband before the "Can you speak English" incident. In Ch'un-ch'ŏn, Kyung-soo had taken a boat ride. When his boat bumped into another one, and the stranger in the other boat—accompanied by a woman—had asked for a light. Viewers of the film will probably not be sure that the stranger in the boat and the man in front of Sun-young's gate were indeed the same person (Hong Sang-soo deliberately cast a nondescript man, not a professional actor, to play the role of the husband). Kyung-soo also is not sure. "Perhaps I was mistaken," he says, before cynically adding, "All Koreans look alike." Are Koreans alike only in physical appearance? What about other qualities, such as behavior? Could this statement be interpreted to mean that the gap between one Korean (the husband) and another (Kyung-soo) is also indiscernible? Questions such as these are left unanswered in the film.

Though *Turning Gate* invokes a legend or myth that directly refers to the external conditions circumscribing the fate of the film's protagonist, the myth does not facilitate a transcendent understanding of life; rather, it implies an objective social condition that suffocates any form of idealism or desire. Kyung-soo's relentless pursuit of Sun-young leaves the two in limbo. In order to help her choose between Kyung-soo and her husband, she and Kyung-soo visit a female fortuneteller. The woman proclaims her verdict like a blind prophet at the climax of a Greek tragedy, forcefully stating that Sun-young should choose her husband over Kyung-soo. This female *mudang* (a shaman who communicates with the local spirits) is incisive in a situation in which there is no clear line between right and wrong. Kyung-soo is truly in love, declaring that there is "nothing else that I would want in a woman." But it is unethical for him to love a woman who has a family with another man. The mudang's analysis is simply too cruel for him. She predicts that Kyung-soo's future will be cursed with emptiness, wandering, and physical danger, while Sun-young's husband will enjoy a life filled with prospects for career advancement, wealth, and popular respect.

It is intriguing that the mudang's verdict about the present is reached through her clairvoyance about the future after analyzing the past—that is, the birthdays of Kyung-soo, Sun-young, and Sun-young's husband (who of course is not at the fortunetelling session). Present, past, and future are once again jumbled together. Ironically, the supernatural and the premodern must be invoked in order to resolve a conflict between the ideal (love) and the practical (marriage) at a time when no other productive mechanism can be found to arrive at a decision. The powers of the supernatural, of clairvoyance, and of the future put the lid on the coffin in which rests the ideal love Kyung-soo seeks.

Though Kyung-soo's ego is bruised and his quest for the meaning of life can never succeed, his failure gives us a glimpse of what Georg Lukács, according to Fredric Jameson, once called "the most basic image of human freedom": "the *momentary* reconciliation of matter and spirit toward which a hero strives in vain [my emphasis]."[10] Kyung-soo's obsession and stubbornness have at least temporarily made him a hero who will strive for the unity of transcendental ideals and a pragmatic life, despite the probability that he will fail miserably in this pursuit. In the process, he will have fallen short of "becoming human," a project that was cursed from the beginning and acknowledged to be unrealizable. By portraying a man who has been thoroughly humiliated, however, the film succeeds in reverberating with the redemptive message that life still needs to be lived—even when its meaning remains undiscovered.

After all, disappointment produces a pivotal moment in any given quest. As several characters plead during the film, "It is difficult to be human, but let's try not to become monsters." This repeated plea, directed at Kyung-soo and also by him at others, is at once a comic line and a critique. *Turning Gate* thus realizes a theme that is extremely rare in stories today, and almost extinct in contemporary films: that of a hero who achieves meaning only in opposition to his context and who is hurt when he seeks integration, whether into a society or true romance. By portraying this awkwardness, Hong Sang-soo draws out a story of human experience in which truth, however futile, is still worth striving for.

Woman Is the Future of Man

In *Woman Is the Future of Man*, two friends, Hun-joon (played by Kim Tae-woo) and Mun-ho (Yoo Jitae), reunite when Hun-joon returns home after earning a master's degree in film production at an American university. As he has done several times before, Hong has borrowed the title of his film from a Western literary or art source. Like *The Day a Pig Fell into the Well*, a title derived from a short story by John Cheever, and *Virgin Stripped Bare by Her Bachelors*, named after a painting by Marcel Duchamp, the title of *Woman Is the Future of Man* comes from a line of Louis Aragon's poetry that Hong Sang-soo found on a French postcard.[11] Despite the film's title, which suggests that the future is reflected in woman, it is mainly the past that Hun-joon and Mun-ho attempt to access through a woman, Sun-hwa. As in Hong's other films, time refuses to stay within a linear framework, and the temporal rhythms in *Woman Is the Future of Man* constantly weave in and out of the past. Because Sun-hwa is essentially a sign of the men's past and present simultaneously, she is also virtually their future.

Toward the beginning of the film, Hun-joon visits Mun-ho. Heavy snow has covered the lawn of Mun-ho's impressive house in P'yŏngch'ang-dong, a district in Seoul well known for its mansions built by the heads of old-money chaebŏls. The film immediately contextualizes these two protago-

38 Hun-joon asks a Chinese waitress to be in his film: is she a germ, a gem, or a *chŏm? Woman Is the Future of Man.*

nists as sons of Korea's affluent class—people who could afford an education and career in the fine arts and film. Hun-joon and Mun-ho go to a Chinese restaurant for food and drinks. Hun-joon's goal is to make films in Korea, but he faces an uncertain future. At one point during their conversation, Mun-ho, who has just been made a professor of studio art, becomes upset about a past event: Hun-joon had apparently given Mun-ho's wife a hug when the couple had paid him a visit in the United States. Mun-ho growls at Hun-joon: "Why did you try to embrace my wife?" Hun-joon tries to defend himself by retorting that it really wasn't much of a *kkyŏantta* (an embrace or a hug). Mun-ho refuses to buy the poor excuse and bursts out: "Shut up! Do you actually think that you are a *miguk nom* (Yankee, or American, bastard) or what?"

Though Mun-ho's reaction is excessive, he legitimizes his anger by asserting that Hun-joon is a national traitor who has violated a thousand-year-old Confucian code of conduct that forbids any type of physical contact between two people of the opposite sex. Is Mun-ho an upholder of traditional Confucian values for blurting out a derogatory term (miguk nom) that contains such strong nationalist or xenophobic views? This scene shows not that Mun-ho is a principled man who strongly defends the traditional values of Koreans, but that he is an egoist who will freely adopt a nationalist cliché in order to camouflage his own insecurities. In other words, miguk nom is only an inscription, a sign capable of emitting anything but its real meaning. But are the two characters aware that they both are placed in the inevitable knighthood of "becoming-miguk nom," fully in effect among Korean elites today who have jeopardized the essence of whatever Koreanness their ancestors may have had in their possession? Is Mun-ho simply suspicious of Hun-joon's intentions, and will he do anything to ward off this threat against his wife, or is his intention to warn his friend that he has adopted obnoxious, American-style manners that are not appropriate in Korea? This multiplying ambiguity reaffirms the repeated circuit of eroticism and death that often overwhelms unsubstantiated rhetoric in Hong Sang-soo's films. Here, one needs to be reminded that hypochondria is always accompanied by the threat of death, so that the actual potential for death becomes unlikely. This circuit that moves from eroticism to death and back again has the potential to continue eternally until love or death actually does arrive.

Mun-ho storms out of the restaurant. Hun-joon, dumbfounded, is left alone. It is at this moment that a plainly dressed waitress carrying a noodle dish enters the frame. Hun-joon glances at her and suddenly asks, "Are you interested in acting?" He introduces himself as a film director and explains that he usually casts as his actors "real, ordinary people" he meets. The young server, without a single word of excuse, tells him that she is not interested and walks away. This awkward encounter between Hun-joon, the film's protagonist, and the restaurant worker introduces a foreign character—a first for a Hong Sang-soo film. When the server leaves Hun-joon's table, the camera follows her with a pan that captures her talking with another woman standing at the cash register. The film provides no subtitles for the Korean audience, despite the fact that the two women are speaking Mandarin, not Korean. It is only because of this exchange that the audience comes to realize that the woman is ethnically Chinese.

Sudden outbursts of anger, the awkward solicitation of women, and sneaky defensiveness against unanswerable questions are familiar in Hong Sang-soo's films. His characters face repeated obstacles that generate "persistent disorientations" and a "sense of being lost in the world."[12] Yet this particular scene shows a postcolonial characteristic that plagues and doubly alienates the Korean intellectual, who arguably belongs neither in the West nor in the East. Hun-joon's character is exposed to attacks throughout the film because his identity is unstable after having been stretched beyond a single national subjecthood. He has just been yelled at for having temporarily forgotten that he is a Korean. Having returned home from the United States, Hun-joon finds himself not only situated between the past (America), the present (the Chinese restaurant), and the future (Korea), but also stretched through and across different registers of textuality, nation, and language, none of which remain stable, and each of which is wrapped up in a series of endless and constantly expanding contradictions.

Earlier, in a vain attempt at self-promotion, he had told Mun-ho that his faculty advisor in graduate school had complimented him on a film he had made. "You know what he called it?" Hun-joon asks, then answers his own question: "A germ." "What is a *chŏm* [a dot]?" Mun-ho asks Hun-joon. Both Hun-joon, a Korean who has returned from his studies in the United States, and Mun-ho, a Korean who has never studied abroad, have mispronounced the word "gem" as "germ." To Mun-ho, "gem" and "germ"—the former signifying purity and the latter its opposite—sound the same (like chŏm), since the Korean language rarely uses the "r" sound. After he is told that "germ" means *posŏk* (a precious stone), Mun-ho snickers and asks if the English word for *posŏk* isn't "treasure." "No," Hun-joon tells him, "treasure" in Korean would be *pomul*, not *posŏk*. The English word "gem" disappears not only in a mispronunciation that confuses it with "germ," but also in the gap between the two Korean signifiers pomul and posŏk, losing in the process the initial signified that was intended to flaunt Hun-joon's talent.

This contentious discursivity created through language persists in the intermittent insertion of Mandarin, spoken by the waitress and the restaurant's proprietor, both of whom are *hwagyos* (Chinese immigrants to Korea). The Chinese restaurant featured in the film belongs neither to a nation nor a reality. The restaurant's wide windows, which display the street as if it were a moving portrait, position the restaurant as a dreamy space devoid—at least for the time being—of the weariness of a native intellectual who has returned from an American metropolis, only to find that job prospects for him at home are dim.

This particular scene lays bare one of the symptoms of Korean society's vexed relation to its ethnic Other. The ethnic landscape of transnational Korea, which is caught between the rest of Asia and the United States, is located somewhere between legibility and inscrutability. The desire shown by the Korean libertines Mun-ho and Hun-joon for the Chinese girl, who is precious because of her gemlike, uncanny ordinariness (or purity), prompts me to note that Chinese subjecthood in Korea has in the past been both conspicuous and inconspicuous. One needs to look no further than O Chŏng-hŭi's short story "Chinatown." The impulse to represent the Other implies the cultural disenfranchisement of the anxious Korean and, in this instance, loops a narcissicism around Hun-joon's own ontological nausea.

That nausea is similarly invoked in Jean Eustache's *The Mother and the Whore* (1973),[13] in which Veronica, a Polish immigrant worker in France, is seduced by Alexandre, an idle Parisian intellectual. It is itself, in the Korean film made about thirty years after, a displaced symptom that engages the body of the Chinese girl without being either conscientious or self-reflective. Hun-joon's strong desire for the Chinese girl and the way her subjectivity is reduced to his need for an actor for his film is an obvious move to construct an ethnic Other in order to help overcome the internal turbulence he feels after his friend claims that he speaks and behaves as if he were a Yankee bastard. Therefore, Hun-joon's scopophilic glance, which will later be repeated by Mun-ho, incubates in these intellectuals a self-deluding otherization of a kind that could be described as the "metropolitan transfiguration of the colonial dilemma"[14] — a state that could be said to resemble Albert Camus's racialized construction of the French imagination through stereotyped representations of North Africans in his novels.

After the Chinese restaurant worker rejects the offer of a role from a disillusioned Korean intellectual, she leaves the restaurant. Hun-joon gazes at the woman as she waits in the street for her ride to arrive. The narrative, initially stymied by the Chinese woman's refusal, gets further off track with the small talk that follows. Hun-joon's gaze, which has been reoriented around the sight of the woman outside, effects a complete break from the present. The film loops into a flashback sequence that features Hun-joon's youth, and the two Korean libertines end up reliving their memories. Does the refusal of the Chinese woman precipitate this radical break from the present to a time when innocence and youth could be grafted onto past college days, when Hun-joon still believed in the purity of women? When he thought of women as gems, and not germs? The intellectual's attempt to find an authenticated place in the world by photographing an ordinary and therefore uncontaminated Chinese woman is thwarted, and all he can do is comb through the memories of his unsullied past.

But even here he finds a young Korean woman, Sun-hwa (played by Sung Hyunah), to be both precious and contaminated. In other words, everything from the past, the present, and the future can be a gem, a germ, or a chŏm. Later, Sun-hwa's sexual relationship with both men, one married (Mun-ho) and the other single (Hun-joon), is exposed, angering Hun-joon. The three separate, and Mun-ho joins his students, who are playing soccer on a school playground. This is the only moment in the film where the protagonist takes part in a group scene, and—as happens in all of Hong Sang-soo's films—he will soon face expulsion from, or public humiliation by, the group.

Echoing *The Day a Pig Fell into the Well*—in which the protagonist, a B-grade writer, is humiliated at a gathering after having had too much to drink—Mun-ho is placed at an art student soiree where drinks flow freely. He is the only faculty member present. "Now whose turn is it? My question is always the same," he says. Turning to one of the female students, he continues: "Tell us the last time you had sex, when it was, with whom, and what it felt like." This question, which is part of the "truth or dare" game they are playing, reaffirms Mun-ho's duplicity in chastising Hun-joon earlier for giving his wife a Yankee-style hug, and also his own inevitable transformation into a miguk nom. Despite a collective protest by the other students, the student he asked decides to answer in a surprisingly frank manner, telling the entire group that she had had sex just two days earlier in a filthy motel room with a person she hardly knew, and that the experience wasn't anything to write home about. Her confession arouses strong disapproval from her peers. By forcing an unmarried woman to talk about her sexual activities, an invisible taboo has been broken. The only way to mollify this public outrage would be to identify the culprit and make him pay.

Mun-ho thus becomes the *homo sacer*, a person who, according to Giorgio Agamben, "is banned, may be killed by anybody, but may not be sacrificed in a religious ritual."[15] A male student across from Mun-ho snickers, "Hey, Teach, don't you think you are a bit *chŏjil* [低質, literally low-grade or vulgar]?" Nervously trying to placate this student, Mun-ho responds: "What are you? If not a chŏjil, what are you? A *kojil*?" Here the joke is that kojil is the Korean pronunciation of both the Chinese characters 痼疾 (chronic disease) and 高質 (high class). Here again, we are introduced at a critical moment to the confusion that arises when one spoken signifier has two different meanings—much like the earlier confusion between "gem" and "germ," both of which a Korean would pronounce as "chŏm." Could a person be both high class and a chronic disease?

Even this punning use of kojil to mean both disease (germ) and high class (gem) is not sufficient to surprise the angry student into laughter. He

39 Mun-ho is fellated by the female student he harassed. *Woman Is the Future of Man.*

brushes off his teacher's question by reiterating his position: "I just said what I said because I thought that you were being a chŏjil, that's all. Not that I think that I'm a kojil." Through his stubborn willingness to further insult the teacher and implicitly challenge him on the legal basis of sexual harassment, the student swiftly moves Mun-ho from desire, to impotence (symbolic or real), and death, finally arriving at paranoia or hypochondria. Though Mun-ho unleashes his own rage, making barely coherent, profanity-laced accusations in response, he cannot regain his standing. He sinks further and further into an abyss of suffering as a teacher accused of sexually harassing his own student. One by one, the other students jump on the bandwagon, verbally stabbing their already slain teacher. "But how do you go on living when you believe in nothing?" exclaims a student. Another howls: "But do you think you are the only one struggling with [agonies of life]?"

Mun-ho has been thoroughly disgraced by this public humiliation, but he must follow the circuit running from pleasure to pain and displeasure in order to be revived. In the film's final scene, Mun-ho is approached in the street by the sexually active female student, who suggests that they check into a motel together. In a crummy motel room, the student volunteers to "suck him off" and proceeds to do so. But before Mun-ho, who earlier had ejaculated prematurely and thus failed to satisfy Sun-hwa, can reach orgasm, the kojil student (somewhere between a nonpervert and a pest) interrupts by calling the female student on her cellphone from right outside their room. Mun-ho, trying to seem cool, becomes frightened that he will be officially charged with sexual harassment and suggests that they coordinate their alibis. Once again he becomes a germ and a gem, moving nervously between a man of principle who openly discusses his true desires and a paranoid hypochondriac worried that a student will sue him (for either harassment or adultery, which still remains prosecutable in Korea).

Tale of Cinema

Hong Sang-soo's films are notorious for the ways in which they shun family, schools, and other social institutions. Most of his films take place in unpopular coffee shops and restaurants, private motel rooms, and on unattractive streets where his characters loiter endlessly. This revulsion against the social is particularly pronounced in *Tale of Cinema*, which marked Hong's debut as a producer of his own films (something which became necessary after he could not secure financing beyond a French distribution deal with MK2). The decentering of subjectivity, through which the protagonist becomes humiliated, serves as an underlying theme of *Tale of Cinema*, as it does in his other films.

In *Tale of Cinema*, Hong's two male protagonists, Sang-weon (played by Lee Ki-woo) and Dong-soo (Kim Sang-kyung, who had played Kyung-soo in *Turning Gate*), are constantly being placed in awkward positions they attempt to evade, which only pushes them deeper into an abyss of humiliation. Both Sang-weon and Dong-soo assume the role of *flâneur*, wandering through the city looking for excitement, only to end up endangering themselves. The hero of *Turning Gate*, Kyung-soo, tries desperately to steal a glance at a woman's legs, then tries even more desperately to deny that he had done so. In *Tale of Cinema*, smoking brings about a similar rupture between private and public.

The film begins, unbeknownst to the audience, with a film within a film. Dong-soo is at a theater in Seoul that is hosting a retrospective of the films of Director Lee, his colleague and best friend at film school. The film-within-a-film's plot begins by showing the lanky teenager Sang-weon, who has just graduated from high school, wandering through the old downtown of Seoul after having had an argument with his older brother. Sang-weon spots a girl (Young-sil, played by Eom Ji-won), a former classmate who had

40 Unfortunately, young Sang-weon is unable to have sex with Young-sil. *Tale of Cinema.*

dropped out of school after being sexually harassed by her teacher, working at an optometrist's. She tells him that they could go on a date as soon as she finishes her shift. After killing time waiting for her by watching a play called *Omoni* (mother), Sang-weon finally meets her. Young-sil confesses that she is smitten with Sang-weon (she asks repeatedly, "Would you like me to be your mistress?"), and they decide to spend the night together in a motel room near Namsan Tower. They fail to complete the sex act, however, because she suffers acute pain whenever Sang-weon attempts to penetrate her.

Sang-weon's libido, the life force or procreative drive, is frustrated. The failure of sex, in Freudian terms, signals the impossibility of all creative and life-producing drives.[16] The juxtaposition of Sang-weon's bizarre dream of a white woman in a nightgown offering him an apple with his futile attempts to have sexual intercourse with Young-sil emphasizes his increasing anxiety over the physical obstacle to pleasure. This stifling of libido, this incapacity to enjoy sex, sparks a death wish that the impulsive Sang-weon cannot resist. Once again, Hong Sang-soo is able to extract the intolerable from the insignificant by translating a seemingly trite sexual experience into a horrifying double suicide attempt. Throughout the night, the two go from one pharmacist to another, buying as many sleeping pills as they can. But fortunately all's well that ends well. Young-sil wakes up in the middle of the night, crawls into the bathroom, and vomits, emptying her stomach. She places an emergency call to Sang-weon's family using his cellphone, and he is rescued by his uncle.

Tale of Cinema thus continues the theme of associating sex with death. In the film-within-a-film, the young couple's failed attempt to have sex causes them to overdose on sleeping pills, which leads to yet another failure: their attempted suicide. This continuing entanglement of sex and death shows that obsessions with eroticism and the termination of life are crucial linchpins in the process of abandoning exteriority and accountability and purifying the individual mind—a place without materiality, immune to the intrusions of capital. In *Turning Gate*, Hong's protagonist Kyung-soo lusts after the perfect woman he has finally managed to find; but as soon as he acknowledges that lust, he cannot act upon it and becomes impotent. In Hong's work, explicit drives toward eroticism and death are always tempered with impotence (inability to have sexual intercourse) and hypochondria (inability to endure pain and to face death cowardly). This is why Hong Sang-soo's films lack the urgency found in the more somber works of Ingmar Bergman, though the films of both directors tend toward an abandonment of the social.

This withdrawal from the social is also captured remarkably by a scene in the middle of *Tale of Cinema* when Dongsoo, who has just seen the film-within-the-film about the double suicide, runs into a friend from his film school days and joins him and his family at a Chinese restaurant. The old classmates cover topics ranging from their dying friend who's in a coma (Director Lee) to memories of *kalbi jjim* (beef rib casserole) they had eaten together many years ago, when Lee was still healthy. Though the lunch is satisfying, Dongsoo's departure from the group is anything but graceful. After the meal, Dongsoo's friend offers him a ride. The ride lasts only a few minutes, however, because Dongsoo asks to be let out almost immediately. He has violated one of those new social rules that have caught on globally in the last few years: avoid smoking in other people's cars, especially around children. When Dongsoo pulls out a cigarette and begins to smoke, he is violating the code of decency that regulates behavior in a public space. I use the word "violating" to emphasize not only Dongsoo's will to fulfill his desire to smoke despite other people's health concerns, but also the primacy of family and especially children, which typically supersedes the desires of the individual. After being asked to put out his cigarette for the sake of the children, Dongsoo begins to feel uncomfortable. The cam-

41 Dong-soo would rather walk and smoke than get a ride in a friend's car but not be able to smoke. *Tale of Cinema*.

era focuses on his discomfort through a medium close-up of his face, which is held for a good ten seconds. Unable either to protest that he should be free to smoke or to comply with the "no smoking" rule in his friend's car, he has no choice but to get out and walk on an unforgiving winter day.

Dongsoo's abrupt departure and voluntary exile from the comfort of the car, rejecting his friend's generosity, prompts us to think about the structure of inclusion and exclusion in a society. Networks of friends, community, and family—and even the nation—rely on regulated codes of ethics that discipline aberrant behaviors and actions. Dongsoo's smoking and—as revealed in a conversation he has later that evening with friends—his binge drinking are signs of irrational indulgence that sum up his negative, self-destructive nature. The fact that his friend, Director Lee, has respiratory problems and is dying at the hospital helps remind us of the unhealthy nature of smoking. For the moment, however, without the assistance of a car, friends, or families, Dongsoo revels in walking.

Being a pedestrian in Seoul is radically different from being what Walter Benjamin describes as "a man of leisure [who] can indulge in the perambulations of the *flâneur* only if as such he is already out of place."[17] "In Paris," Hannah Arendt notes, "a stranger feels at home because he can inhabit the city the way he lives in his own four walls. And just as one inhabits an apartment, and makes it comfortable, by living in it instead of just using it for sleeping, eating, and working, so one inhabits a city by strolling through it without aim or purpose, with one's stay secured by the count-less cafés which line the streets."[18] If Paris, as suggested by these two Ger-mans, successfully erases the city's boundary between inside and outside by providing a smooth passage for pedestrians, Seoul's sidewalks cannot be said to invite a similar kind of comfort. Parked and moving cars perpetu-ally invade the sidewalks because of crowded roads and a shortage of public parking. Construction equipment, excavations, and men at work also fre-quently disrupt the flow of foot traffic on sidewalks in Seoul, which is con-stantly undergoing repair and redevelopment. Along with the masses of pedestrians endlessly snaking along the sidewalks, these conditions make the experience of pleasant strolling and loitering in outdoor cafes virtually impossible. As a result, the interiorization of the exterior—and the inclu-sion of exiles or foreigners as well—is difficult to achieve in Seoul.

Dongsoo has chosen to take his walk on a frigid Sunday afternoon. There are hardly any other pedestrians, and there is no reason for him to hurry, for he has no friends, no family, no job obligations, and perhaps no will-power. On the street, he catches sight of the actress who played Young-sil (which is also the actress's name) in the film he has just seen, entering the same optometrist's office as shown in the film. He asks bluntly and un-expectedly whether she is making a "pilgrimage" tour. Though they have just met, Dongsoo not only asks for her phone number, but also asks her to star in the film that he is working on—which may or may not get made. She is amused by both requests, but they are destined to meet again later at a dinner to raise money for the terminally ill Director Lee.

"Should we die together? If we knew we could only live another half a year, we could love each other intensely," Dongsoo says later, after having sex with Young-sil. This statement is intriguing for it presumes that the reason for the failure of true love is that we do not know when we are going to die. In other words, the unpredictability of life makes us wander from one desire to another. Hong Sang-soo's films generally feature char-acters who suffer from nagging injuries or health problems. In *Woman on the Beach*, for instance, there is a scene in the middle of the film where Kim Jung-rae (played by Kim Seung-woo) suddenly falls down while jogging on the beach. He has inexplicably pulled one of the "unused muscles" in his right leg, and he drags his foot in pain for the remainder of the film. In *The Power of Kangwon Province*, Jae-wan complains to the main protagonist Sang-gwon that he has dermatological problems. "Use less soap," is the ad-vice that Sang-gwon offers to his dear friend. Soo-jeong in *Virgin Stripped*

Bare by Her Bachelors constantly avoids meeting her boyfriend Jae-won at a motel room, using her poor health as an excuse, and Dongwoo in *The Day a Pig Fell into the Well* visits a clinic to get a shot as a precautionary measure against venereal disease. Each of these ailments provides comic relief from the otherwise serious, everyday matters (such as unemployment, adulterous situations, sexual advances in romantic relationships) in which the characters are embroiled. The proliferation of hypochondriacs—who are constantly entering and exiting clinics, hospitals, and pharmacies to treat their inconsequential or nonexistent medical problems—forces us to think that the fear of death or pain, not unlike the desire for sex and love, is slightly inflated in Hong Sang-soo's films.

In *Tale of Cinema*, death or the death drive is no longer treated in the grossly exaggerated way it was in previous Hong Sang-soo films. Dongsoo suggests to Young-sil that they plan a double suicide because that would be the only way their love could remain genuine. But is love between the two bound to be more successful if death looms around the corner? Would the pleasure principle then be completely freed from the constraints of reality (the need to save for retirement, the familial duty to reproduce, and so on)? Or would the prolongation of hedonistic sex, like drug use, also be considered an avoidance of reality, and thus the same as death—at least in the domain of the social? What remains clear is that love is intimately tied to death—not as its binary opposite, but as its mutually dependent Other, with the two sharing common ground in their opposition to the reality principles that govern the conventions and rules of any social community. Young-sil shrugs off this question because she fails to grasp the sincerity of Dongsoo's offer of sex and death at the same time. She has granted him his wish to have sex with her, but she does not seek a future with him beyond this one-night stand.

When Dongsoo visits him in the hospital, Director Lee, who has difficult breathing even with the aid of a respirator, begs: "I want to live. I don't want to die." Lee, who is in some way Dongsoo's alter ego, struggles to say these simple words. This statement is a reversal of hypochondria that is marked within a Hong Sang-soo-ian twist of fate, as Lee's shrill desperation, sweaty face, and terrified eyes all suggest that death and the pain associated with terminal illness (though we are never told what his illness is) is neither a trifle nor a joke. Death is frightening; it is absolute, real, and irreversible. Dongsoo leaves the hospital, and on the street, he remarks in an earnest voice-over: "I need to think more. Thinking can make me even quit smoking. Only thinking can rescue me from dying." He then reaches for a cigarette.

Hong Sang-soo in the Age of Hallyu

Despite their lack of box office success, Hong Sang-soo's films continue to inspire page after page of critical reviews in the local press because their imagery interrogates, critiques, and seeks to unsettle the rigid ways in which humans continue to live, talk, work, and shun their families. Yet especially during the hallyu era, Hong's work has continued its downward spiral in terms of box office receipts. None of his films—including his most successful one, *Turning Gate*, which was widely released and sold about 250,000 tickets in Korea[19]—made a profit for the investors. Despite theatrical and DVD releases of *Woman Is the Future of Man* and *Woman on the Beach* in the United States, Hong's international box office figures have not exactly been something to write home about either. His films suffer not only from the decline of art house moviegoers in recent years, but also from the widespread prejudice against modernist Asian films in general. Though online American DVD rental outlets have been flooded by recent releases of over 100 Korean titles, most of these are genre films that specialize in horror, action, and melodrama.

In an effort to construct a unique vision of aesthetic practice, Hong Sang-soo gestures toward what could become the guiding ideal of Korea's contemporary art house cinema: seeking in the arts a space where culture cannot function as capital. Hong's films claim no obvious kinship with the genres that appeal mostly to teenagers. While genre films have to have a clear beginning, middle, and end, Hong's texts instead focus on the aimless peregrinations of intellectual characters and the endless, monotonous loops such journeys tend to create. In a moviegoing environment in Korea that is increasingly subject to pressure from mass media and the consumer marketplace, maintaining prestige solely on favorable reviews and awards from film festivals is difficult. Hong is often charged with snobbery, based on his rejection of commercial genre forms as well as the political realist narrative codes employed by, for instance, Lee Chang-dong and Bong Joon-ho. In addition, Hong's blunt treatment of sexuality has added to his growing reputation of being obsessed with sex. But Hong's work is never a good aphrodisiac. Not only do his films lack the salaciousness that usually underpins deep-seated Confucian repression, such as that displayed in the work of Hong's predecessor Jang Sun-woo, but they are also too closely aligned with death (both symbolic and physical)—especially the films he made after *Virgin Stripped Bare by Her Bachelors*.

Mainstream audiences tend to consider themselves decent and reasonable; they do not want to be challenged by the revelation of stronger impulses toward domination, selfishness, and deceit. For example, US Republicans continue to insist that going to war with Iraq was a "noble" thing to do and a genuine attempt to make the world into a better place.[20] Audiences who are likely to attend Somang Presbyterian Church services (purchase Rick Allen books), vote for Grand National Party candidates (vote for Tea Party candidates), and subscribe to *Chosun Ilbo* (watch *The O'Reilly Factor*) crave more patriotic images that can reassure them that the insecurities of nomadism and alienation are fabrications of the mind, not real social situations. It is not surprising, then, that the films of Hong Sang-soo are devoid of commercial value in both Korea and abroad, in an age when the spirit of experimentation and pursuit of sexuality even in art house films have waned. Hong's images insist that they cannot represent anything beyond what is being projected within the cinematic frame: life's frailty poised between life and death, between truth and deceit, and between the egotistical mind and love for others. Hong Sang-soo's characters, as attested to by his films, are slowly being transformed, and will persist only as long as the plane of life on which he exists remains fundamentally unchanged: sooner or later, human desire, the human's will to live, and his or her nation's destiny, will all be thwarted.

six

Virtual Trauma

Lee Chang-dong's *Oasis* and *Secret Sunshine*

The international emergence of Lee Chang-dong (Yi Ch'ang-dong) was per-haps inevitable since his works, staples at international film festivals over the past fifteen years, have proven to be a good deal more accessible to Korean audiences than those of other modernist filmmakers of his gen-eration—a list that includes Hong Sang-soo, Tsai Ming-liang, and Abbas Kiarostami.[1] Lee Chang-dong started out as a novelist, entering the film-making world in the mid-1990s, when he joined in Park Kwang-su's assis-tant director team as one of the writers for two of the most pivotal hallyu films: *To the Starry Island* (*Kŭ sŏm e kagosip'ta*, 1993) and *A Single Spark* (*Arŭmdaun ch'ŏngnyŏn Chŏn T'ae-il*, 1996).[2] Born in 1954, Lee was almost forty when he began his career in film. He quickly established himself as one of Korea's most talented directors and is now a major figure not only in the Korean film industry, but also internationally. His first two films, *Green Fish* (1997) and *Peppermint Candy* (2000), featured critiques of Korean so-ciety told through the eyes of two young male protagonists who slowly be-come enmeshed in dark underworlds. *Green Fish* depicts the rise and fall of Mak-tong (played by Han Sŏk-gyu), whose gutsy acts win him praise from his mafia boss before he is killed by the hand that had fed him. *Pepper-mint Candy*, possibly the most ambitious film Lee has made, covers twenty years in the life of a man ruined by his experiences in the military, law en-forcement, and the business world. Fueled by powerful performances and a unique narrative structure that tells the story in reverse chronological order, and providing a strong social critique, *Peppermint Candy* was widely praised both in Korea and abroad. Lee's next two films—between which he sandwiched a two-year stint (2003–4) as the minister of culture, tour-ism, and sports in the cabinet of the liberal Roh Moo-hyun government— garnered him even more international recognition. His third feature, *Oasis* (2002), won the prize for best director at the 2002 Venice Film Festival and was one of the most popular films on the international film festival circuit during the early 2000s. Lee's fourth film, *Secret Sunshine* (*Milyang*, 2007), also won prizes at over twenty international film festivals, including the award for best actress at the 2007 Cannes International Film Festival. *Poetry* (2010) won the best screenplay prize at Cannes.

This chapter argues that *Oasis* and *Secret Sunshine* continue to exploit the subject of trauma, not as a symptom at the national scale, but as one that has been privatized. Throughout the relatively prosperous and peaceful period of liberal government rule (1998–2009), political traumas such as the Korean War (1950–53) and the Kwangju massacre (1980) became distant memories in the public consciousness. The only notable Korean contemporary filmmakers other than Lee who continue to make films that consistently explore the narcissistic condition of the self are Hong Sang-soo and Kim Ki-duk. However, Lee Chang-dong's cinematic vision is markedly different from those of Hong and Kim. Hong's and Kim's characters are almost always defined by their complete alienation from a society dominated by money and the need to earn it. Hong's shiftless intellectual characters typically find themselves cast out of lives that are made conventional by workplace, family, and social norms; Kim's characters normally exist in lowlife communities and dilapidated red-light districts on the fringes of metropolitan society. In addition, Hong's characters, as the previous chapter argues, are released from the three-part structure of genre plots, and his films instead resemble the open-ended free form of the *shishosetsu* (Japanese I-novel), whose characters "inhabit a space unbothered by life's constraints."[3] The reverse is true of Lee Chang-dong's films: they resoundingly accept the Aristotelian model of a beginning, a middle, and an end and treat the individual—who is an ideological allegory of society at large—with care, as if the hero's struggles represent a microcosm of the cultural clash imperiling a nation.

Just as reliance on a classical, three-part narrative structure does not make a director a creator of commercial films, neither does rejecting that structure make a director's work an art film. As explained above, Lee Chang-dong served as an assistant to Park Kwang-su, who, during the late 1980s and the 1990s, made films that often depicted an antihero pitted against an entire community in an isolated setting such as an island. In Park's films like *Black Republic* (*Kŭdŭl to uri ch'ŏrŏm*, 1989) and *To the Starry Island*, the main settings are, respectively, an isolated mining town, where labor unrest is making the entire community uneasy, and a small island off the western coast of Korea at the beginning of the Korean War. Such monumental historical events brought forth the reluctant heroes of Park Kwang-su, whose obsession with the metaphor of islands continued with his film *Uprising (Yi Che-su ŭi nan*, 1999), which is set on the island of Cheju-do. Lee Chang-dong, on the other hand, wryly depicts romance—which, according to Northrop Frye, is "a wish fulfillment or Utopian fantasy that aims at the transfiguration of the world of everyday life in such a way as to restore the conditions of some lost Eden, or to anticipate a future realm from which the old mortality and imperfections will have been effaced."[4]

Lee simulates the realist perceptions of Park's metaphoric island by recreating isolated spaces—for example, the predevelopment Ilsan in *Green Fish* and the small riverfront town in Kyŏngki-do in *Poetry*—but he emancipates his films from realism by almost always adding romance to them, thus including an additional layer of fantasy that sweetens his stories and distances them from the everyday banality of realism. By adding romance, Lee's films can afford to make only limited use of the scenic representation of a landscape—rural or urban—that in realist cinema almost always evolves into stock shots. Thus he restores the mythical narrative form that enables him to tie his dramas to the quest-driven, folkloric world. This resuscitation of quest romance in a realist art film genre is of course in the "context of" what Fredric Jameson calls "the gradual reification of realism in late capitalism."[5] Lee's films inarguably engage the cultural condition of Korea around the beginning of the twenty-first century, when the distinction between capital, machines, and human bodies has almost evaporated, reaching the point where, according to Gilles Deleuze and Félix Guattari, "machines and agents cling so closely to capital that their very functioning appears to be miraculated by it."[6] Though Korea in this century has moved far beyond the romanticism of, for instance, Yi Mun-yŏl's novels, which were popular during the 1980s, love has ironically once again become the key means by which the schizophrenic breakdowns of late capitalism can be at least temporarily halted, and the possibility of Utopian transformations of real social conditions can be registered as a subtle but discernible tremor. The mass demand for romance novels and stories has ensured an appropriate reception for Lee Chang-dong's films, resulting in a compromise between commerce and art in the theatrical marketplace.

Oasis's Greenfinches and Sparrows

The desire to tie romance to the realist form is not a subject that Lee avoids. Discussing the difference between cinema and novels in an interview given in Korea, he stated: "I realized that fantasy is what makes films different from, let us say, novels . . . Since love is a fantasy where only two people share a unique experience, I thought it would be natural for it to become one of the elements used for *Oasis*. Love, because it is special, becomes a subjective experience, which often clashes against its objective surroundings. So I wanted the viewers to be placed on the boundary between this subjective viewpoint [that is often a fantasy] and the objective perspective [one that is based on the realistic everyday]."[7] Set in that context, this chapter explores two questions. First, how does Lee exploit fantasy as one of the organizing principles of *Oasis*'s thematic concerns? If the film is about probing various boundaries—between fantasy and reality, making a film and watching it, people with disabilities and people without them, the signifier (language or visual sign) and the signified (its intended meaning), subject and object, the self and the Other (a nuanced separation that is heightened by the film's employment of hand-held cameras and the elimination of a conventional shot–reverse shot structure)—what kind of meaning do such juxtapositions achieve? The second question is how does language, or the lack of it, become a crucial element underpinning the film's theme? If *Oasis* does resist a unified subject by creating or naturalizing the ruptures listed above, what kind of gendered position is rendered by the disruption of language?

In *Oasis*, Jong-du has just been released from prison, where he had been serving a sentence of two and a half years for killing a road sweeper in a hit-and-run accident while driving under the influence. At the age of twenty-nine, he has neither the skills nor the mental capacity to make it in the real world. After failing at a job delivering food for a Chinese restaurant, he becomes an apprentice at his older brother's auto shop. One of the first places he visits on his day off is a flimsy apartment building in a working-class neighborhood on the outskirts of Seoul. He visits the family of the road sweeper who had been killed in the accident in order to offer an apology. The family, however, refuses to accept it. It is here that he meets Kong-ju, a disabled woman with cerebral palsy who is both compassionate and intelligent. It turns out that she is the road sweeper's daughter. Though they quickly fall in love, neither of their families believes that they are capable of loving each other—or anyone else for that matter. In a crucial scene, Jong-du brings Kong-ju to his mother's sixtieth birthday party. It is here that the audience learns that Kong-ju's father's death had been caused not by Jong-du but by Jong-il, Jong-du's older brother. Though the accident had nothing to do with Jong-du, he had volunteered to take the

fall for his family because they needed Jong-il's steady income and therefore could not afford to have him incarcerated. Meanwhile, the film reveals that Kong-ju has also been exploited by her brother and his family.
A new, spotless apartment, subsidized by the government for people with
disabilities, had been awarded to Kong-ju, but her brother has moved into
it, leaving her behind, alone, in the old crummy apartment.

When Jong-du and Kong-ju make love for the first time in Kong-ju's
apartment, her brother and sister-in-law pay an unannounced visit. The
lovemaking is mistakenly identified as a rape. Because Kong-ju, when
angry, becomes physically incapable of making sense to others, she becomes an unreliable source of testimony to the police. And because Jong-
du has a criminal record and has been disowned by his own family, whatever he says carries hardly any credibility with the authorities. With the
two lovers incapable of communicating the truth, Kong-ju's sister-in-law
becomes the only person whose testimony is officially accepted, and she
testifies on Kong-ju's behalf that she had been "sexually assaulted" by
Jong-du. The final scene suggests that Jong-du is again serving a sentence
for a crime that he has not committed. But despite the couple's separation,
Jong-du's voice-over in an epistolary exchange addressed to Kong-ju suggests that their love remains strong.

In a crucial scene that takes place at his mother's birthday party, held
in a restaurant, Jong-du begins to tell a story from his childhood. Seated
awkwardly between his uncle and his girlfriend, Kong-ju, he begins: "When
I was little, loads of greenfinches used to live behind our house. I used to
think they were sparrows. But Dad told me they were greenfinches. He
also said that you can tell greenfinches apart from sparrows because they
have 'bells' under their necks. [In Korean, the greenfinch is called *pangulsae*, literally bell bird.] So I stood below a big tree to look for the bells on
their necks. I truly thought that they had bells." Before Jong-du finishes
his story, he is interrupted by his older brother, Jong-il, who says: "Why
are you telling this story now? Tell me why? I can't figure out what goes
on inside that head of yours." To Jong-il's evident exasperation an answer
to this question is not available. Jong-du himself does not know why he
has told the story. Instead of answering, he begins to laugh and cry at the
same time. Foregrounded in the frame is Jong-du's girlfriend, Kong-ju, an
unwelcome guest whose condition makes it difficult for her to pick up her
food. Her father was killed by Jong-du's older brother, and she has already
been asked to leave because the accident is not something that the family

wants to be reminded of. Yet Jong-du has insisted on her staying, and she remains in the restaurant, trying desperately to fit in.

The story of misidentified birds is critically placed between two of the film's most climactic scenes: the previous scene, in which the viewers learn Jong-il, not Jong-du, had been responsible for the killing of Kong-ju's father; and the subsequent scene, a fantasy in which Kong-ju miraculously stands up from her wheelchair at an empty subway station and sings "*Naega manil*" ("If I were . . ."), a popular ballad composed and originally sung by the socially committed folk singer Ahn Chi-hwan. Yet the story's meaning is unclear at first. Why is Jong-du telling the story at this particular moment in the narrative? Does the story about the confusion between green-finches and sparrows simply serve to reaffirm Jong-du's naiveté, something that we already know? And what about his tears? Franco Moretti has succinctly stated that "tears are always the product of *powerlessness*."[8] If so, is Jong-du crying because the story reminds him of his father, someone who is missing from the party and presumably dead? If tears crystallize the irrepressible state of childhood trauma and a sense of powerlessness, it is clear that the confusion created between the signifier of pangul and its signified (actual bells) that does not match its utterance still lingers, affecting Jong-du emotionally. His failure to recognize the chasm between words and their referents has marked him as a person who is trapped in that stage of childhood where the difference between image and language, or between fantasy and reality, is not clearly demarcated. Therefore, Jong-du's desperate search for birds with bells around their necks ties into not only the subsequent sequence, where his dream of his speech-impaired girlfriend singing a beautiful song becomes a reality, but also the previous one, where the audience finds out that Jong-du was not the person responsible for the hit-and-run accident that caused the death of his girlfriend's father. It is because he has failed to grow up that Jong-du can become a martyr for his family despite the abuse he receives from them, especially from his undeserving brother. Perceived until this point in the film as an irresponsible and immoral man with a criminal record, Jong-du is now freed from the negative judgments that the viewers had made about him.

Jong-du's story directly underscores the triadic relationship between fantasy; the masculine symptom of perpetual, ongoing trauma that I have called the "male lack";[9] and the linguistic crisis between an utterance and its essence, a central theme in Lee Chang-dong's *Green Fish*, *Peppermint Candy*, *Oasis*, *Secret Sunshine*, and *Poetry*. As all of his titles indicate, Lee is motivated by the irony that words do not always capture the essence of their meaning. All of his films are sign objects that stutter between something that is, for example, symbolic of a fictional fish, a piece of candy, or a ray of sunshine, on the one hand, and the impossibility of capturing the essence of a sign that resists that very symbolization, on the other hand. *Green Fish* employs the metaphor of a fictional animal to allegorize the never-ending crisis of a male subjectivity trapped between images and words, and between fantasy and reality. Just as a green fish or a bird with bells cannot exist except in linguistic form, the characters in Lee's films continue to inhabit a world that is half-dream and half-real. Mak-tong's dream of "owning a small restaurant with a family" in *Green Fish*, for instance, becomes impossible in the real world, which is tainted with crimes and violence and juxtaposed against the film noir–like nocturnal surface of *Green Fish*. Only when Mak-tong dies does his dream of a family restaurant become a reality. In *Peppermint Candy*, the actor Sŏl Kyŏng-gu is cast in the role of Yŏng-ho, who first as a soldier and then a cop is forced to witness and participate in the brutal crackdown on students and civilians during the military dictatorship of the 1980s. He is able to regain his innocence only when he commits suicide. In Lee Chang-dong's latest film, *Poetry*, President Kang, played by Kim Hee-ra (son of Kim Seung-ho, one of the beloved actors from the golden age of Korean cinema of the 1960s), is an aged, retired invalid suffering from a speech impediment; he can communicate only through writing and hand gestures. The film's main character, Mija, is a caretaker and an amateur poet who shows early signs of Alzheimer's and constantly forgets very simple words.

The transition between reality and fantasy is much more transient, contingent, and fluid in *Oasis* than in *Peppermint Candy*, which moves backward in time.[10] Perhaps underscoring this flexibility is Lee Chang-dong's altered opinion of nostalgia and his obsession with the recovery of things that have been lost. In his first two films, the protagonists are led down the path to self-destruction by their desire to recover their purity. However, his last three films display Lee's renewed faith in human recovery and redemption. *Oasis*, for instance, begins when Jong-du is released from prison and ends with him back in his cell. But the state institution that Jong-du has been forced to enter is not a metaphor for death, as the army had been for both Mak-tong in *Green Fish* and Yŏng-ho in *Peppermint Candy*. Neither is the impending and inevitable incarceration of Mija's teenaged grandson in *Poetry*—for repeatedly participating in gang rapes of his classmate—a metaphor for death. There is an ironic aspect here. When the grandson is taken away by the plainclothes policemen at the end of the film, the audience is assured that he will be decently treated while justice is served because the head of the policemen who have come to arrest the kid turns out to be a generous friend of Mija's and, like her, a poet.

According to D. N. Rodowick, the narrative structure of fantasy is fundamentally paradoxical because of its simultaneous expression and prohibition of desire.[11] Taking this as my cue, I have come to consider fantasy not as an antithesis to realism, but as a step toward realistic representation. In *Oasis*, Lee Chang-dong explicitly uses fantasy sequences to heighten the realistic drama. For instance, while on a date with Jong-du, Kong-ju sees a young couple playing around on the other side of the bus. The film cuts to a medium shot of Jong-du, and Kong-ju, no longer disabled, stands up without difficulty and smacks him on the head with a water bottle. Jong-du fails to realize what has happened, and, when he sees Kong-ju laugh, he asks—in a close-up shot—"What's so funny?" This fantasy sequence, which has apparently taken place in Kong-ju's imagination, is disclosed only to Kong-ju (and us, the viewers), not to Jong-du.

During the second fantasy sequence, Jong-du and Kong-ju, who are thrown out of a restaurant, return to the auto repair shop and order Chinese food delivered. Here, Jong-du finally understands and enters into Kong-ju's fantasy, making it possible for them both to enter a special, private world. Reality surely has yet to collapse—the characters are presented in a rundown auto shop that is covered with sordid wallpaper and features a disordered arrangement of cheap metal furniture and worn-out sofas. Yet the couple draws magical power from a romantic love that permits them to move between reality and fantasy. What is also extremely significant in this scene is that the fantastic is signaled by the return of language for Kong-ju. While waiting for the food, Jong-du receives a phone call from his sister-in-law, who inquires about some money missing from her purse. Still in her wheelchair, Kong-ju bumps into Jong-du, who is talking on the phone. Unable to gain his attention, she gets up from the wheelchair and, miraculously, begins to parrot his half of the phone conversation. Dancing around him, she now has full control of her linguistic faculty. She mimics him: "*Kǔrǒk'e malhamyǒn andoyjo!* [You can't be saying that!] *Kǔrǒk'e malhamyǒn sǒphajyo!* [You are saying that to hurt me!]" It is not coincidental that the first time Kong-ju speaks is in a fantasy that takes place when Jong-du is being verbally attacked by his sister-in-law. Her parrot-

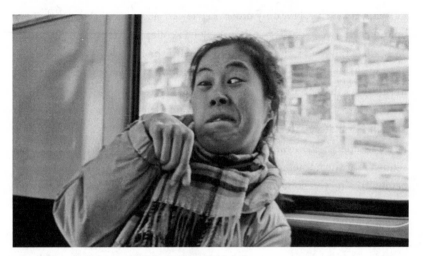

42.1 Kong-ju, severely disabled, dreams of . . .

42.2 . . . standing up in the bus. *Oasis.*

like mimicry of his desperate self-defense playfully reimagines the nature of words that in reality are acerbic, combative, and hurtful.

Kong-ju's full use of her body forces Jong-du to drop the phone. She bumps into him hard, and his phone conversation is over. Outraged, he yells, "Look what you made me do!" We have seen an event that originated in reality (a phone call) be supplanted by fantasy (Kong-ju's use of her hands to force Jong-du to drop the phone), forcing the viewers to combine a reality and a fantasy that would, under normal circumstances, be mutually exclusive. Not only must the viewers accept that the fact that the boundary between reality and fantasy has collapsed (the reality in which Jong-du is talking on the phone merges with the fantasy in which Kong-ju gets out of her wheelchair and walks), but Jong-du must also participate in Kong-ju's illusion in order to fully realize their romantic union.

The third fantasy scene is the one previously discussed, which takes place immediately after the two are thrown out of the birthday party at a restaurant. In the deserted subway station, Kong-ju, who earlier in the sequence at the noraebang (karaoke) had been unable to sing a single note, begins to sing the song that she had not been able to manage earlier on. Taken down from Jong-du's back, she continues to sing: "Dearly beloved, do you know what my heart feels?" She places Jong-du on the seat of her wheelchair and slowly dances around him.

The use of fantasy can further the goal of realism, rather than thwarting it. Rather than being situated at a remove from a system of truth and reality, fantasy can be present in the same plane as reality, converging with it at a point where the two realms become equally "uncanny." The term "uncanny" (*unheimlich*, which literally means "unhomely") comes from Freud. He pointed out that the uncanny encompasses not only what is novel and unfamiliar, but also its opposite—what is *heimlich* or homely, familiar, friendly, congenial, and so forth. The uncanny is thus something that belongs to these two sets of different, but not necessarily contradictory, ideas. The uncanny is, on the one hand, something familiar, and on the other hand, that which is concealed and kept out of sight. Freud offers several accounts of uncanniness, such as occasions when one "doubts as to whether an apparently animate being really is alive and, conversely, whether a lifeless object might not perhaps be animate."[12] Modern, civilized society had produced various mechanisms of repression, which, Freud noticed, had emerged in fiction as the uncanny.

In the discussion of colonial and postcolonial films in chapter 2, I proposed that the haunting images of impaired Korean bodies are figurations of national *ressentiment*. Much as the ambiguities between life and death and between the animate and the inanimate heighten the frightening effects of postcolonial horror films, *Oasis* uses the uncanny to underscore its melodramatic effect. But if, for instance, the doctor with a limp (a bright mind in a dysfunctional body) in *Epitaph* (2007) or the female ghost (a pure spirit in a contaminated body) in *The Public Cemetery of Wolha* (1967) are both allegories for the sickly national body, the doubleness of

Kong-ju—both a severely disabled woman who has already created an uncanny impression on the film's audience, and her imagined, non-disabled
Other, who is fully capable of determining the movements of her body and
even of singing a melody—and of Jong-du—both a child mentally, and a
man, physically—develops without national allegories and inches toward
a schizo model famously proposed by Deleuze and Guattari in their *Anti-
Oedipus*. This *double of the self* is essential not only to Kong-ju, but also
to the film's production of pathos for the audience. What is possible in
cinema through the fantasy of an *uncanny doubling of the self* is impossible
in reality, with Kong-ju trapped in her wheelchair no matter how much
the text has naturalized the appearance of her imagined Other. Not unlike
"the severed limbs, a severed head, a hand detached from the arm, feet
that dance by themselves"[13] that often constitute the essence of a horror
film, the intimate scenes in *Oasis* stem from a sense of the uncanny—itself
stemming from proximity to fantasy, the temporary relief earned by our
repressed ego, which normally is governed by the reality principle.

Fantasy is also often closely associated with disavowal in the works of
feminist psychoanalysis—that is, with something that seeks to demystify
and deny a woman's difference, or her "castration." The uncanny therefore
has a subversive and purposeful potential. Though Kong-ju's double identity mobilizes a mode of fantasy in *Oasis*, her female subjectivity exists
only on a plane that is regulated by the division of fantasy from reality. In
other words, Kong-ju is disabled in reality, and her freedom from her disabilities is permitted only in the space of fantasy, where she literally becomes what her name signifies: a princess (kongju), capable of becoming
a pangulsae and having at her disposal a loyal servant. Moreover, her two
conditions are not interchangeable, especially in a world whose govern-
ing principle is reality, reinforced by law, morality, religion, and language.
This world is where the two characters are at a serious disadvantage. In Lee
Chang-dong's films, the mythological world eventually ends up yielding to
the world unencumbered by fantasy, and *Oasis* is no exception.

The film's narrative structure is in some ways even more problematic.
Kong-ju's fantasy has been constructed not only as the means by which
she is able to reconcile with her Other, but also as something based on
male desire. Kong-ju, alone toward the beginning of the film, becomes intensely upset when her brother and his family move out of her apartment
and leave her by herself. She looks at herself in a small hand mirror before throwing it away in an act of self-disgust. Only later is she able to see

herself in the mirror again. In Lee Chang-dong's first two films, men were the ones who placed themselves in endless reconfigurations that allowed them to reexperience the mirror stage; this time, the director has chosen a woman as his narcissistic subject. The problem is that between the gesture of disavowal suggested by the discarding of the mirror and a subsequent act of reconciliation with the self (Kong-ju looking at herself in the mirror again) comes what is perhaps the film's most disturbing scene: the real, attempted rape of Kong-ju by Jong-du. This violent scene, which takes place before the two fall in love, may have been engineered by Lee Chang-dong both to make Jong-du a man capable of sexually expressing his virility and to make his incarceration in the final scene seem not entirely groundless, but instead it infelicitously aligns Kong-ju's search for her identity with masochism, the male gaze, and violence.

Oasis's Schizo

In contrast to Kong-ju, who has been denied even a fantasy identity that is autonomous from the male gaze (despite the fact that, on the surface, she has an active role in the fantasy), Jong-du emerges as a character who manifests himself within the realm of fantasy. Jong-du, still mentally a child, often refuses to think before acting. *Oasis* is thus as much a film about Jong-du's transcendent redemption as it is a romance. Jong-du's recovery of masculine subjectivity might provide a narrative movement that follows a discernibly linear and perhaps irreversible continuum, but this continuum continually obfuscates the truth. Because of this ambiguity, the resolution of the castration complex—which is pivotal in restoring not only a masculine subjectivity, but also in providing a heteronormative closure to the melodramatic narrative—remains doubtful. Jong-du has no intention of moving past previous traumas, and he becomes a subject without a fixed locus who therefore moves easily between fantasy and reality. His refusal to mature is precisely what defines him as a subject capable of naturalizing the Deleuzian schizo, who is thus spared from symbolic castration.

In a famous passage from *Anti-Oedipus*, Deleuze and Guattari write: "A schizophrenic out for a walk is a better model than a neurotic lying on the analyst's couch. A breath of fresh air, a relationship with the outside world . . . while taking a stroll outdoors . . . he is in the mountains, amid falling snowflakes, with other gods or without any gods at all, without a family,

43 Jong-du cannot think before he acts. *Oasis.*

without a father and a mother."[14] In this classic critique of Freud's Oedipus complex, Deleuze and Guattari frame their schizo subject as someone who bolts off the couch and walks around without the need for either gods or family. Throughout his career, Lee Chang-dong has explored the theme of prioritizing the individual's free will over the family's values and self-sacrifice. Jong-du enters the world alone in the opening sequence of *Oasis*, "borrowing" a cigarette from a stranger and unable to find his family, which had moved without informing him. Though he is eventually able to locate them, he can hardly be pressed back into the family, which operates according to principles of exclusion that apply to schizos, like him, and to the disabled, like Kong-ju. His relatives continually try to restore him to the order of the Lacanian name-of-the-father and submit him to the law of language and the Christian way. For instance, he is severely scolded by his brothers when he brings Kong-ju to the family celebration at a restaurant. When his younger brother tells him, "Think before you act!" Jong-du responds by saying, "I don't know what you're talking about." Jong-du has already rejected the notion that reason is a precondition for his existence. In another scene, he decides to run away from the police detention center when a police officer temporarily unlocks his handcuffs at the request of a pastor who has visited him to help him pray. For Jong-du, acting is not preordained by thought or fear of God. By acting without thinking, he rejects both the Cartesian *cogito ergo sum* that constitutes the mind as separate from the body and the Freudian psychoanalytic tradition of translating dreams into language. For Jong-du, language, the body, and the mind are not instruments of reason, but rather things that combine to create a history of instability and madness—that is, the antithesis of reason. The putative lack of respect that he shows to his elders—and thereby to the hierarchical structure of power—is thus closely associated with the irreconcilable bond between the mind and the body.

Disobeying his brother's command, Jong-du refuses to kick Kong-ju out of the party. He tells Jong-il, "We are hungry." Kong-ju, a guest at the party, deserves to be given the courtesy of being served. Communication continually breaks down between Jong-du and his brothers, not because Jong-du does not have the faculty of hearing or speaking, but because his brothers' verbal rationales, which demand that he act a certain way, always fail to create a logic that he finds acceptable. Things ought to be simpler; when one is hungry, one ought to eat. When one is sexually aroused, one needs to seek physical union with another. When one is sorry, one should apologize. But as the film points out, each of these acts—eating, fucking, and even apologizing—pushes both Jong-du and Kong-ju deeper into trouble. Earlier in the film, Jong-du tries to offer an apology for the death of Kong-ju's father, an act that falls outside the realm of law and the Lacanian name-of-the-father as represented by his older brother. But such an apology is unnecessary; the law had already tried and convicted him.

The use of language as an important motif in the film is possible because it forms the basis of social organization as a system of difference (between the self and the Other, reality and fantasy, and private and public) that "polices individuality by making it part of a transindividual, intersubjective system: precisely what we call society."[15] The failure of Kong-ju's linguistic faculty, and of Jong-du's sense of social decorum and communication skills (at a Chinese restaurant, his older brother tells him that he should first listen to what the other party has to say before allowing himself to speak) are directly linked to the film's theme, which, as Lee Chang-dong has stated, has to do with the erosion of boundaries in the "system of difference." In a system of language, nothing will come of silence, and nothing can be achieved through the ineffable. So the failure of language (expressed through bodily, vocal, or psychological impairments) leads the audience to consider all boundaries ambiguous, and this very obfuscation becomes a potential source of disruption to the social system, which favors the articulate—no matter how dubious what is articulated might be. As mentioned above, the sister-in-law, who had stolen Kong-ju's apartment from her, is the only person whom the police deem to be trustworthy; both the accused and the putative victim are forced to remain mute.

Jong-du is not completely severed from the genealogy of characters that Lee Chang-dong has created, ranging from Mak-tong in *Green Fish* to Kim Yŏng-ho in *Peppermint Candy*. The bandaged hand of Mak-tong, the limp of Kim Yŏng-ho, and the runny nose of Jong-du are all synecdoches that designate the phallic lack of these characters. By this, I mean that these characters, who suffer from male insufficiencies, are trapped somewhere between childhood and adulthood. However, something remains categorically unique about Jong-du that separates him from these other protagonists. While Yŏng-ho and Mak-tong become increasingly afraid of their "ugly" reflections, Jong-du remains unconcerned about the gap between himself and the world around him. He remains somewhat satisfied with his identity as a delinquent who refuses to grow up. Neither purity nor essence is lost because Jong-du remains incorruptible—unlike Yŏng-ho and Mak-tong, whose obsessions with lost innocence lead them to self-destructive abomination and sin. Jong-du, who is neither desperate nor obsessed, is released from the kind of guilt and shame that crippled and destroyed Lee Chang-dong's previous leading characters. Jong-du is becoming an animal in a sense, like Georg in Kafka's *Metamorphosis*. Deleuze and Guattari describe in their two volumes on capitalism and schizophrenia, *Anti-Oedipus* and *A Thousand Plateaus*, a special sort of morphing human—motivated by both brute instincts and modern civility—that, in its denial of stability, underscores many of the contradictions of capitalism. Jong-du is also schizo and thus, according to this model, departs from the Freudian model of psychological pathology. He is a schizo because he is an affective and alternative mode of experimentation at the level of sensation, perception, and feeling that gestures past normative indices governed by law, ethics, religion, and family principles. Whether with a girl or his family, Jong-du embodies the schizo spirit that points to an uncontrollable force of wild intensity. He chatters, eats, drinks, and fucks as if there were no tomorrow.

If it weren't for today's society—which is well known for its tendency to pathologize any kind of deviant or excessive behavior and to tie that behavior to the repression of Oedipal desires or the absence of Christian faith—such a draconian ending, with Jong-du back in prison and separated from Kong-ju, would not have been possible. The origins of Jong-du's transgressions are unclear. Unlike Lee's earlier works (*Green Fish* and *Peppermint Candy*), neither economic poverty (class) nor a violent police force (state) can effectively explain the narrative of the traumatized individual (an allegory for the nation) in *Oasis*. But even if *Oasis* has managed to untie itself—as I believe it has—from the narrative of post-traumatic recovery and failure that dominated Korean cinema for at least the 1980s and 1990s, does it also succeed in decentering the male lack that still stands as Korean cinema's fundamental leitmotif? And can a man be spared self-destruction only by remaining a schizo, whose ego does not patrol the border between unconscious desire and a consciousness governed by law? The purity or essence of the film is still drafted from the fantasy that a true hero—who ought to separate good from evil for the audience—is someone with an impulsive understanding of what is good and what is evil. But Jong-du is someone who dispenses with society, offering a glimpse of a universe in which the being and the real world edge closer to the laws of nature, natural impulses, and redemption.

Here, once again, the story of the greenfinches and sparrows may serve as a relevant point of interlocution where fantasy is integrated into the very structure of reality. Jong-du's failure to separate fantasy (birds with bells under their necks) from reality, the romantic fantasy of the two misfit lovers as the ideological basis of the film, and the hand-held camera style that departs from the conventions of realist long shots and long takes all ironically confound the unanswerable resistance of the Lacanian real. *Oasis* begins with Jong-du's release from the prison and ends with him back inside after having failed to reintegrate into his family. Also in the opening sequence, Jong-du finds himself at a police station because he has eaten a meal in a restaurant without having any cash to pay for it, and, toward the end of the film (perhaps extending the theme of eternal recurrence), he is once again inside a police station. The uncanny spatial repetition of the prison ironically stages the world outside the prison (family, work, and society) as a fantasy world, turning the relationship between fantasy and reality inside out. The film's last scene, which shows Kong-ju doing her daily chores in her apartment while Jong-du reads his letter to her for the viewers, is a case in point. The end of the film discloses that the real (Jong-du's confinement in prison) is both fundamentally unrepresentable (he is visually absent) yet realizable as a repressed unconscious (his voice can be present only through his physical absence).

Sunshine's Secret

Secret Sunshine (*Milyang*) begins when Shin-ae (played by Jeon Do-hyun) gets lost on a local road on her way to Milyang, a small town in the conservative southeastern province of Kyŏngsang, where the film takes place. Her nondescript silver Hyundai Avante has apparently broken down and sits on the shoulder of a narrow road next to rice paddies. As she sits and waits for the tow truck to arrive, the camera surveys her surroundings, which include scattered houses, wet paddies, rows of vinyl greenhouses, unimposing mountains, and a small stream—all typical of Korean rural landscapes. *Secret Sunshine* will not feature the fourteen-story concrete apartment buildings that have feverishly covered not only metropolitan areas but also many of Korea's rural areas over the past two decades. "I don't exactly know where I am," Shin-ae repeats to the person on the other end of the phone. This later turns out to be "Chairman" (*sajang*) Kim (played by Song Kang-ho), the owner of a car repair center in Milyang. "*Salrŏ wattagoye* [you came to live here]?" Kim-sajang asks in the thick local accent that, without exception, transforms the suffix -*yo* into a -*ye* that sounds humorous to urban Koreans. He is surprised by Shin-ae's intention to settle in his small town. Milyang's population, as Kim mentions, has been plummeting, and the town no longer attracts people like Shin-ae, a good-looking woman in her thirties from the city who wears a navy blue shirt over a J. Crew T-shirt and a tight pair of jeans (in contrast to the local *ajumma*s [married women whose femininity has vanished] who wear loud-colored shirts with baggy, unrevealing, pajama-like pants).

Secret Sunshine is the first film directed by Lee Chang-dong that systematically refuses to transform its plot and characters into allegories of Korea's history. As mentioned above, his previous films—*Green Fish*, *Peppermint Candy*, and *Oasis*—included a slew of plot devices and metaphors anchored in historical events. For instance, Kong-ju's speech impediment in *Oasis* can easily be interpreted as a metaphor for the denied civil rights of socially marginalized people in Korea. As a matter of fact, it could be argued that the entire film is a text about the social tension between privileged people (the family members of Kong-ju and Jong-du) who take advantage of the marginalized, and often silenced, physically disabled. Other metaphors used by Lee Chang-dong—an oasis, for example (a space of romance between two socially disenfranchised people in the midst of a

44 Shin-ae meets "Chairman" Kim in Milyang. *Secret Sunshine.*

harsh, desert-like environment); the unexposed film left in Yŏng-ho's camera in *Peppermint Candy* (the impossibility of recovering the innocence of
youth because of the Kwangju massacre); and the willow tree in *Green Fish*
(Mak-tong's idyllic pastoral life that is destroyed in the end)—symbolize a
ray of hope during Korea's passage through its era of harsh authoritarian
rule. However, in *Secret Sunshine*, Shin-ae's trauma—revealed through a
conversation with her brother to be the death of her husband (and Joon's
father), and later the death of Joon—cannot be directly traced to social
issues such as the historical disenfranchisement of women, political dis-
senters, the disabled, or the poor, forcing us to interpret the text without
the conveniences of political allegory.

Such an ahistorical engagement with his subject allows Lee Chang-dong
to explore three aesthetic ideas for the first time. The first idea is woman as
a non-phallic figuration, shifting violently between the subject of mourning and the object of melancholia. The second is the substitution of the per-
sonalized motivation of religious faith for a desire for political agency and
representation. (Christianity did make a distinctive mark in *Peppermint
Candy* through Yŏng-ho's wife and in *Oasis* through Jong-du's mother and
sister-in-law, but because those characters were supporting actors rather
than leads, religion was a minor supplement to the main thematic concerns of national history or social justice. During the second half of *Secret
Sunshine*, church emerges as a significant channel through which the traumatized Shin-ae seeks to end her melancholia after Milyang, her dead husband's *kohyang* [hometown], failed to serve that function in the first half

of the film.) The third idea is the snatching of historical specificity away from the narrative (in this film, there is no monumental historical marker such as the torture of political prisoners, the Kwangju massacre, or the 1997 "IMF crisis" that can serve as a powerful backdrop to the main drama). This reconstructs the unique space of Milyang as what Deleuze terms an "any-space-whatevers" (*l'espace-quelqu'un*),[16] which serves to anchor any of the cinema's naturalist tendencies. Just as the farcical naturalist stories of Luis Buñuel could take place in any bourgeois community, Milyang—released from the weight of Korea's national history—achieves a sense of nonspecificity; its conservative, xenophobic community, which turns against a young woman seeking to move there, could be found anywhere.

In his books on cinema, especially *Cinema 1: The Movement-Image*, Gilles Deleuze discusses naturalism several times. He argues: "Naturalism is not something that is opposed by realism; but, on the contrary one that accentuates [realism's] features by extending them in an idiosyncratic surrealism."[17] Deleuze's discussion of naturalism illuminates Milyang's position as a very precise milieu that does exists, but—as is the case with all of Lee Chang-dong's settings—is also an isolated space (like an island or an oasis) that has minimal contact with the outside world and that therefore constitutes a filmic space of fantasy not too different from the artificial milieu of the small town that constantly pops up in Hollywood's imagination. Milyang's small-town commercial street, which runs right in front of Shin-ae's newly opened piano center, reminds us of the anonymous frontier towns that are featured in Westerns directed by Howard Hawks, Nicholas Ray, and John Huston, and that have been appropriated by European filmmakers such as Luis Buñuel and, more recently, Lars von Trier.[18] The isolation of the geographical milieu—free from external interventions of law and ethics—is imperative to naturalist stories that follow the trajectory of decline, degradation, and destruction in a primal world divided simply between brutish aggressors and victims crying for pity and mercy.

Shin-ae's presence in a rural town is made more conspicuous by the fact that most of the immigrants to Korean rural areas in recent years have been women from China and Southeast Asia who marry Korean farmers.[19] It is difficult for any Korean to imagine that a Korean widow, one with the radiant beauty and professional piano-teaching skills of Shin-ae, would settle in a rapidly declining rural town such as Milyang, even if it were her deceased husband's kohyang. But, just as Jong-du seeks to return home after being released from the penitentiary (his site of trauma) at the beginning of *Oasis*, Shin-ae is attempting to find a new home to replace the one where she lived when her husband died (her site of trauma).

However, there is a fundamental difference between the two characters. Throughout *Oasis*, Jong-du remains unconcerned about setting an agenda for his post-traumatic recovery. He never seeks to acquire a marketable skill or find a job that might help him to mature; enable him to distinguish between word, image, and meaning; and finally produce a family of his own. Shin-ae, on the other hand, seeks acceptance in the community by running a piano center for schoolchildren, looking for high-yield investment opportunities, being a good mother, and, when her son dies, becoming a dedicated member of the church. In addition to running the piano center, Shin-ae attempts to earn additional respect from others in the community as a land speculator. "Is there any good piece of land for me to buy?" Shin-ae asks Kim-sajang and others. However, such questions mark her as a carpetbagger presumptuously seeking to exploit the naiveté and poverty of the defeated local people, and her goal invites their suspicions. Though the two films seem miles apart stylistically, the thematic tension of *Secret Sunshine* is not unlike that of Lars von Trier's *Dogville* (2003), a controversial film that pays homage to the American Western and whose plot pivots around the chasm between conservative small-town dwellers and a fugitive woman (played by Nicole Kidman) who seeks asylum among them. Shin-ae is not a pioneer, like so many heroines of American Westerns, but she is inauspiciously conspicuous among the local, overweight women who chatter in a thick Kyŏngsang accent. She also recommends—to people living in a town named after "secret sunshine"—a sunlit way of life," which is not dissimilar to a mandate by Japanese colonial officials that required Korean citizens to maintain clean, orderly settlements.[20] Because Shin-ae is college educated, uses a standard metropolitan accent, and does not (initially) attend the church, she cannot easily assimilate with the other women in Milyang. Her isolation will lead to attitudes of inadvertent superiority on her part, and outright contempt on theirs.

The film is divided into two parts—in the first part, Shin-ae has to adapt to the ways of her new community after the death of her husband; in the second, she has to learn how to cope with post-traumatic symptoms resulting from the death of her son—linked by the subject of death and mourning. If *Oasis* is a film about love between two socially marginalized people, *Secret Sunshine* is a story about how individuals cannot help being blindsided by disasters, no matter how hard they try. Not only will Shin-ae find herself the subject of public ridicule and an object of proselytization among women who loiter in beauty parlors and attend Bible study sessions, but she will also eventually lose her son in a kidnap-and-ransom scheme. Stripped of the false veneer of wealth and the privilege of having a son, Shin-ae lives like human wreckage in her devastated, empty house.

Do You See What I See?

Shin-ae's relocation efforts have profound consequences for the little town of Milyang. It remains unclear why Shin-ae settled in this town, especially after her vague preoccupation with "buying a plot of good land" turns out to be only a pretense for gaining more respect from her unhelpful, callous neighbors. She does say that Milyang was the hometown of her deceased husband. But the simplistic interpretation—that her settling in Milyang is somehow a tribute she is obligated to pay in order to properly follow the virtuous path of mourning her husband—mischaracterizes Shin-ae. It is almost impossible to understand the insensitivity shown by the small-minded people of Milyang (other than Kim-sajang, who has genuinely fallen for Shin-ae and expresses his unrequited love) except as yet another expression of Korea's phallocentrist agenda, which punishes the unvirtuous woman. The film is clearly about the binary opposition between the pride of Shin-ae, an educated outsider, and the prevailing xenophobic attitudes of the town, which used to be a common plot device for many Enlightenment novels (*kyemong sosŏl*) and films such as Sin Sang-ok's adaptation of Sim Hun's *Evergreen Tree* (*Sangnoksu*, 1961).[21] But the film by Lee Chang-dong reveals neither the full circumstances of her husband's death nor the public perception of Shin-ae. In this sense, *Secret Sunshine* turns its back on the system of "allegorical interpretation in which the data of one narrative line are radically impoverished by their rewriting according to the paradigm of another narrative."[22] If Shin-ae's mourning and post-traumatic recovery are part of a feminist or other agenda, that agenda certainly remains invisible—as if it were a kind of secret sunshine.

Shin-ae changes neither her haughty attitude nor her agonistic world-view despite the irritating derision of the owner of the clothing store and the persistent proselytizing efforts of her pharmacist neighbor. Only when her son is abducted and murdered—by the teacher of his after-school debate program, as it turns out—does her pride succumb to local pressure.

Reversing her initial rejection of Christianity, Shin-ae—struck by the deaths of both her husband and her son—begins to communicate with God and revives her life as a devout Christian, a move that is welcomed by the local pharmacist and her community of worship. "It's like falling in love. You know the feeling of being happy when you know that someone is in love with you and protecting you? That's the same kind of feeling I am having—knowing that God is in love with me and protecting me," explains Shin-ae to a group of women who have yet to convert to Christianity. Once secular and practical, Shin-ae has become one of the most faithful of believers.

At this point, three-quarters of the way into the film, Shin-ae seems to have been relieved of all of her previous agonies. But the worst has yet to come for Shin-ae, in this film that refuses to settle for a Utopian denouement. Instead, Lee Chang-dong proposes that the penchant to create false gods originates from humans' denial of their fallibility. Shin-ae announces to her cronies at church, who now include Kim-sajang, that she has one more mission left: forgiving the sin that the heinous debate teacher has committed by visiting him at the penitentiary and offering him her mercy in person. This is ultimately the only objective left to Shin-ae: sacrificing herself in order to further her principles as a Christian and to elevate her status to that of a martyr. "Didn't God ask us to 'Love thy enemy'?" asks Shin-ae, in response to the loud protest around her. She insists on making the day trip to the penitentiary in order to visit the man who had destroyed what had been left of her family.

However, when the debate teacher appears on the other side of the thick, transparent divider in the penitentiary's visiting room, Shin-ae, once confident and ready to offer mercy as if she were a god herself, begins to tremble. The prisoner, in an orange uniform with a number stitched across his chest, looks unbelievably ravishing: unblemished, rosy hued, and both physically and psychologically healthy. "You look much better than I had imagined," Shin-ae begins, her voice shaking. "I'm sorry," responds the debate teacher, without an ounce of meekness. "No, there's nothing wrong with your being healthy. Even someone who has committed the most terrible sins deserves his health, thanks to our mighty God," she replies. When she says "God," the murderer looks up. Shin-ae no longer has the courage to look straight into the eyes of the person whom she had hoped would be begging for her mercy. She makes her offer: "The reason

45 A murderer behind bars. *Secret Sunshine.*

46 Will Shin-ae be able to forgive him? *Secret Sunshine.*

I have come today is to offer you the greatest gift of grace and love from God." To this generosity, the once unrepentant criminal replies: "Thank you so much. To hear the word of 'God' from Joon's mom brings such joy in my heart. I also happen to have found faith. After arriving here at the penitentiary, I have begun accepting God as my savior."

The reaction shot of Shin-ae while the prisoner says these words reveals that Joon's mother can no longer contain her discomfort. "God has come to this man who has committed so many sins. He has made me kneel before him, made me repent my sins, and he forgave me," the prisoner continues. His continuing confession about how he wakes up praying and spends his entire day as if God were with him, giving him strength, cannot be easily tolerated by Shin-ae, whose notion of possessing and dispensing godlike mercy has been undermined. Denied the role of a sacrificial martyr who has overcompensated for her loss and suffering, she returns to the familiar role of a victim mired in self-hate. She collapses in the parking lot at the penitentiary, unable to climb into Kim-sajang's car.

The play between presence and absence that was discussed previously in relation to the ending of *Oasis* (when the locked-up Jong-du becomes spiritually present though he is physically absent) motivates *Secret Sunshine* as well. "How can I place my belief in things that I can't even see?" Shin-ae once retorted, when urged by her pharmacist neighbor to place her faith in God. In his classic "Mourning and Melancholia," Sigmund Freud makes an important distinction between the two psychological conditions. "Mourning," he explains, "is regularly the reaction to the loss of a loved person."[23] He continues: "In one set of cases it is evident that melancholia too may be the reaction to the loss of a loved object . . . In yet other cases one feels justified in maintaining the belief that a loss of this kind has occurred, but one cannot *see* clearly what it is that has been lost, and it is all the more reasonable to suppose that the patient cannot consciously perceive what he has lost either."[24] The melancholic, unlike the mourner, "may know *whom* he has lost, but not *what* he has lost in him."[25] Shin-ae's conversion to Christianity, Lee Chang-dong may be suggesting, is based on guilt for failing to believe in the dead, inanimate, or invisible being. Thus, it is not coincidental that only when her son is murdered and joins her husband in death, she decides to place faith in God despite the fact that he or she is still unseen. Also, among the many things that Shin-ae has lost is the veneer of self-esteem and pride that covered her vulnerability ever since her arrival in Milyang. She withdraws further from mourning, which is the pained reaction to the loss of a beloved Other, and instead digs deep into self-reproach and mental delusion, reaffirming Freud's position that "in mourning, it is the world which has become poor and empty; in melancholia, it is the ego itself."[26] Her ego, in other words, has become poor and empty toward the end of the film.

After her collapse in the parking lot, Shin-ae's ego and self-esteem are diminished to the point of emptiness. She soon signals her renewed refusal to accept God by throwing a rock through the window where a prayer meeting is being held. She even plays a cynical pop song ("It's all a big lie") over the loudspeakers at a public outdoor sermon. In these actions, Shin-ae not only denies God, but she also rejects any last shreds of self-respect she may have had. Joon, her son and perhaps even an extension of herself—and consequently, her god—has become completely invisible. Her wave of self-hatred escalates even further when she tries to seduce one of the church elders and then Kim-sajang, who until then has demonstrated undivided loyalty to her. Both attempts end up as disastrous failures. Shin-ae may be physically alive, but psychologically she might just as well be dead. She pensively strokes the sharp edge of a knife against her wrist while peeling an apple, an act that leads to her screaming in the streets of Milyang, her shirt drenched in blood in a rather poor attempt at suicide.

This severe case of melancholic disorder allows neither respite nor reconstitution of Shin-ae's fractured (for having lost her son) and then bruised (for having failed to offer mercy to his murderer) soul until the film's coda. After a lapse of some years, Kim-sajang and Shin-ae's brother greet her at a mental institution. Her brother has to hurry back to Seoul; so Shin-ae asks Kim-sajang to help her get a haircut. He gleefully takes her to a beauty salon where, unbeknownst to everyone around her (the meeting is known only to the audience), she unexpectedly runs into the daughter of the very man she loathes. A former delinquent juvenile, the daughter of the debate teacher is now a hairdresser who has been dealt Shin-ae as a customer. Unsure whether she can now forgive the daughter, who had never been directly involved in her father's crimes but surely had abetted them, Shin-ae bolts out of the salon during the middle of her cut. Back home, with Kim-sajang, Shin-ae tries to finish trimming her own hair by looking at her reflection in a mirror.

Shin-ae's cutting of her own hair in a small courtyard through the use of a mirror (which serves a different function here than that of a narcissistic instrument, its role in *Green Fish* and *Peppermint Candy*) and a pair of simple scissors (no longer the sharp instrument employed in a suicide attempt, but rather one that helps restore self-esteem) suggests that, even in *Secret Sunshine*, metaphors are not completely cut off from the complex narrative network of representational objects and central themes. Though the act of cutting her own hair could be construed as a metaphor of independence from the mental institution (Freudian psychiatrist), the danger posed to herself and others (police surveillance), the daughter of the killer (urge to revenge), family care (her brother who has already left for Seoul and Kim-sajang, a proxy spouse), and her need for religion (God), it is hard to imagine that she could ever be able to live without all of the above—that is, without psychiatrist, police, enemy, husband, and God. As I argued above, this is a radical departure from *Oasis*, in which Jong-du resists such institutions and apparatuses as a way of avoiding a Freudian prescription for post-traumatic recovery. Shin-ae's idyllic, solo act of cutting her hair suggests that there is room for a kind of grace in her future. She does have a courtyard of her own and a desire to look decent to others. And while it is unclear whether Shin-ae can truly be independent of religious faith and a husband, both her mourning and melancholia could come to an end as she moves toward forgiving the murderer, his family, and—most important—herself. After all, couldn't a solo haircut be interpreted as a metaphor for the cessation of melancholic self-accusation and a discernible gesture toward post-traumatic recovery?

Shin-ae stands at a crossroad. Neither an arbiter of tradition and modernity in the tradition of Im Kwon-Taek's films (a role that has been asked of women throughout the literary and cinematic history of Korea), nor a woman stuck between social justice and injustice of the type characterized by Kong-ju in *Oasis*, Shin-ae is instead a volatile woman who simply moves between a regressive pathology of melancholia (a state of trauma) and passive expectation of new loss (pretrauma) as she seeks to resume her life trapped in the cyclical means of reproduction, wealth accumulation, and social acceptance.

Conclusion: Trauma-Free Jong-du and Pretraumatic Shin-ae

Lee Chang-dong's films would never have been made without the influence of Western literature and cinema, but, as Kobayashi Hideo claimed in 1933: "What is crucial is that we have grown so accustomed to this Western influence that we can no longer distinguish what is under the force of this influence from what is not."[27] As I have argued throughout this chapter, *Oasis* and *Secret Sunshine*, the third and fourth feature films directed by Lee Chang-dong, have kept up with the current tide of Korean films by moving discernibly away from the codification of political and national allegory. Yet Lee's perspective, especially as revealed in *Secret Sunshine*, is organized under a series of Freudian metaphors and ideals that has had a long and sometimes contentious relationship with feminist theories. This strategy of aestheticization, which often seeks to reconstruct a narrative of post-traumatic recovery, is almost always reserved in the literary imagination as the exclusive realm of women. Hysteria, depression, and melancholia are often pathologies associated with women rather than men. Previously, together with his male protagonists, Lee Chang-dong sought to promote a single fundamental theme: that of an individual's struggle to snatch freedom from police or gangsters (*Green Fish* or *Peppermint Candy*). Such themes having become anachronistic, Lee has proceeded with films that are vital explorations of individual experiences with crisis and the recovery of the human spirit. Stories depicting male melancholia, trauma, and recovery have begun to dominate recent world cinema, with such award-winning titles as Julian Schnabel's *The Diving Bell and Butterfly* (2007), Paul Thomas Anderson's *Magnolia* (1999), and Tsai Ming-liang's *The River* (*He Liu*, 1997). In the Korean film industry, Hong Sang-soo remains the only auteur concerned with the subject of male hysteria.[28]

Though *Oasis* confirmed that Lee Chang-dong is drawn to the Kafka-esque schizo who bolts out of the Freudian armchair and takes a walk in the fresh air, away from money-driven economies and repressive family laws, his *Secret Sunshine* hesitates to free a woman from the analyst's armchair. The post-traumatic female victim is trapped in a cycle of loss and recovery because she cannot withdraw from the domain of law, capital, and family ethics. Nor can she escape from hysteria, self-appointed divinity, and loss of family. Rather than being freed from trauma, she is relegated to the domain of Freudian analysis. Trapped in an endless cycle of checking into and out of mental institutions, the woman (Shin-ae), in my mind, suffers an even more pathetic fate than the man (Jong-du), who moves in and out of prison for crimes (hit-and-run and rape) that he didn't commit. Therein lies the paradox of the gendered allegory of Korea that still exists today.

Oldboy is one of a slew of Korean films distributed in the United States (a list that includes *Chunhyang*, *Memories of Murder*, *Spring, Summer, Fall, Winter . . . and Spring*, *Tae Guk Gi: the Brotherhood of War*, *Take Care of My Cat*, *Tell Me Something*, *Untold Scandal*, and *Way Home*), but—unlike the others—it has been met with surprisingly negative reviews.[1] Manohla Dargis, a critic at the *New York Times*, acknowledges *Oldboy*'s director Park Chan-wook as "some kind of virtuoso [of cool]," but she also writes that the film is "symptomatic of a bankrupt, reductive postmodernism: one that promotes a spurious aesthetic relativism (it's all good) and finds its crudest expression in the hermetically sealed world of fan boys."[2] Disappointed by the all-too-apparent nihilism that *Oldboy* putatively promotes, Dargis argues that the film fails to undertake the kind of tangible philosophical inquiries that Sam Peckinpah and Pier Paolo Pasolini explored in their films during the 1960s and 1970s. The criticisms of Dargis and others like her undoubtedly dampened *Oldboy*'s chances to perform well at the box office.[3] Despite the fact that *Oldboy* won numerous international awards, including the Grand Prix (the second prize) at the Cannes Film Festival in 2004, and despite the cult status it has achieved among young fans of action films since its video release, the film managed to generate only mediocre theatrical box office receipts in the United States.

I begin this chapter with Dargis's critique of Park Chan-wook's work because it indicates a number of vantage points from which *Oldboy* must be considered when discussed in an international context. Like *Sympathy for Mr. Vengeance* (*Poksu nŭn na-ŭi gŏt*, 2002) and other Park Chan-wook films, *Oldboy* does not conjure up the kind of humanist themes that Dargis implies are properly associated with art-house films such as those directed by Ingmar Bergman, Andrei Tarkovsky, and Krzysztof Kieslowski as well as Pasolini and Peckinpah. Instead of preaching values of tolerance and salvation, Park's protagonists plot revenge, brandish sharp metal instruments, and impatiently wait for their turn to spill someone's blood. Moreover, the exaggerated male icons featured in Park Chan-wook's films seem to be direct copies of Japanese manga characters or the Hong Kong action heroes created by John Woo and Tsui Hark. These contrast with the realism of Park Chan-wook's predecessors in Korean cinema such as Park Kwang-su or Jang Sun-woo—who, as I have argued elsewhere, have demytholo-gized the masculinity of Korean cinema.[4] While many of Dargis's points are valid, she fails to note that Park is not the only filmmaker recognized by Cannes in the recent past who has been uninterested in asking epistemo-logical questions about life. Cannes winners Lars von Trier, Wong Kar-wei, and Quentin Tarantino have similarly created distance from philosophical or political issues, seeking instead to leave their viewers with an indelibly "cool" impression of violence. In addition, Dargis's review sidesteps the controversy surrounding filmmakers like Peckinpah, whose intentions and philosophical depth have been continuously questioned by critics. Jetti-soning some of the exaggerated claims made by critics such as Stephen Prince, who celebrated Peckinpah's "melancholy framing of violence," Marsha Kinder proposes instead that Peckinpah was the first postwar nar-rative filmmaker in America who "inflect[ed] the violence with a comic exu-berance."[5] Peckinpah choreographed scenes of explicit violence as if they were musical numbers and was considered a pioneer in American cinema. However, the question of whether or not the violence used in his films truly inspires philosophical questions or simply feeds an orgasmic viewing experience of the kind that has spawned the films of Quentin Tarantino or Park Chan-wook is a serious one. I contend that as filmmakers, Peckinpah and Park Chan-wook are, for better or worse, similar rather than categori-cally different.

In the films of Park Chan-wook's "revenge" trilogy—*Sympathy for Mr. Vengeance* (*Poksu nŭn na ŭi kŏt*, 2002), *Oldboy* (*Oldŭboi*, 2003), and *Lady Vengeance* (*Ch'injŏlhan Kŭmjassi*, 2005)—one can trace the emergence of a postmodern attitude, holding not only that the grand ideologies (such as humanism, democracy, and socialism) are faltering or already collapsed, but also that the image is just that: an image. Though Hong Sang-soo—as I argued in a previous chapter—also tends to produce images that deny the metaphoric plane and refute the hidden agenda, Park Chan-wook's image here is that which is not an impression of reality, but a perception of mat-ter that approximates the verisimilitudes of both space and time, which may not have anything to do with reality. This renders a sense of the "un-knowable" that troubles reviewers like Dargis, who have criticized Park's films for having failed to produce social criticism. But is this all there is to the debate? Is there no history, no significant meaning, or no profound idea behind Park's images? How conveniently indescribable is the "unknowable"?

The aim of this chapter is threefold. First, I will try to identify the ways in which the main tropes of Park Chan-wook's work—including a flattened mise-en-scène, the commodified body, the mystification of spatial markers, and the disjointed juxtaposition of images and sound—all aim to explore the potential of cinema in ways that may have vexing epistemological implications. Second, I invoke the Nietzschean *ressentiment* in examining Park Chan-wook's assertion that personal vengeance is a plausible kind of energy in a society whose law and ethics have been dictated by the combined interests of liberal democracy and capitalism. This may give us room to rethink Park's allegorical presentations of the "unknowable." Third, in the conclusion, I will entertain the question whether or not the post-political or antihistorical ideas of Park Chan-wook can still be read politically in the Korean historical context—just as Peckinpah's work, when contextualized in the American sociopolitical context, was perceived to refer to the violence of Vietnam and the civil rights movement.

Plot of the "Unknowable"

Loosely adapted from an eight-volume manga (*manhwa* in Korean) mystery novel of the same title,[6] *Oldboy* follows in the footsteps of other Korean films—such as Yi Jang-ho's *Alien Baseball Team* (*Kongpo-ŭi oein kudan*, 1986) and Kim Young-bin's *Terrorist* (1995)—that have adopted the narratives and style of manhwa into live-action films. Before Park Chan-wook, the most prominent among the directors who adopted a manhwa approach to filmmaking was Lee Myung-se (Yi Myeong-se), whose films during the late 1980s and the 1990s stubbornly departed from the realist trend of the New Korean Cinema. Most of Lee's films—including *Gagman* (1988), *My Love, My Bride* (1990), *First Love* (1993), and *Nowhere to Hide* (1999)—have insisted on a cinematic worldview that treats live-action characters as animated ones, thus presenting a distorted vision of the real world. Thus some similarities can be drawn between the works of Lee Myung-se and those of Park Chan-wook. However, it should be noted that Park's cynicism differs radically from Lee's heavily thematized romanticism. Park's films have had such a powerful impact that they have led the Korean film industry to consider manhwa as a treasure trove of original creative property. *Oldboy* was followed by the box office blockbuster films *200-Pound Beauty* (2006), adapted from a graphic novel by Suzuki Yumiko and directed by Kim Yong-hwa, and Choi Dong-hun's *Tazza: High Rollers* (2006), which was originally a manhwa series created by Yi Hyŏn-se.

As noted above, *Oldboy* is the second film in Park Chan-wook's revenge trilogy, which has been successful both in the Korean market and on the international film festival circuit.[7] In these films, vengeance is carefully restricted to the realm of the personal, rarely ever entering the public domain: it is always aimed at other individuals and almost never against state institutions. This in itself is hardly original. However, in all three films, the police play only a perfunctory role. This erasure of authority accomplishes several things. First, it emphasizes the fact that the heroes and villains operate outside the domain of the law. They mercilessly abduct, kill, blackmail, threaten, unleash violence, and engage in reprisals without any reference to a public judicial system of the kind that typically occupies a central position in dramas dealing with individual liberty and freedom. Examples of this mode can be seen in realist films such as Park Kwang-su's *Chilsu and Mansu* (1988) and Lee Chang-dong's *Peppermint Candy* (*Pakha sat'ang*, 1999), which foreground the police as sources of corruption or social malaise, who meet both personal and public acts of transgressions with violence.

Second, it enables *Oldboy* to suggest a mythical, ahistorical world—beyond the mundane realities of a legal system—in which figures such as the protagonist Dae-su and the villain Woo-jin roam free. Philip Weinstein writes about something he calls "beyond knowing," a common symptom of the modernist narrative, which "tends to insist that no objects out there are disinterestedly knowable, and that any talk of objective mapping and mastery is either mistaken or malicious—an affair of the police."[8] Although it is difficult to classify Park Chan-wook's films as modernist, they do exploit such Kafkaesque devices by deliberately rejecting "objective mapping and mastery" and consequently aim to dispel the "knowing," sometimes even after the lights are turned on at the theater. Park unwaveringly refuses to claim the "knowable," despite having been labeled as superficial by several prominent critics.

This unknowable attitude can also be seen stylistically in Park's reconstitution of the visual plane, which deliberately rejects realist depth of field and instead opts for a flattened mise-en-scène that relies heavily on wide-angle lenses and reduces the distance between the camera and its subjects. These techniques, which deny any density beyond surfaces, once again underscore the relentlessly superficial domain of the unknowable. Also complementing the unknowable is the deletion of landscape in films such as *Oldboy*. As discussed in chapter 2, if—as argued by the critic Karatani Kojin[9]—the discovery or emergence of landscape is absolutely vital to the structure of our modern perception, is the erasure of landscape essential in shaping a postmodern perception? Instead of nature, the features of this flattened space are the dilapidated concrete cells, meaningless television images, anonymous Internet chats, and chic restaurants and penthouses that are symbolic of Korea's postmodern environment. Even when a pastoral space is depicted in *Oldboy*, its saturated color scheme yields not a realist portrayal of Korea's countryside, but an anonymous, artificially generated, neobucolic space.

Third, in Park Chan-wook's realm of the unknowable, the police are useless. Park's visual invocation of pastiche helps readdress and essentially efface Korea's modern history—which is marked by the tyranny of uniformed men. There is one notable exception to this absence of police in *Oldboy*. At the beginning of the film, the protagonist—Oh Dae-su, played by Choi Min-sik—appears in a scene that takes place in a police station. Jump cuts centrally figure Dae-su, who is drunk and unruly. He has apparently been brought into the station after having caused some disturbance—in short, he is a public menace. This sequence is shot with a minimum of effect. The realistic lighting and natural acting style differ radically from the saturated colors and highly choreographed action sequences that constitute the bulk of the film. Although this police station sequence lasts for more than two and a half minutes (a significant duration in a feature-length film that only runs 120 minutes), uniformed policemen rarely appear in the frame. Only their voices are heard, presaging the absence of police throughout the film. Although Dae-su verbally insults the police, going so far as to urinate inside the station, the authorities allow him to leave unscathed. The police act as if they were from the twenty-first century, even though this scene is set in 1988. Dae-su's obstreperous acts may be trivial, but as films like Park Kwang-su's *Chilsu and Mansu* and Hong Sang-soo's *The Day a Pig Fell into the Well* (1996) have proved to audiences time and again, South Korean authorities rarely overlook even the slightest disagreeable incident caused by unruly drunks.[10] Made fifteen and eight years, respectively, after the release of these other films, *Oldboy* shows the police as having lost their teeth. In this postauthoritarian era, it is not surprising that abuses of power by figures of authority are no longer the central concern of the drama.

Dae-su, an ordinary salaryman with a wife and a toddler daughter, is released from the police station only to find himself locked up minutes later in an anonymous cell. No particular reason for his incarceration is cited, and no indication is given as to the duration of his confinement. Days and nights pass, and Dae-su is forced to repeat the same routine every day. Having no one to talk to, he watches television and masturbates, inhales the Valium gas pumped into the chamber that puts him to sleep, eats the fried dumplings (*gunmandu*) provided for him, rigorously performs martial arts training exercises, and starts to dig an escape route through the wall with the tip of a hidden spoon. In other words, he eats, sleeps, masturbates, and works as if his life inside a prison is a microcosm of life outside. Before he can escape, however, he is released. Fifteen years have passed since the night of his kidnapping and confinement. Not only is his imprisonment unexplained to him or to the audience, but neither is his release. When he wakes up after a session of hypnosis conducted in his cell, he finds himself on the rooftop of an apartment building.[11]

Fifteen years of solitary isolation have transformed Dae-su, who first appeared as an unruly charlatan at the police station. No longer an ordinary man, he now speaks in a succinct monotone that accords him a godlike, transcendental status. During the film, several characters ask, "Why do you speak that way?" His sentences are almost always in present tense — not future, conditional, or past — and they lack any modifying clauses. The erasure of the past and future tenses marks Dae-su as a man who is devoid of history, thus achieving for him the status of atemporality. This makes him even more mysterious: a man who shows neither his age nor basic human emotions. The lack of emotions makes Dae-su seem larger than life. Furthermore, years of martial arts training while imprisoned have given him a seemingly superhuman agility and strength that he puts to use as a ruthless warrior in search of vengeance. While in captivity, Dae-su had helplessly watched as news reports framed him as the prime suspect in the murder of his wife. After his release, he finds out that his supposedly orphaned daughter, Bora, had left for Sweden. With no family to rely on and no authority figure to appeal to, Dae-su finds himself utterly alone.

The only person he can turn to is his new friend, Mi-do (Kang Hye-jeong). The first place Dae-su visits after being released from his private cell is a sushi restaurant called Jijunghae. He is served by Mi-do, a young woman who has become a sushi chef despite the discriminatory belief that women's hands are too warm to maintain the proper coldness of raw fish. The two quickly trade lines that mutually invoke a feeling of uncanniness—as noted above, Freud defines this as the feeling of "something familiar ["homely," "homey"] that has been repressed and then reappears."[12] Dae-su has a wallet filled with 100,000 won bills (each worth about $100), and he quickly orders and consumes an entire octopus, served by Mi-do to him uncooked and cut up. Dae-su loses consciousness when Mi-do reaches out to grab his hand and tell him: "I think I am quite unusual. My hands are very cold." As the film later reveals, Mi-do is actually Dae-su's grown-up daughter, Bora, who had supposedly been given up for adoption to a Swedish family.[13]

Dae-su overcomes his initial suspicions of Mi-do, who takes him home, and the two of them work as a team to investigate the man behind the arrangement to keep Dae-su in captivity for fifteen years. Feelings grow between the two. Mi-do promises Dae-su that she will serenade him with the 1990 hit song "Pogosip'ǔn ǒlgul" ("Face I Want to See Again") when she is sexually ready for him. This promise—naturally involving a future action—ironically restores Dae-su's temporality and historicity—something that he has been denied ever since his release from the cell. Mi-do and Dae-su move closer to their imminent copulation (future action), which ironically enables Dae-su to move closer to the reason behind his incarceration as he recovers a memory from his high-school days (past). When Dae-su rescues Mi-do from the thugs who threaten to kill her soon afterward, she sings him her siren song, sending Dae-su into dangerous waters. The two of them do not know that they are beginning an incestuous relationship. And only when their incestuous relationship materializes will Dae-su be given the reason behind his imprisonment.

The only clues with which Dae-su has to work in tracing the origins of the crime committed against him are the taste of gunmandu (Chinese dumplings) he was fed during the entire period he was locked up, and a small piece of chopstick wrapping paper that was accidentally found in one of the dumplings. The paper is printed with the characters ch'ǒngryong (blue dragon)—two characters of the restaurant's name. After combing through Seoul, where literally hundreds of Chinese restaurants contain both characters in their names, Dae-su finally locates Jach'ǒngryong (Purple Blue Dragon), the restaurant whose dumplings match the taste of those he ate every day in his cell.

This in turn leads him to the "business group" that specializes in illegal abductions and detentions. Only a few days elapse before Dae-su is confronted with the film's villain, his high-school classmate Woo-jin (Yu Ji-tae). Both Dae-su and Woo-jin had attended the Evergreen (Sangnok) High School, a Catholic school located in the Korean countryside. Even after identifying the man responsible for his long imprisonment, Dae-su still fails to understand what could have motivated Woo-jin to commit such heinous crimes against him. After further investigation, Dae-su remembers an event from the past that had completely evaded him during his captivity. This is shown in a flashback, during which he remembers his younger self. The young Dae-su is wearing a high-school uniform and watching a girl riding a bike. It is his last day at Evergreen High School before he transfers to another school in Seoul. Soo-ah (Yoon Jin-seo), the pretty female student whom he has been watching, attracts young Dae-su's interest even more when they meet briefly on a bench. For no apparent reason other than curiosity, he follows Soo-ah and discovers a dark secret about her: she is sexually intimate with her own brother, Woo-jin.

"It wasn't my dick that impregnated my sister. It was your tongue," Woo-jin explains when the two finally meet. One of the most intriguing points of *Oldboy* is that linguistic communication almost always falls outside the sphere of rational dialogue. Verbal miscues, infelicitous remarks, and gaps between signifiers and signifieds not only produce misunderstandings between two individuals but also help create a world that is "beyond knowable." Was Soo-ah pregnant or not? Once rumors began spreading that she fooled around with her brother and had become pregnant with his child, she committed suicide. After his sister's death, Woo-jin suffered from heart disease and was forced to replace his heart with an artificial one. What first started as innocuous chatter in high school between Dae-su and a friend about Soo-ah's illicit affair resulted in Soo-ah's death and Woo-jin's cardiac arrest. This led Woo-jin to seek revenge against Dae-su, who could not remember having done anything that would have merited fifteen years of incarceration.

A final showdown between the hero and his former captor would, in a commercial film, normally favor the victim. But in a sense it is Woo-jin who has the last laugh during this confrontation. Once his revenge is complete, Woo-jin descends from his penthouse in an elevator, where he puts a gun to his head and pulls the trigger. His death is dramatic, but it could be argued that his heart had already died many years earlier. The only thing that had kept him alive was his desire to seek revenge for his sister. Woo-jin had wanted Dae-su to sleep with his own daughter, as Woo-jin had once slept with his own sister. Woo-jin's revenge was complete once Dae-su, to protect Mi-do from the knowledge that he is both her lover and her father, voluntarily cuts off his own tongue. Once this happens, Woo-jin has no intention of seeking a further extension of his life. Having once been resuscitated through technological means (his artificial heart), Woo-jin claims his subjectivity through completing his revenge, not forgoing it.

Ressentiment

Memory is a crucial site for contestations between individuals and the state.[14] The question of whether or not a person—usually a male, in films—can remember the site of his trauma is directly linked to the question of whether he can achieve a salient form of subjectivity. Many films made during the period between the heyday of the Minjung Democratization Movement in the late 1980s to the inauguration of President Kim Dae-jung in 1998 centered on the demand that official histories, especially of the Korean War and postwar human rights violations, be revised. The personal recollections found in many films from this period—such as Chang Kil-su's *Silver Stallion* (*Ŭnma nŭn oji annŭnda*, 1991), Jang Sun-woo's *A Petal* (*Kkonnip*, 1995), Park Kwang-su's *A Single Spark* (1996) and Lee Kwang-mo's *Spring in My Hometown* (*Arŭm taun sijŏl*, 1998)—are crucial to this overarching preoccupation with representing alternative histories that work against hegemonic, distorted representations of the state. Given that public history is at stake, these recollections accompany an objective that reaches far beyond the realm of the individual. For instance, in *A Petal*, a traumatized girl who lost her mother during the 1980 Kwangju massacre must remember what happened and articulate what she saw on the fateful day when her mother was among those killed by the soldiers. The girl's personal memories cannot be disassociated from the public need for a witness who can narrate the truth about Kwangju and contest the official, state-authorized history, which denies that there were any civilian casualties.

The girl from Kwangju is briefly able to remember the day in her hometown where the soldiers ruthlessly opened fire on demonstrators gathered to protest the never-ending military rule, but she quickly relapses into mental disorder. The viewers of *A Petal* are offered the truth about Kwangju, but in *Oldboy*, like Park Chan-wook's other vengeance films, memory remains in the domain of the personal and never ventures beyond it. Dae-su's recollection of himself witnessing the incestuous relationship between Woo-jin and his sister has absolutely no implications beyond a personal matter — its only purpose is to identify the essence of the resentment, the root cause of the revenge that has demanded such a high price from him.

Since Park Chan-wook's trilogy identifies vengeance as the reactive action of resentment, Nietzsche's concept of *ressentiment* may serve as a useful reminder of how to better read these works. In *On the Genealogy of Morals*, as well as in other works, Nietzsche uses the concept of resentment to further elucidate the relationship between master and slave, and also between good and evil. The dreadful power of resentment, Gilles Deleuze wrote as he summarized Nietzsche, is that it is "not content to denounce crimes and criminals, it wants sinners, people who are responsible."[15] Deleuze, following Nietzsche, explains that society ends up acquiring the sense of the evil and good as opposites of each other from the idea of *ressentiment*: "You are evil; I am the opposite of what you are; therefore I am good." This derivation of morality ("slave morality," according to Nietzsche) justifies the spirit of revenge, which is conditioned by a hostile world. In this sense, even destructive energy has the potential to become creative, good energy.

All of the main characters in Park Chan-wook's films rely on this Nietzschean (or Old Testament) idea of slave, and therefore inferior, morality. They continuously assert that vengeance is neither evil nor unethical. Woo-jin tells Dae-su: "Revenge is good for one's health." "Health" in this statement implies not only physical health, but also mental health. Woo-jin's acquisition of incredible amounts of wealth, though unexplained in the film, is tacitly understood as the fruit of the drive for revenge he conceived while in high school. Analogously, Tae-ju (played by Kim Ok-bin) in *Thirst* (*Pakjwi*, 2009), Kŭm-ja (Lee Young-ae) in *Lady Vengeance* and Park Dong-jin (Song Kang-ho), the factory owner in *Sympathy for Mr. Vengeance*, all seek revenge because they are good, not because they are bad. Is revenge, according to Park Chan-wook, an ethical decision that ironically produces a judiciously responsible subject, not a savage one? Must one seek revenge, rather than forgoing it, to reclaim subjectivity? Are these questions even relevant in Park Chan-wook's entertainment films?

Nietzsche and Deleuze seem to agree that revenge is not antithetical to salvation. Deleuze echoes Nietzsche's idea that no religious value, including those of Christianity, can be separated from hatred and revenge. Deleuze writes: "What would Christian love be without the Judaic power of *ressentiment* which inspires and directs it? Christian love is not the opposite of Judaic *ressentiment* but its consequence, its conclusion and its crowning glory."[16] In the closing sequence of *Sympathy for Mr. Vengeance*, Park Dong-jin shudders and sheds tears before brandishing his knife in front of his daughter's killer Ryu (Shin Ha-kyun). Park says: "I know you are a good guy. So you understand that I have to kill you, right?" Herein lies the paradox of Park Chan-wook's vengeance trilogy—revenge comes not from hatred, but from love and pity. Park Dong-jin's tears are genuine, and he seems to believe that Ryu had no choice but to abduct his daughter in order to pay for his sister's medical bill; the daughter's killing was inadvertent. Like the acts of terror (kidnapping and demanding ransom) that in Park Chan-wook's films are sometimes seen to be good and at other times bad, revenge in his films is not always bad. In fact, it is almost always good, if it is executed with good intentions. Revenge, as such, is both harmful and beneficial; consequently, in *Oldboy*, the sharp distinction between good and evil disappears. Derrida once similarly deconstructed Plato's *pharmakon* by showing that this term possesses not a singular but a double meaning, both "remedy" and "poison."[17] Park Dong-jin chooses to remain faithful to his feelings of resentment, a choice that leads him to react violently against Ryu, as if he is unleashing Platonian pharmakon.

Even though Park Chan-wook's violence is not categorically severed from salvation and love, we must ask whether a film such as *Sympathy for Mr. Vengeance* is truly Nietzschean. The open acknowledgment that the enemy is good cancels out the possibility of Nietzschean *ressentiment*, since resentment vanishes once the other is reevaluated and found not to be evil. The question of what he is seeking justice for becomes a complicated one. Is Park Chan-wook suggesting that the famous New Testament credo of "love thy enemy" can be just as good when it is reversed into "kill thy brother," a story also found in the Bible (the Old Testament)? What is the point of this if Park does not believe in God? Is "kill thy brother" just a playful, if perverse, speech act and nothing more? Even if an act of violence committed against the virtuous is allowed by a postmodern sentiment that negates any cogent correlation between the signifier (the subject's violent act) and the signified (the accomplishment of justice against evil), the conclusion Park Chan-wook comes to does not make Nietzschean theory any more relevant. What is the point of giving Park Dong-jin a line

47.1 Ryu shudders in the same river where Park Dong-jin's daughter drowned. *Sympathy for Mr. Vengeance.*

47.2 Park tells Ryu: "I know you are a good guy." *Sympathy for Mr. Vengeance.*

telling Ryu that he is good, and then to have Ryu executed seconds later? The moment a person finds someone else to be good, the excitation that arises out of resentment and hostility should lose its power. Once the subject abandons resentment and revenge, he or she, according to Nietzsche, is capable of achieving a sovereign identity based on a superior sense of morality (*Übermensch*, or superman) rather than a slave one. Is Park Dong-jin then killed for failing to adopt an alternative perspective that is endowed with superman-like power to recognize values beyond good and evil? Are the deaths of Ryu and Park Dong-jin, who both fall into the pitfall of mediocrity by trying to be good and avenge the loss of victims, simply affirmations of Park Chan-wook's cynicism, which deliberately contradicts Nietzsche's firm belief that each human being is capable of becoming an *Übermensch*? In other words, does Park Chan-wook believe that humans prefer to be pitiful beings and thus choose not to abandon *ressentiment*—maintaining the inferior mentality often associated with slaves?

Body: An Eye for an Eye, a Tooth . . . for a Wad of Cash?

In the Western philosophical tradition, the body is often seen in opposition to speech and language. Even if it is ineffable and unintelligible, however, the body is the perfect articulation of the unknowable discourse. A healthy, virus-free, whole body rarely appears in Park Chan-wook's films, and often the failed heart, the infected liver, or severed body parts constitute the mechanisms Park uses to naturalize the alliance between the logic of capitalism and the postmodern commercial genre of thriller. Bodily pain or dismemberment is such an important characteristic of Park's revenge trilogy that through this recurring motif, the three films achieve what I think of as an aesthetic, ethic, and politics of the body. In the films, bodies are often dismembered, and human organs such as kidneys or hearts become detached from the body. They are either sold for profit or replaced with healthier, or artificial substitutes. They are acquired, bartered, relinquished, and redistributed—sometimes legally, but more often outside the law. The body falls far short of sacred in a postmodern capitalist society, which configures the body's function is configured quite differently than precapitalist ones did. A healthy body is a mandatory prerequisite to feeling sensations, including pleasure. In nomadic societies, the body was regarded as belonging to the earth; in imperial societies, it belonged to the despot; and in the capitalist societies that Park depicts, it belongs to capital. Debunking the mantra of the Confucian society, which posits the familial collective—and consequently the nation—as being organically linked to individual bodies, the bodies in Park Chan-wook's films are regarded as commodifiable, their organs usually quantifiable in terms of monetary value.

Oldboy furthers *Sympathy for Mr. Vengeance*'s theme of living flesh and organs that are metaphors for—and make explicit—the extreme conditions of late capitalism by attaching price tags to body parts. Park Cheol-ung (played by Oh Dal-su), the president of the underground business that specializes in private incarcerations, is a minor yet important character in the film. When Dae-su identifies the Chinese restaurant that made the dumplings he ate in his cell, he is able to locate Cheol-ung. Dae-su tortures

48.1 "One tooth for every year I spent in your cell."

48.2 "A tooth for a tooth." *Oldboy*.

him by tying him up and starting to take his teeth out with the aid of a claw hammer. After taping Cheol-ung's face Dae-su tells him: "[I'm going to take out] one tooth for every year I spent in your cell." By the time Dae-su has removed six teeth, Cheol-ung surrenders and gives Dae-su the leads he wants. The next time Dae-su and Cheol-ung meet, the power dynamic between the two has been reversed. Dae-su has fallen into a trap set by Cheol-ung and is on the verge of having the same number of teeth—six—extracted with a claw hammer. Before Cheol-ung is able to exact his revenge, however, he receives a phone call from Woo-jin asking him to stop, in exchange for a briefcase filled with cash. Cheol-ung reluctantly agrees on this exchange and gives up his revenge for this undisclosed amount of cash. Park Chan-wook sets the price of six teeth at a briefcase filled with cash.

Cheol-ung accepts this money, and it turns out that he also trades his right arm for a building that Woo-jin owns. Although only a minor character in the film, Cheol-ung's decisions to trade parts of his body for financial gain are not insignificant. In recent Korean history, sacrificial acts such as workers immolating themselves or cutting off their own fingers to protest human rights violations or to express nationalist views have become common. Cheol-ung's willingness to sacrifice parts of his body for money deliberately scoffs at and renders profane the sacred and political condition of corporeality. In Park's films, the body of an individual is almost a site of transgression that moves from "serv[ing] to protect the entire community"—to use René Girard's description of sacrifice[18]—to being a crude repository of private assets, in which each body part can be exchanged for money in order to help realize capitalistic goals.

Space: "There Is Too Much *Buchu* in Your *Gunmandu*"

In realism, the use of provincial accents clearly marks identity and boundaries that in turn provide a sense of knowability and familiarity. Modernism tries to take away that sense of familiarity. For instance, Kafka's novels erase specific national and regional markers and thus are deliberately elliptical and anonymous. The spaces in these nonrealist novels become uncanny, unbound by the specificity and particularity of each setting.[19] Postmodern novels like those of Haruki Murakami and, arguably, films like *Oldboy* achieve a similar sense of the unknowable or the uncanny, but these works register a different kind of impact than Kafka's. The fried dumpling and the chopstick wrapper inscribed with the restaurant name "blue dragon" invoke a sense of easy familiarity for many Koreans. However, this very ubiquity of the dumpling and wrapper—which may be global phenomena like McDonald's or Starbucks—leads the viewer into the anonymity of unfamiliar territory. The search for a restaurant that both produces the dumpling with the correct taste and has a name including the characters "blue dragon" is a complicated one. It is disconcerting to search for something that is both ubiquitous and anonymous, but also extremely specific. Compounded by the sense of global anonymity, the postmodern space of *Oldboy* remains outside a specific locale or time. All of the spatial configurations depicted in this film—such as Cheol-ung's private cell enterprise, Dae-su's high school, the cyber chat room shared by Mi-do and Woo-jin, Mi-do's sushi restaurant, and Woo-jin's suite at the top of a high-rise building—are framed within postnational, ahistorical, or artificial realms.

Earl Jackson Jr. states: "The way Oh [O Dae-su] tastes each gyoza, comparing that taste with his specialized knowledge of the gyoza he has eaten for fifteen years, seems a darker parody of the Japanese trope of gourmet nostalgia, exemplified most vividly in popular culture in the film *Tampopo*, on the quest for the perfect ramen."[20] With both globalization and modernization in full swing, Seoul has actively participated in the global, border-crossing culture. Chinese food, particularly *jajangmyŏn* (black-bean-paste noodles),[21] was the only ethnic cuisine to which the general Korean populace had access during the 1960s and the 1970s, but the food quickly lost its exoticness and became part of Korean culture.[22] The use of gunmandu (*gyoza*) in *Oldboy* as the primary evidence that leads Dae-su to his captor is significant not only, as Jackson suggests, because it transforms taste from a high-brow pursuit in the vein of *Tampopo* into a survival skill, but also because it erases the kind of regional identity that is often clearly marked by taste.

"Tell the kitchen that there's too much *buchu* in your gunmandu," Dae-su tells the delivery boy from the restaurant that bears the name Purple Blue Dragon and produces dumplings with the taste that he had grown accustomed to during his fifteen years in captivity. Excessive use of buchu, or thin spring onions, has made it possible for Dae-su to track down the organization that Woo-jin has hired to lock him up. But what is the significance of Dae-su's statement? First, it is both a complaint and a kind of compliment. He had grown sick of buchu over fifteen years, but if it had not been for the excessive use of buchu in the dumpling, Dae-su would never have been able to find the company that had held him captive. Even though gunmandu has a standard, anonymous taste anonymity in Korean culture, the excessive use of buchu in the Purple Blue Dragon's dumplings made them sufficiently unique for Dae-su. Second, the buchu statement could be read as cynically reducing one of the most important modern periods of Korean history into a vacuous, insignificant one. Because he had been locked up alone in the private jail, the dumpling is Dae'su's only significant memory from the critical years between 1988 and 2003, when South Korea became a democracy, as well as one of the most economically successful and technologically advanced countries in the world. Dae-su does not remember the deaths of nu-

49 "Tell the kitchen that there is too much buchu in your gunmandu!" *Oldboy*.

merous demonstrators throughout this period of democratization, or the workers fired during the so-called IMF-bailout crisis. What matters most to him is the unforgettable taste of excessive buchu that he has struggled to find again, so he can put his trauma behind him. And to me the unpacking of history into gunmandu is the defining moment of "virtual hallyu."

The gunmandu is one of many references used in the film that makes space both familiar and unfamiliar. The sushi restaurant where Mi-do works while wearing a kimono, for instance, is called Jijunghae, which means the Mediterranean Sea. The high school that Dae-su and Woo-jin attended, Evergreen (Sangnok) High School, lacks any regional identification in its name, though most Korean high schools, like those in the United States, are named after their towns or districts. Since all of the high-school friends Dae-su visits to find out about Woo-jin speak in thick regional accents, the viewer can be sure that Evergreen High School is located in the provinces—but where, exactly? Do the regional accents offer us any other clues? *Oldboy* makes it clear that these characters do not speak standard Korean, but simultaneously pushes the accent's spatial identity past the familiar, rendering it anonymous. As a result, the relationships of the characters in the film to spatial coordinates become unclear. Our sense of "what is what" has become so disengaged that even when a provincial accent or the taste of a food is invoked, it only adds to the mystification. *Oldboy*'s effective underscoring of the sense of the unknowable makes globalization almost synonymous with anonymity. The abandonment of the knowable suggests the end of epistemology, achieving instead a postmodern condition marred by schizophrenia.

Language: "Face I Want to See Again"

Park Chan-wook's vengeance films typically use two modes to disrupt narrative linearity: the use of balletic action sequences that become attractions in and of themselves; and the use of performative language. In *Sympathy for Mr. Vengeance*, much of the dialogue is in sign language because the protagonist, Ryu, is mute. Park Chan-wook's work has almost always paid particular attention to mutes. As I discussed in chapter 2 (Asako's aphasia in *Epitaph*) and chapter 6 (Kong-ju's speech impairment in *Oasis*), the evaporation of language produces a regime of censorship—both social and allegorical. But of all the films that have featured mutes and characters with speaking disabilities, only two stand out as instances that employ linguistic handicap as a political metaphor: Park's contribution, "Neverending Peace and Love," to the human-rights omnibus film *If You Were Me* (*Yŏsŏt'kae ŭi sisŏn*, 2003) reenacts the true story of a female Nepalese migrant worker in Korea, who is diagnosed as mentally disabled and forcibly institutionalized in a mental hospital for years for simply not speaking a word of Korean. In *Thirst*, for instance, the climax comes after a sequence in which the paralyzed Mrs. Ra (played by Kim Hye-suk)—who is unable to speak or move her body—finds a way to communicate to the rest of the family by blinking her eyes. Ironically it is Evelyn, her Filipino daughter-in-law who speaks limited Korean, who understands Mrs. Ra best.

Voice, as I will discuss in detail below, is an important element of human identification, subjectification, and sexual fetish. A person who cannot speak loses agency in the domains of society, morality, and sexuality. This psychosocial function of the voice, rather than its secondary use as a political metaphor, is what motivates Park Chan-wook's work. *Sympathy for Mr. Vengeance*'s creative use of subtitles and intertitles, which feature characters other than Ryu speaking aloud while using sign language to Ryu, help the audience to understand the narrative. However, such performative use of bodily gestures and linguistic images complicate the communicative channels of language. The vocal punctuations of sound, the variety of titles, and the movements of bodies and the expressions on faces force us to wonder if Park, in making *Oldboy*, was influenced by modernist filmmakers like Jean-Luc Godard, who explored the possibility of pure visuality and sound in cinema. In the third and final film of Park's revenge trilogy, *Lady Vengeance*, the villain is an English teacher who sometimes communicates in English, and the heroine's daughter—a Korean girl who

50 If you blink, it means "yes." A long blink means "no." *Thirst.*

lives in Australia with her adoptive parents—speaks only English. When English is spoken in the film, Park slows down his characters' speech so that Korean subtitles can appear word by word, choreographed in the exact rhythm and order as the spoken English words, so that the audience can witness the process of translation laid bare.

In *Oldboy*, Dae-su undergoes a dramatic transformation after being locked up for fifteen years. As mentioned above, one significant change is signaled through his voice. Not only does he speak in a terse monotone after he is freed, but he also speaks through voice-overs.[23] What makes his voice so unusual is that it detaches itself from the social and the personal, becoming transcendental. If Woo-jin's artificial heart metonymically underscores his heartlessness and ruthlessness, Dae-su matches Woo-jin's inhumanity through the transformation of his voice. Even before Dae-su loses the battle with Woo-jin—and, as a consequence, loses his tongue—it is possible to perceive him as a quasi-mute. Michel Chion notes that, according to Jacques Lacan, voice—along with the gaze, the penis, the feces, and nothingness—is ranked as an objet petit a, a part object "which may be fetishized and employed to 'thingify difference.'"[24] Sexual differences, prohibition, and the law can all be established through the voice. However, Dae-su's transcendental voice (sometimes heard only through voice-over narration) rises beyond the law and society. Here Park Chan-wook's use of voice radically departs from, for instance, Lee Chang-dong's use of Kong-ju's unspeakable body in *Oasis*. I argue that it is through the extraordinary voice, artificially permed hair, and superathletic body of Dae-su that the audience engages in the sensationalized tension between human and nonhuman. If the origin of modern literature and film was embedded in the new discovery of landscape and nature, as I discussed in chapter 2, not only have they become irrelevant in *Oldboy*, they have also ostensibly been replaced by this supernatural, indestructible being positioned between god and human. This provides a strong sense of the unutterable or the unspeakable, underscoring the film's invocation of the taboo that remains at its heart. Since Dae-su has achieved a nonhuman voice, the audience assumes that a mundane code of ethics, with all of its prohibitions, does not apply to him—that is, until the very end of the film, when we learn that he has slept with his daughter. It is at this moment that his voice departs from the transcendental and becomes human again—the precise moment that he decides to cut out his tongue.

In addition, the medium of television emerges as a penultimate postmodern instrument through which the film concretizes the relation between subject and space as dysfunctional. As Dae-su is forbidden from communicating with anyone during his imprisonment, his only access to information is through a television set placed in his cell. Before he is released, Dae-su tells the audience that television is capable of being everything from "a clock, a calendar, a school, a home, a church, a friend, to a lover." When he states that television is like "a friend," the image on the television in his cell features classic 1931 footage of *Frankenstein*. The visual image chosen as the linguistic signifier of "a lover" is an image of Min Hae-gyeong, a popular singer from the late 1980s and the early 1990s, singing "Bogosip'ŭn ŏlgul" ("Face I Want to See Again"), which will later again enter the narrative as Mi-do's siren song. But can an image on television (or subsequently the real daughter) be classified as a real lover? Is Min Hae-gyeong, who dances only on the television monitor—untouchable, unable to interact with the imprisoned Dae-su, and therefore unaffective—capable of becoming Dae-su's lover? Being equipped to address every desire and fantasy, but without being able to deliver on any of them, is like simultaneously dreaming the perfect dream and one's worst nightmare. This contrasts with more traditional realist takes on alienation such as Hong Ki-sŏn's *The Road Taken* (*Sŏnt'aek*, 2003), a Korean film that was released the same year as *Oldboy*. Both are dramas about men unfairly put in jail. An irreconcilable gap, however, remains between Kim Sŏn-myŏng, the protagonist of *The Road Taken*, and Oh Dae-su: the former is a prisoner convicted by the state for believing in an ideology (Marxism) deemed subversive to the state; the latter is a prisoner put away by a private man for having been a "loud mouth." Despite having been locked away for over thirty-five years—setting a world record for the longest-serving political prisoner—Kim, who is sometimes in solitary confinement, has comrades in adjacent cells around him who are equally unfortunate. They have no television or any other electronic devices to keep them entertained; yet they celebrate birthdays, play games, communicate through secret codes by tapping the wall, and plan political actions together. In contrast, Dae-su spends all of his time with his only surrogate friend: the television—not unlike the average postmodern person, who spends far more time communicating electronically than face to face. Like the gunmandu, Min's dance to the samba beat of the Korean song "Face I Want to See Again" underscores an anonymously global pop culture that has lost its genuine regional authenticity while perfectly accommodating the clichés of the medium of television.

Postmodernism, which is predicated on the pleasurable use of the difference between the signifier and the signified, is also conditioned in *Oldboy* through the use of voice-overs and other creative juxtapositions of image and sound. Deleuze lauds Jean-Luc Godard's achievements, claiming that Godard is "definitely one of the authors who has thought most about visual-sound relationships."[25] Deleuze continues: "[Godard's] tendency to reinvest the visual with sound, with the ultimate aim of . . . restoring both to the body from which they have been taken, produces a system of disengagements or micro-cuts in all directions: cuts spread and no longer pass between the sound and the visual, but in the visual, in the sound, and in their multiplied connections."[26] Deleuze insists that the visual and the voice are often taken from human bodies in film, but as soon as they are processed and textually manipulated through a machine—the camera, sound recording devices, and other postproduction gadgets—they do not remain natural to the body. What Godard wants to accomplish could be considered the cinematic equivalent to cacophonous sound, but achieved through the potentially disjunctive relationship between sound and image. Park Chan-wook aims at something similar: his soundtracks are designed to go beyond the boundary of the real and expand the chasm between the human and his or her vocal signification. Park reappropriates and makes self-referential the unnatural relationship between sound and image that Godard experimented with in his films, as well as the relationship between the real and its representation that narrative cinema had seamlessly sewn together over the years in order to produce admittedly coy comic gags and "cool" effects. But has the contradiction between image and sound, or between reality and its representation, not already manifested itself as humorous and playful (for example, in the silent days of cinema)? In other words, isn't this unnaturalness natural to the medium of cinema?

Conclusion: "Just Look at the Surface"

"If you want to know all about Andy Warhol," Warhol famously told the press, "just look at the surface of my paintings and films and me, and there I am. There's nothing behind it." One of my favorite scenes in contemporary Korean cinema comes from the end of *Sympathy for Mr. Vengeance*, when Park Dong-jin, the factory owner whose daughter had been kidnapped, is stabbed multiple times by members of a terrorist organization called the Revolutionary Anarchist Alliance. "Who the hell are you guys?" Park demands. Instead of giving a verbal answer, the anarchists pin a prepared note to Park's chest with a knife. If this were a film by Godard, for instance, such an abrupt and incoherent insertion of violence would have been welcomed as an allegory of class conflict. However, *Sympathy for Mr. Vengeance*, like Park Chan-wook's other films but unlike Godard's work, is a tightly structured, entertainment film in which every scene is tied to the causality and clear rationale of the whole. Did Park Chan-wook think that he could afford one Godardian moment at the end? There are a number of superfluous possible answers to Park Dong-jin's final question: the public one (class hostility), the private one (revenge for Ryu's girlfriend, who was also an anarchist), none of the above, and all of the above. The final scene refuses to give us an answer. Park Chan-wook is thus able to maintain the premise that representation (which assigns certain mimetic symbols to reality) is untenable—and, therefore, that it is impossible to excavate any kind of agency from it. After all, can anyone other than the original members of Monty Python extract any meaning behind the excessive buchu? While gasping for his last breath, Park Dong-jin tries desperately to read the note pinned to him. Without the strength to move his body, he can only tilt his head, but the note remains beyond his range of sight. The credits soon roll, and every viewer can air his or her frustrated sigh.

EIGHT

The End of History, the Historical Films' Beginning

Korea's New *Sagŭk*

South Korea witnessed the establishment of its two-party political system and the domination of big, global corporations during the first decade of the 2000s, the period that arguably sealed the triumph of neoliberalism around the world and brought about Francis Fukuyama's conservative "end of history."[1] Lost has been the ethical urgency, in other words, that places the past in the context of the Hegelian continuum of humanity's progression toward Utopian ideals.[2] As I have argued throughout this book, South Korea, despite its ongoing political crisis marred by the recalcitrant presence of Communist North Korea, has flirted with a sense of various kinds of ends (ideology, modernism, socialist democracy, the egalitarian welfare state, and so on). The affirmation of neoliberalism's victory in South Korea was the effective outcome of these ends, with neither conservatives nor liberals pushing agendas to slow Korea's embrace of the capitalist system that tolerated the growing gap between classes and the increase of corporate power.

Because almost every feature film can be completed only with the aid of a capitalist who seeks to profit from his or her investment, cinema is an institution, not just a set of expressive objects made by unique individuals. According to the law of supply and demand in the capitalist marketplace, every film that costs more than 10 billion won (approximately $800,000) at its most fundamental level must create a realm of fantasy that reconstitutes individuals within a specific political economy and its contradictions. The old framework of different genres is no longer enough; instead, the realm of fantasy must rearticulate what Fredric Jameson calls "metageneric production." This mixed-genre trend typified Hollywood cinema of the 1970s, which used "the pregiven structure of inherited genres as a pretext for production which is no longer personal or stylistic in the sense of the older modernism."[3] Realization of this "metageneric production," which also utilizes technology-driven high production values and a non-reflexive expression of historical impulse that freely manufactures nostalgic images of the past, has created a new sense of postmodern film auteurship in South Korea since the beginning of the century—an auteurship that mediates between the fantasies desired by the masses and reinvented modernist dreams by ambitious directors such as Park Chan-wook, Kim Jee-woon, Bong Joon-ho, and Choi Dong-hun. Despite their prolific efforts during this period, which insisted upon the importance of craftsmanship in filmmaking, I claim that the historicism that they collectively imagined throughout the heyday of Korean cinema failed to reawaken auteurist shock values. At the end of the last millennium, these filmmakers vied to set a new standard for cinematic visions through their reproductions of North Korea (Park Chan-wook's *JSA*), colonial-era Korea (Kim Jee-woon's *The Good, the Bad, the Weird*), and contemporary, hyperurban Seoul (Park Chan-wook's *Oldboy*, Bong Joon-ho's *The Host*, and Kim Jee-woon's *Bitter Sweet Life*). The visual pastiche that these films collectively reconstructed breaks free of the restraints of both realist cinema and modernist austerity, but it ultimately asphyxiates history.

In the United States, Hollywood has successfully spatialized and congealed the fantasies of its mass audiences by visualizing innumerable iconographies that range from remote Western landscapes, small provincial towns in horror films, glossy war scenes of rural Vietnam, and decayed urban skyscrapers that are repetitively destroyed in many disaster and superhero films. All these spaces—including the deserts of Arizona and Nevada that frequently served as sets for both Westerns and sci-fi films, and the rice paddies in Thailand that were the background for the apocalyptic American vision of the Vietnam War—can be construed as the "ultimate and defining moment of the twentieth century," or what Slavoj Žižek calls "the direct experience of the [Lacanian] Real as opposed to every social reality."[4] But what exactly are the generic landmarks of Korean cinema over the last decade that visually fulfilled Korea's passion for its own "Real"? The visual conceptualization of the real had, first, to acknowledge and mourn the end of history and the futility of interpreting it for humankind's pursuit of Utopian ideals.[5] Second, Korean cinema's iconography also needed to ironically celebrate the triumph of neoliberalism and South Korea's ascendancy as an economically powerful nation capable of manufacturing its own hidden kernel of truth, which does not totally mimic Hollywood's. Third, it needed to maximize the potentials of cinema—an imitative art that, to borrow a term from André Bazin, "mummifies"[6] the

Table 2. Annual box office admissions in South Korea

| | KOREAN FILMS | | |
	ADMISSIONS (MILLION)	SHARE OF THE KOREAN MARKET	ADMISSIONS PER CAPITA
1998	12.59	25.10%	0.29
1999	21.72	39.70%	0.50
2000	22.71	35.10%	0.41
2001	44.81	50.10%	0.96
2002	50.82	48.30%	1.07
2003	63.91	53.49%	1.32
2004	80.19	59.33%	1.65
2005	85.44	58.71%	1.75
2006	97.91	63.80%	2.00
2007	79.39	50.00%	1.61
2008	63.54	42.13%	1.28
2009	76.47	48.77%	1.54
2010	68.29	46.52%	1.35

Source: 2010 data from KOFIC.
Note: In 2007, South Korea's population was forty-nine million.

present moment for posterity's sake, even if this means that the most essential architectural symbol of Korea, the Kwanghwa Gate of the Kyŏngbok Palace, must be recreated through computer graphics.[7]

When the national distribution system for films stabilized in the early years of the twenty-first century after years of volatility,[8] the Korean film industry saw the need to refashion its own virtual cinematic space. Modern films in Korea (as in most countries) largely depend on glossy images generated by 3-D technology, computer graphics that place human characters somewhere between live-action and animation, and visuals and narratives reminiscent of video games. Consequently Korean cinema—once its industry infrastructural potentials were heightened through the expansion of the number of theatrical screens, the unbelievable jump of annual movie ticket sales per capita from 1.1 (1998) to 3.2 (2007), and the increase

FOREIGN FILMS			TOTAL	
ADMISSIONS (MILLION)	SHARE OF THE KOREAN MARKET	ADMISSIONS PER CAPITA	ADMISSIONS (MILLION)	ADMISSIONS PER CAPITA
37.59	74.90%	0.81	50.18	1.10
33.00	60.30%	0.70	54.72	1.20
41.91	64.90%	0.89	64.62	1.30
44.55	49.90%	0.94	89.36	1.90
54.31	51.70%	1.13	105.13	2.20
55.56	46.51%	1.15	119.47	2.47
54.98	40.67%	1.13	135.17	2.78
60.08	41.29%	1.23	145.52	2.98
55.49	36.20%	1.13	153.40	3.13
79.38	50.00%	1.61	158.77	3.22
87.29	57.87%	1.76	150.83	3.04
80.32	51.23%	1.61	156.79	3.15
78.51	53.48%	1.55	146.81	2.92

of export revenue—sought its own virtual iconographies that, at their core, functioned as signs of Korea's virtuality and reality (see table 2).

If the Korean cinema of the 1980s and the 1990s could counter Hollywood action and sci-fi films only with erotic films that advertised half-naked female bodies in the commercial marketplace, and art-house films that featured troubled intellectuals, the subject of the remasculinized Korean films of the early 2000s sought to continue to cultivate their own metageneric locations in sci-fi or superhero films. The most expensive Korean film of the early 2000s was Jang Sun-woo's *The Resurrection of the Little Match Girl* (*Sŏngnyang p'ali sonyŏ ŭi chaerim*, 2002). The director—whose earlier sexually charged films, such as *To You, from Me* (*Nŏ ege narŭl ponenda*, 1994) and *Lies* (*Kojinmal*, 1999), challenged the repressive ideological principles of neo-Confucian Korea—was put at the helm of a sci-fi

Table 3. Annual Korean film production cost

	PRODUCTION COST (A)		PRINT AND ADVERTISING (B)		TOTAL PRODUCTION COST (A + B)**
	PER TITLE*	PERCENTAGE OF TOTAL PRODUCTION EXPENDITURE	PER TITLE	PERCENTAGE OF TOTAL PRODUCTION EXPENDITURE	PER TITLE
1996	0.9	90.0%	0.1	10.0%	1.00
1997	1.1	84.6%	0.2	15.4%	1.30
1998	1.2	80.0%	0.3	20.0%	1.50
1999	1.4	73.6%	0.5	26.4%	1.90
2000	1.5	69.7%	0.65	30.3%	2.15
2001	1.62	63.5%	0.93	36.5%	2.55
2002	2.45	65.9%	1.27	34.1%	3.72
2003	2.84	68.3%	1.32	31.7%	4.16
2004	2.80	67.3%	1.36	32.7%	4.16
2005	2.73	68.4%	1.26	31.6%	3.99
2006	2.58	64.2%	1.44	35.8%	4.02
2007	2.55	68.5%	1.17	31.5%	3.72
2008	2.07	68.8%	0.94	31.2%	3.01
2009	1.56	67.5%	0.75	32.5%	2.31
2010	1.42	65.7%	0.74	34.3%	2.16

Source: 2010 data from KOFIC.

* 10 billion won (approximately $1 million). The exchange rate between the South Korean won and the US dollar has fluctuated from approximately 800 won to the dollar (1996) to approximately 1,200 won to the dollar (2010).

** Though the total cost per film seems to have decreased steadily from 2006, this is due to the fact that the average figure now also includes many independently produced, low-budget films routinely released in theaters. While *Wônang sori* (*Old Partner*, 2009,) a documentary film about a friendship between an aging cow and a septuagenarian farmer, was a surprising hit and sold over three million tickets, most of the films that cost under $1 million to make do not last more than a week in theaters. Average production costs of commercial feature films have continued to rise.

project that was initially budgeted at around $4 million. Not surprisingly for a figure whom I have previously called an exemplary filmmaker of an "exile cinema," who has long suffered from a "state of unbelonging" in his own country,[9] Jang managed to spend over $12 million, bankrupting Tube Entertainment, the film's main investor. At a time when the average film cost only about $2 million, the final budget of this film was unsustainable (see table 3).

A messy plotline; inappropriate use of B-movie aesthetics, such as the deliberate use of cheap props—including a toy fish gun and overdone gangster outfits—and a synthesizer soundtrack, in a big-budget sci-fi film; and, most important, the director's uncompromising attitude of an auteur rather than the creator of an entertainment film—all were identified as critical factors in the film's failure. Though *Little Match Girl* had a disastrous theatrical run, its opening sequence does manage to emblematize the postmodern figure of the elusive little match girl—the objective of the game-within-the-film—who, by selling lighters in the street from a basket, invokes Korea's memory of colonialism.

The little match girl (played by Im Un-gyŏng, who rose to stardom via billboard advertisements for TTL cellphones) assumes the figure of nuŭi tongsaeng (younger sister), discussed in chapter 2, not unlike Kim Sin-jae's character in Ch'oe In-gyu's *Angels on the Streets* (*Chip opnŭn ch'ŏnsa*, 1941), who is caught between the fear of losing her virginity and the desire to modernize. The objective of the game-within-the-film is for Joo, the main character, to seduce the little match girl and then allow her to die peacefully. The peaceful death represents both Korea's fear of forgetting its troubled past and the need to put its painful past to sleep. The first two legitimate big-budget sci-fi films released in the first decade of the new millennium, both unsuccessful at the box office, were *Little Match Girl* and *Lost Memories 2009* (2002), whose plot also involved a continued Japanese occupation of Korea into the twenty-first century. This is probably not a coincidence, since the trauma Koreans suffered from the Japanese colonial era remains an enigmatic but seductive kernel. Throughout the decade, big-budget films set during the colonial era—such as *Blue Swallow* (2005), *The Good, the Bad, the Weird* (2008), and *Modern Boy* (2008)—were released, only to lose money for their investors.

The colonial capital of Keijo, the evacuated cities of the Korean War era, and the forest that stretched along the border with North Korea all vied to serve as milieus of South Korean cinema's "Originary World"—the world

51.1 Postmodern nuŭi tongsaeng (younger sister) in *Little Match Girl*.

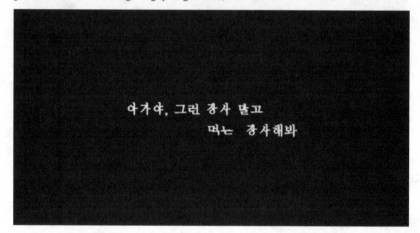

51.2 *During Little Match Girl's opening sequence, dialogue is replaced with silent film–like intitles and the song "Tears of Mokp'o," from Korea's colonial period.*

that, in the words of Gilles Deleuze, is "recognizable by its formless character . . . [and] pure background."[10] After a fleeting revival of interest, they all failed, for they could not live up to the expectation of visualizing a space that can free itself from the politicized semiotics of present realities such as the "Tokdo Belongs to Korea" Campaign (a symbol of border dispute between South Korea and Japan), or the intensification of the Left-Right conflict after the sinking of the South Korean Naval Warship Cheonan and the bombing of the Yeonpyeong Island off the coast of Incheon (a symbol of border dispute between Communist North and Capitalist South). What

52 The iconic nuŭi tongsaeng of colonial-era cinema: the actress Kim Sin-jae, shown here in *Angels on the Streets*.

spaces were left to exploit in a non-Hollywood film industry, with limited resources and audiences for its own metageneric productions featuring local actors? In other words, what could Korean cinema offer to counter the callisthenic bodies that somersault through the bamboo groves, or the samurai swords that criss-cross alongside rice paddies—traditional features of Hong Kong and Japanese cinema? Korean cinema around 2005 proposed its own "Originary World" that allows viewers to diagnose the frail conditions of civility and the cruelty of the present: using the Kyŏng-bok Palace and its association with Chosun-era history as the main setting for premodern period pieces that probe Koreans' own brand of love stories and action dramas, which cut across the regional, ideological, and class barriers that have plagued Korea for the past hundred years. For decades, sagŭk (史劇), films set in the pre-modern era, fell out of public favor and existed only on television as a pastime mainly targeted at retired men. They were neither witty nor spectacular. The only notable sagŭk films produced during the 1990s were Park Chong-won's *Eternal Empire* (1995) and Im Kwon-Taek's *Ch'unhyang* (2000), which did well at international film

53 Comedy actor Park Chung-hoon plays General Kye Baek in *Hwangsanbeol*.

festivals but had woeful results at the Korean box office. Though Im Kwon-Taek is often misperceived as a sagŭk filmmaker, most of the films he made during the 1980s and the 1990s were set during the colonial or early modern era, and not in the premodern one. The last time sagŭk made headlines was in 1986, when *Ŏudong* (starring Yi Po-hŭi) and *Pyŏn'gangsoe* (starring Yi Tae-gŭn) successfully marketed the half-clad bodies of female stars in order to attract male audiences. Since then, no sagŭk has even reached the quarter-million admissions mark, a barometer of moderate commercial success throughout the late 1980s and the 1990s.

In 2003, two films were released in October, a typically slow season, within two weeks of each other. First was E J-yong's *Untold Scandal*. Two weeks later, on October 17, Lee Joon-ik's *Once upon a Time in the Battlefield* (*Hwangsanbŏl*) opened in theaters, to be met with critics' raspberries and audiences' derision for its inaccurate depiction of the Battle of Hwangsanbeol in AD 660 between Silla Kingdom (Korea's southeast) and Baekje Kingdom (Korea's southwest), led by General Kye Baek. Not only did this comedy sagŭk, the first of its kind in decades, lampoon the modern regional conflict between the southeastern Chŏlla Province and the southwestern Kyŏngsang Province by forcing southeastern Silla characters to use a thick, modern Kyŏngsang provincial accent to distinguish themselves from their southwestern Baekje rivals, who indiscriminately use meaningless filler (*kŏsigi*, meaning "that thing"), between almost every word in Monty Python–like sketches.

Not only was this directorial decision to use modern regional accents seen as a way of inauthenticating history but it was seen also as a cheap way to exploit regional dialect—which had become popular at the time through the successes of *Marrying the Mafia* (*Tusabu ilch'e*) and *My Wife Is a Gangster* (*Chop'ok manura*) that were originally released in 2001 and had spawned sequels throughout the decade. Despite the reactions of irritation that it initially provoked, *Once upon a Time in the Battlefield* ended up in the box office top ten films of that year, selling 2.8 million tickets nationwide. It also restored the then-floundering career of its director, Lee Joon-ik, who achieved even greater success with another sagŭk set in the Chosun Dynasty. That film, *The King and the Clown* (*Wang ŭi namja*, 2005), compared by the *New York Times* with *Brokeback Mountain* despite Lee's protest,[11] surprisingly became one of only five Korean films released during the first decade of the 2000s that sold more than ten million tickets.[12]

Its initial critical reception was not nearly as disastrous as that of *Once upon a Time in the Battlefield*, and *Untold Scandal*—starring Bae Yong-jun, fresh from the success of the television drama *Winter Sonata*, set new standards for sagŭk, with its plot adapted from a French libertine literature (Laclos's *Les Liaisons Dangereuses*), its unprecedented use of baroque music for the soundtrack, and its convenient exploitation of the Chosun-era setting in order to include explicit sex scenes and deflowering schemes. *Untold Scandal* sold more than 3.5 million tickets nationwide and, along with *Taejanggŭm* (*Jewel in the Palace*), which featured the female chef-cum-doctor in the Chosun royal court and aired on television around the same time, created a new heyday of sagŭk in Korean film and television.

The two premodern films—*Once upon a Time in the Battlefield* and *Untold Scandal*—transformed the landscape of commercial films in Korea by becoming unlikely blockbusters and changing the perceptions of investors who had thought that period films were not commercially viable in Korea. The cultural repercussions of these two sagŭk titles extended well beyond 2003. Sagŭks were no longer required to get the historical details right and baroque music actually became the norm, not the anomaly, of their soundtracks.

Lee Joon-ik became one of the hit filmmakers of the decade with the enormous success of *The King and the Clown* and another martial-arts drama set during the 1592 Japanese invasion of Korea, *Like the Moon Escaping from the Clouds* (*Kurumŭl pŏsŏnan tal ch'ŏrŏm*, 2010). In addition, Kim Dae-woo, who wrote the screenplay for *Untold Scandal*, emerged later in the decade as

54 King Sŏnjo flees the burning Kyŏngbok Palace in *Like the Moon Escaping from the Clouds*.

one of Korea's most talented writer-directors through two successful *sagŭk* films: a fictional romance between the queen and an erotic genre writer, *Forbidden Quest* (*Ŭmran sŏsaeng*, 2007), and a *Shrek*-like revisionist interpretation of the classic tale of *Chunhyang*, *The Servant* (*Pangjajŏn*, 2010). The successes of these period films raise a question: do the deconstruction and demise of historical authenticity in these films suggest that there is no need for representation, historical analysis, or an investigation into the current systematic failures that legitimize the increasing gap between the rich and the poor?[13]

In Choi Dong-hoon's *Jeon Woo-chi: The Taoist Wizard* (2009), among the largest grossing films of 2010 after being released during the Christmas season in 2009, Ch'orong, Woo-chi's sidekick dog who is able to magically appear human, asks his master: "If Woo-chi were to choose the fame and status in the world suggested by Confucian literature rather than the solitude recommended by Taoism, wouldn't that be meaningless like a dream? If he's not aware of that, he surely wouldn't know how to distinguish illusion from reality?" This question sums up the film's quixotic plot, which— at a dizzying pace—transports the characters (and the viewers) from the Chosun Dynasty to the present, from a Southeast Asian beach resort to a dressing room on a movie set in contemporary Korea, and from the monochrome mountains of a traditional Korean landscape painting to the spectacularly colored billboard selling the latest in menswear on a congested Seoul street. The dog's question also complements Woo-chi's rather poignant question: "What is life, if not a dream? If it can't be a dream, what's the use of having a Taoist wizard like me around?" Woo-chi's disappearing

55 Woo-chi arrives at the Kyŏngbok Palace, where the king is bowing in greeting.
    Jeon Woo-chi.

act, along with Korea's ability to fantasize such wizardry, the film seems
to argue, has been kept imprisoned for centuries, until now. "Speed creates pure objects," writes Jean Baudrillard,[14] discussing America's fascination with cars and the American desert. The sheer speed of time, which
first impacted the New Hollywood during its multiplex era and created the
consumer base of young audiences, fascinated filmmakers in the United
States, Hong Kong, and elsewhere. The themes of forgetting preferred to
remembrance, the postmodern fascination with amnesia, and the super-
ficiality of a pure object that flattens every traumatic bit of history has
finally branded Korean cinema. Through its sagŭks, a new chapter in search
of the most persuasive special-effects visual imagery for its metageneric
production has been launched.

The multiple traditional spaces that *Jeon Woo-chi* engenders—the
Kyŏngbok Palace; the phallus-shaped mountains of traditional landscape
paintings, with white rings of clouds just below their peaks; and the dimly
lit *sarangbang* (guesthouse usually occupied by men) chambers where de-
mons hide under the skins of *yangban* aristocrats—all morph into hyper-
urban forests composed of thin, glass-surfaced buildings, mental institutions, Catholic churches, and sets for movies and fashion photo shoots,
which are all common sights in contemporary Seoul. We have come full
circle: the virtuality rendered in this new sagŭk is a Korea that insists on
blurring the boundary between the way things really were and the way
things are remembered, or the way things now appear in our consciousness. The Deleuzian "powers of the false,"[15] which suggest finding a third

path beyond true and false, here meet the subversive trope that was raised in the original *Tale of Chŏn U-ch'i*, written in the early Chosun period, or in the "Song of Four Seasons," which I discussed in chapter 1. In this world, neither the opposition between true and false nor the one between reality and fantasy can be resolved. Instead, both turn into what Henri Bergson calls the "creative evolution"[16] that allows that very tension to be a joyous *nolabose* (let us play) site.

Even during the phase of late capitalism, the "temptation of the local," Ackbar Abbas explains, remains very strong, as the local is now reasserted as a mark of independence in a place where the "history of colonialism has a hangover effect."[17] Abbas was thinking of Hong Kong, especially the expats who sometimes occupied more marginalized places than the locals of Hong Kong when he wrote this, but South Korea may be no different as it struggles to project cinematic iconographies that both remain as commercially viable as the "gunslingers and railroads" in American Westerns or the "flying swordsmen and bamboo forests" in Chinese martial arts films and address its anxiety about forgetting, given that the country has yet to satisfyingly mourn its end of history. Not only is Korea still scarred and traumatized by its colonial era and the Cold War, but—given the continuing US military presence and occasional threats of war from North Korea—it has yet to claim a true postcolonial and post–Cold War identity. This is why Korean cinema has to resurrect its premodern past, which is surely filled with episodes that are just as humiliating as those of the twentieth century, but which can be rewritten to fill in for the largely undocumented histories of *sŏja* (bastard sons), *nobi* (slaves), *naesi* (eunuchs), *kungnyŏ* (court ladies), and kisaeng, most of which are omitted from the official court documents.[18] That the only South Korean film to be an adaptation of a North Korean novel was also a sagŭk (2007's *Hwang Chin-i*), a love story between a kisaeng and a nobi, is perhaps not a coincidence.[19] Perhaps Bruno Latour was right: "We have never been modern."[20] That the futuristic sets of Korean cinema are found not in the postmodern future but in the metaphysical space of premodern topography may demonstrate the extent to which this space is penetrated by the virtual dream of both a Utopian end of history and the destruction of the corporate capitalist system.

Preface

1 Chris Howard argues that *The Host*, which was released on 620 of the 1,649 screens then available in Korea, exemplifies what he calls the "national conjunction" of the South Korean film industry that draws on patriotic consumerist behavior ("Contemporary South Korean Cinema"). Perhaps so, but patriotic consumerism of blockbuster films exists in most countries capable of producing and releasing their own big-budget action films (for example, *National Treasure* in the United States or *The Red Cliff* in the People's Republic of China).

2 Korea's annual box office statistics can easily be found on the websites of the Korean Film Council (http://www.koreafilm.or.kr) and Box Office Mojo (http://boxofficemojo.com/intl/korea/yearly/).

3 The Korean film industry has never been bold in its attempt to make films in languages other than Korean. Though there have been several attempts to make low-budget English-language films coproduced by Koreans—such as Chin Won-suk's *Too Tired to Die* (1998), Yuk Sang-ho's *Iron Palm* (2002), Gina Kim's *Never Forever* (2007), and Michael Kang's *West 32nd* (2008)—these have not been box office successes in either the United States or Korea and did not produce an environment propitious for larger investments in films with English dialogue.

4 Korean, along with Arabic, Chinese, and Japanese, is categorized by the US Defense Language Institute as a Category IV language, meaning that it is one of the most difficult languages for Americans to learn.

5 The surprising success in reinvigorating commercial activity with vastly improved and more fluid storytelling actually had its roots in the late 1980s and the early 1990s, when Korean students were demonstrating in the streets not only for democratic representation through the popular vote, but also for free access to media and films beyond mainstream productions. The popularity of alternative filmmaking and cinephile culture in the urban sectors of Korea had deeply affected the generation then in college. Bong Joon-ho, Kim Jee-woon, Hong Sang-soo, and Park Chan-wook, who were some of the star filmmakers during the 2000s, represented the "386 generation" filmmakers. Euphemistically named after the computer chip megahertz speed, the "386 generation" refers to the people who reached age thirty in the 1990s, entered college during the 1980s, and were born in the 1960s. They had grown up not only with the Hong Kong and Hollywood action films that dominated the Korean box office

from the mid-1980s to the mid-1990s, but also with modernist films made available through international film festivals, special retrospectives of foreign art filmmakers, and cinephile club screenings that also sprouted up throughout the same period and that helped to inspire these future star directors.

6 The figure of 1.15 trillion won is based on box office sales only and includes neither ancillary market sales nor food concession sales. In comparison, according to the 2009 figures, Korea's newspaper companies annually report about 1.3 trillion won (slightly over $1 billion) total sales. NHN, the company behind www.naver.com, Korea's most popular search engine website, also has annual sales of around 1.2 trillion won. Korea's three biggest television broadcasting companies (KBS, MBC, and SBS) together and the publishing industry boast markets that are twice as big: each annually reports about 2.5 trillion won (slightly over $2 billion) in total sales. The music industry has suffered the most from illegal downloading, and its sales have steadily declined during the 2000s. Its annual sales are now less than 200 billion won.

7 Quoted in Deleuze and Guattari, *Anti-Oedipus*, 24.

8 Fredric Jameson discusses the difficulty, if not the impossibility, of sustaining a national film production, and along with it, "that of national or local culture as a whole" due to the worldwide success of Hollywood films, especially after the demise of the Soviet Union and the socialist alternatives during the latter part of the twentieth century. Fredric Jameson, "Notes on Globalization as a Philosophical Issue," 62.

Introduction

1 Norimitsu Onishi, "What's Korean for 'Real Man'? Ask a Japanese Woman," *New York Times*, December 23, 2004.

2 Norimitsu Onishi, "China's Youth Look to Seoul for Inspiration," *New York Times*, January 2, 2006.

3 In her forthcoming *Tourist Distractions: Traveling and Feeling in South Korea's East Asian Cinema*, Youngmin Choe introduces local sites like Hapchon, where Kang Je-gyu shot *Taegukgi: The Brotherhood of War* (2004) as "transient monuments" or "cinetouristic sites." She describes them as sites that are intersubjectively interwoven through both the past viewing experiences and the present tour travel.

4 The list of scholarly English-language books on Korean films includes Lee, *Contemporary Korean Cinema*; James and Kim, *Im Kwon-Taek*; K. Kim, *The Remasculinization of Korean Cinema*; Abelmann and McHugh, *South Korean Golden Age Melodrama*; Shin and Stringer, *New Korean Cinema*; Gateward, *Seoul Searching*; Parquet, *New Korean Cinema*; and J. Choi, *The South Korean Film Renaissance*.

5 Especially important are Chua and Iwabuchi, *East Asian Pop Culture*; and *Korea Journal*'s special issue on "Positioning the Korean Wave in the Nexus between Globalization and Localization" (45, no. 4 [winter 2005]).

6 By about 2005, Korean soap operas had become so dominant that all of Korea's

neighbors—including China, Taiwan, and Vietnam—had either considered or actually executed bans on foreign television dramas. See Maliangkay, "When the Korean Wave Ripples," 15.

7 According to CNN, South Korea is the world leader in its average broadband Internet speed and the percentage of the people with a high-speed Internet connection (94 percent). See David D. Sutter, "Why Internet Connections Are Fastest in South Korea," CNN, March 31, 2010 (www.cnn.com).

8 Bae Yong-jun's popularity in Japan led to the enormous success of Hur Jin-ho's *April Snow* (*Oech'ul*, 2005) in that country. The film grossed about $30 million in ticket sales alone in Japan, in a stark contrast to Korea, where it flopped badly, grossing only about $5 million.

9 Said, *Orientalism*, 54.

10 Ibid.

11 After Korean film exports earned a record $75 million in 2005, there was an enormous decline, with only $24.5 million reported in 2006 and $12 million in 2007 (Korean Film Council [KOFIC], 2007-*Nyŏn han'guk yŏnghwa kyŏlsan* [Korean Film Annals 2007]). KOFIC received subsidies of approximately $100 million from the government from 2005 to 2007. In 2008, KOFIC was given an additional $400 million to support the local film industry for another three-year cycle.

12 Sin Tong-hun and Yŏm Kang-su, "Kŏp'um ppajin hallyu saŏp, Süt'a momkap-man ttŭiwŏnokko 'hŭich'ŏng [Deflated Hallyu business: turbulence after stars' wages spike]," *Chosun-Ilbo*, December 22, 2008.

13 Yoo In-chon, a former actor and a conservative politician who was appointed minister of culture, tourism, and sports by President Lee Myung-bak in 2008, cut budgets and appointed other conservative figures to key posts in the Korean Film Council (KOFIC), the Korean Film Academy, the Korean Film Archive, and the Korean National University of Arts.

14 Eagleton, *After Theory*, 17.

15 Here I am pointing to the essays featured in Chua and Iwabuchi, *East Asian Pop Culture*, and the special issue on "Positioning the Korean Wave in the Nexus between Globalization and Localization" in *Korea Journal*, both mentioned above.

16 Shim, "Hybridity and the rise of Korean Popular Culture in Asia," 27.

17 Shim's piece curiously cites an obscure essay, "Five Theses on Actually Existing Marxism," by Fredric Jameson, the prominent Marxist literary critic, to point out how modernity and postmodernity cannot be disassociated from capitalist development (ibid., 26).

18 Yi S. "Lingering Impressions of a Mountain Village," 332.

19 Ibid., 334.

20 Terms "peaks of present" and "sheets of past" employed by Deleuze throughout his second book on cinema, *Cinema 2: The Time-Image*, are illustrated by the touch of an inverted cone's peak (present) of the top layer of sheets (of past) that centrally formulates the ideas behind Henri Bergson's *Matter and Memory*. This simple point of contact between the "peak" and the "sheet" as the *actual*

past of this present that incommensurably expands into the *virtual* as the circumference of the inverted cone, as well as the crystallization of memory, gets considerably larger beyond the *actual*. See Deleuze's illustration of what he calls Bergson's "famous cone" in his *Cinema 2: The Time-Image*, page 294.

21 As explained in the preface, the fact that the term "virtual reality" has become one of the most popular concepts today—interchangeable with "artificial," "less-than-real," and "cyberspace reality"—and is commonly understood as "unvirtuous" makes it harder to understand Deleuze's use of "virtual."

22 Nichols, *Representing Reality*, ix.

23 The export figure provided by KOFIC is based on the reports filed by Korean film companies. The export figure is slightly exaggerated because the companies often report optimistic numbers based on agreements on minimum guarantee (MG) figures or advances, which sometimes do not materialize into an actual sale.

24 In 2010, Hollywood's combined annual figure of domestic and international box office reached an all-time high of $31.8 billion. The US share of that was $10.6 billion, or 33 percent. For the past five years of figures of worldwide box office, see Motion Picture Association of America, "Theatrical Market Statistics 2010," 3, http://www.mpaa.org/policy/industry.

25 Lorenza Muñoz, "Coming Attractions: South Korean Films Take a Leap Across Oceans," *Los Angeles Times*, November 5, 2006.

26 Moretti, "Planet Hollywood," 92.

27 After falling to its lowest level in the mid-1990s, the share of the domestic box office that went to Korean films rose continuously throughout the late 1990s and the early years of the twenty-first century, plateauing at around 50 percent from 2005 to the present. Both export figures and the domestic box office sales for Korean films in that period were unprecedented and abnormal.

28 Until 1998, the Korean market share of Korean films hovered around 20 percent. It started to grow in 1999, reaching 35.8 percent in that year compared to the previous year's dismal 25.3 percent; it set a record in 2006 of 63.8 percent. Despite setbacks, the domestic film's market share for the rest of the decade was about 50 percent. See Korean Film Council, *2001-nyŏn Han'guk yŏnghwa yŏngam* [Korean Film Annals 2001], 24; *2007-nyŏn Han'guk yŏnghwa yŏngam* [Korean Film Annals 2007], 36; and *2010-nyŏn Han'guk yŏnghwa kyŏlsan* [Korean Film Summary 2009], 8. For more details, see table 2 in chapter 8.

29 The domestic film market share in Korea was within the 50–65 percent range from 2003 to 2007. Among the twenty-seven nations in the EU, only France and Sweden have a significant domestic market share in cinema (37 percent and 32 percent, respectively, in 2009). During the first decade of the century, France was the only nation to stay within the 35–45 percent range. All the other major EU countries—including Germany, Spain, England, and Italy—have reported figures of well below 25 percent for domestic market share. See European Audiovisual Observatory, "European Union Cinema Attendance up 4% in 2006," February 21, 2007 (http://www.obs.coe.int/about/oea/pr/berlin2007

.html.en); and "EU Admissions Approach the 1 Billion Barrier Again in 2009," February 11, 2010 (http://www.obs.coe.int/about/oea/pr/berlinale 2010.html).

30 In the days before multiplexes, Korean audiences often had to tolerate the aroma of dried cuttlefish, narrow seats with dirty white covers, barely audible soundtracks, and ragged projection in old, rat-infested theaters.

31 Korea's gross domestic product (GDP) per capita increased from $3,368 (1987) to $21,653 (2009). (Not adjusted for inflation and converted US dollars applying market exchange rate.) See "GDP Per Capita at Current Prices," World Bank, World Development Indicators, April 25, 2011, available at google.com/public data.

32 The annual national average admissions per capita rose from 0.68 (1997) to 3.22 (2007) in Korea. Though this is roughly only half of the comparable figure for the United States (6.5 national average admissions per capita in 2009), it was one of the most astonishing rebounds recorded in any nation during this period. In addition, the number of Korean screens jumped from 588 in 1999 to 2,003 in 2010. Of these screens, 83 percent (1,657) were owned by four major multiplex chains (CGV, Lotte, Megabox, and Cinus). See Korean Film Council, 2010-nyŏn Han'guk yŏnghwa kyŏlsan (2010 Korean Film Industry Summary). For the latest US statistics, see Motion Picture Association of America, "Theatrical Market Statistics 2010," 7, www.mpaa.org/policy/industry.

33 Most of the national cinemas that gained international notoriety in the latter half of the twentieth century were European avant-garde cinemas, including Italian neorealism, French nouvelle vague, and new German cinema, which were deeply rooted in formal experimentations with the film medium.

34 Chris Berry, "Full Service Cinema: the South Korean Cinema Success Story (So Far)."

35 It was François Truffaut who, as a young film critic writing for the journal Cahiers du Cinéma in 1954, advocated the importance of the characteristics of a director's work when distinguishing one film from another. Because of the close association of the French nouvelle vague and auteur theory, it was through the work of Truffaut (who later became a director) and Jean-Luc Godard that the term "auteurism" gained its initial popularity. But since then, the term has been widely adopted as a crucial way of looking at and promoting art-house cinema.

36 The American Forces Korea Network changed its name to AFN-Korea in 2001, and because American television studios wanted to protect their content from being freely consumed by Korean viewers, they prohibited Korean cable companies from carrying AFN-Korea. This has made the network virtually inaccessible to most Koreans who watch television through cable subscription.

37 Maliangkay, "Supporting Our Boys," 24.

38 P. Kim and Shin, "The Birth of 'Rok.'"

39 Berry, "What's Big about the Big Film?"

40 Most of these filmmakers are represented by American talent agencies such

as CAA, ICM, and Endeavor and are in constant discussion with Hollywood studios about making English-language features. Remake rights to the films that they have directed have long attracted the interest of many Hollywood studios and companies.

41 Choi Dong-hun, a prominent director of several commercial films (2006's *Tazza: The High Rollers* and 2009's *Jeon Woo-chi: The Taoist Wizard*), once complained to me at dinner that today's actors prioritize their value in the world of product advertisement before their careers in movies, and will therefore sacrifice screen parts that may end up tarnishing their value in product advertisements.

42 Virilio, *The Vision Machine*, 10.

43 South Korea's data from *2010 Korean Film Industry Summary*. The admissions per capita in the United States remained unchanged during this period: 4.8 (1995) annual admissions per capita to 4.7 (2005). Japan's figure is even significantly less: 1.3 annual admissions per capita.

44 The opening of the first multiplex, CGV's Kangbyon 11—inside Kangbyon Technomart, the then new retailer of consumer electronics and computers—on April 11, 1998, was a sensational event. Since then, the number of movie screens in Korea has recorded double-digit growth every year: from 497 screens in 1997 to 2,058 in 2007. CGV's name comes from the initials of three companies, Cheil Jedang (Korea), Golden Harvest (Hong Kong), and Village Roadshow (Australia). Although during the late 1990s, all the Korean conglomerates then investing heavily in the film industry began to withdraw because of the "IMF crisis" in 1997, Cheil Jedang continued its aggressive investment by expanding its CGV franchise and fast becoming the largest financier of Korean films through its subsidiery, CJ Entertainment.

45 The only two films made outside Hollywood and Korea that appeared on the annual top ten gross list in Korea between 1998 and 2007 were from Japan: Iwai Shunji's *Love Letter* (1999) and Miyazaki Hayao's *Spirited Away* (2002). Both were ranked tenth in the year they were released.

46 Though Korean cinema enjoyed a heyday during the 1960s, because of the large budgets required to fully match the sensations of Hollywood blockbusters, the emphasis at that time was on cheap genres such as melodrama, horror, and comedies.

47 The decline of bookstores over the past two decades was not unique to Korea, as print technology proved to be inferior to televisual and computer technology in the critical area of speed of information transmission. But even more than other nations—especially because it has the world's highest rate of high-speed Internet usage—Korea has experienced a radical drop in the sale of books in this century, despite its high literacy rate of 99 percent.

48 Deleuze and Guattari, *A Thousand Plateaus*, 168.

49 Deleuze and Guattari, *Anti-Oedipus*, 240.

50 Baudrillard, *Simulations*, 2.

51 Walter Benjamin's *The Arcades Project*, which began in the late 1920s, crystallizes his fascination with urban gardens, commodification and phantasmagoria of the then capital of the world: Paris. See Benjamin's *The Arcades Project*.

52 See McLaughlin's "Virtual Paris: Benjamin's 'Arcades Project'" for a discussion on Benjamin's frequent use of the term "virtuelle" in his work.

1. Virtual Landscapes

1 Karatani, *Origins of Modern Japanese Literature*, 19.

2 Ibid., 23.

3 Ibid., 29.

4 Marx, "Capital, Volume Three," 441.

5 Virilio, *The Art of the Motor*, 81.

6 Latour, *We Have Never Been Modern*, 99.

7 James, "Im Kwon-Taek," 57.

8 Choe, "Affective Sites."

9 James, "Im Kwon-Taek," 57.

10 Eisenstein, *Nonindifferent Nature*, 355.

11 Lefebvre, "Introduction," xii.

12 Abbas, "Cosmopolitan De-scriptions," 771.

13 Arendt, "Walter Benjamin," 22.

14 Although it is extremely difficult to gauge a nation's xenophobic tendencies through survey data, according to the *World Competitiveness Yearbook 2008*, compiled by the International Institute for Management Development in Switzerland, Korea ranked lowest in the category of "openness of the national culture to foreign ideas" among fifty-five countries surveyed and ranked fifty-fourth in the category of immigration tolerance (Chŏn Su-yong, "Hanguk saenghwal mulga syegye ch'oego sujun" [Seoul prices remain exorbitant], *Chosun Ilbo*, May 19, 2008).

15 Choe, "Affective Sites," 114.

16 Andreotti, *Theory of the Dérive and Other Situationist Writings on the City*, 22.

17 Nancy, *A Finite Thinking*, 23.

18 These quotes are from memoirs of Kafka's friend and Prague-born novelist Max Brod, whose writings also inspired Benjamin on his essay "Franz Kafka." Benjamin, *Illuminations*, 116.

19 Ibid., 137.

20 *Memories of Murder* received the most votes from forty international and local critics who participated in the KOFIC survey for the most outstanding Korean films of the first ten years of the twenty-first century (2000–2009). See Korean Film Council, "Best 5 Korean Films of Last 10 Years."

21 I disagree with Christina Klein when she states that Bong Joon-ho's "shots have their kin not in Hollywood genre movies, but in the films of Im Kwon-taek, the so-called father of Korean national cinema" ("Why American Studies Needs to Think about Korean Cinema," 881). Bong's shots typically employ

wide-angle lenses even when he attempts to depict landscapes, whereas Im Kwon-Taek is well known for his use of long lenses.

22 Quoted in Benjamin, "On Some Motifs in Baudelaire," in *Illuminations*, 167.

23 Jameson says that it is only in the Marxist state that the proletariat, or the individual subject, can achieve the collective unity and be "positioned within the social totality." Within the capitalist grids, this imagination of a subject "positioned within the social totality" is only just that—a repressed fantasy or a "political unconscious." Jameson, *The Political Unconscious*, 283.

24 Deleuze and Guattari, *Anti-Oedipus*, 5.

25 Ibid., 4.

26 This scene was based on a real incident known as the 2000 Yongsan Water Dumping Scandal, in which a Korean court tried, in absentia, Albert McFarland, a mortician with US Forces in Korea (USFK), and sentenced him to six months in prison. Formaldehyde, a form of formalin used to prevent the decay of dead bodies, was dumped down the drain in the Yongsan Garrison in February 2000. Green Korea, an environmental organization, claims that sixty gallons were dumped. The USFK says that it was only 20 gallons and that the formaldehyde had been diluted by running water and was then processed through Seoul's waste treatment process, along with 1.9 million gallons of other sewage and waste that day. McFarland admitted responsibility for ordering the disposal of the unused formaldehyde, but he refused to appear in the Korean court because under the US-Korea SOFA (Status of Forces of America) agreement, a violation of Korean law that happens while on duty and on a US military base has to be tried in a court with US jurisdiction. The USFK did suspend McFarland for thirty days and paid the $4,000 fine levied by the Korean court.

27 Deleuze and Guattari, *Anti-Oedipus*, 75.

28 Ibid., 67.

29 See chapter 6 for a detailed discussion of *Oasis*.

30 For a more detailed discussion of *Sopyonje*, see my chapter on road movies in K. Kim, *The Remasculinization of Korean Cinema*, 60–66.

31 Deleuze and Guattari, *Anti-Oedipus*, 277.

32 Deleuze and Guattari, *A Thousand Plateaus*, 478.

33 Ibid., 510.

34 As Karatani asserts, "discovery of landscape" was not merely an "internal event." Hokkaido—like Korea and Taiwan later—was a new territory for colonialists whose indigenous people, the Ainu, had to be driven away to make room for new settlers and developers. Since the Meiji government had recruited from the West an agricultural scientist who was also a Protestant missionary to develop Hokkaido (which became a prototype for Japan's later colonial policies), the gaze of Meiji-Era writer and poet Kunikita Doppo—also a Christian who spent time in Hokkaido and who was impressed with the sight its capital Sapporo to the point that he had used it to express his interiority—cannot easily be disassociated from the colonialist ideology. See Karatani, *Origins of Modern Japanese Literature*, 40–44.

35 Though Hong Sang-soo is only nine years older than Bong Joon-ho (Hong was born in 1960, Bong in 1969) and though he remains an active filmmaker, Hong is inspired by the modernist works of Luis Buñuel, Robert Bresson, and Eric Rohmer. Bong's commercial aspirations put him in a different category as filmmaker.

2. Viral Colony

1 At this point in Korea's colonial history, *Ch'unhyangjŏn* was, according to Serk-bae Suh, an exemplary hybrid cultural text that had even spawned a 1938 Japanese-language theater production. Murayama Tomoyoshi, a playwright and director and a leading figure of Puroretaria Engekidomei (the Japan Proletarian Theater League), secured a Japanese-language script from the Korean writer Chang Hyŏk-ju. *Ch'unhyangjŏn* was the first Japanese-language theatrical play performed by Japanese actors in the Japanese language based on a Korean literary source, and it had successful runs in several Japanese cities in the spring of 1938. The production also toured Korea that fall. See Suh's "Empire and Nation," 78–153.

2 Although no explicit reason is given for Young-il's illness, all his symptoms point to tuberculosis.

3 Some 213,723 Koreans served in the Japanese army and navy from 1938 to 1945. See Fujitani, "Right to Kill, Right to Make Live," 17.

4 As Thomas Lamarre states: "In Japan (during its war period), as in Germany, France, and England, hygiene and nutrition became a central concern, not only to assure the health of national citizens, but to enable the advance of national armies as well" ("Bacterial Cultures and Linguistic Colonies," 602).

5 Lamarre recounts the postwar history of sciences written by Nakayama Shigeru, who underscored the importance of nutrition and science in the victories of the Japanese military during the late Meiji period. Lamarre quotes Nakayama: "Scientific victory meant military victory; the success of the Japanese army was directly tied to advances in nutrition and hygiene" (ibid., 609–10).

6 Fujitani, "Total War at the Movies," 94.

7 K. Choi, "Impaired Body as Colonial Trope."

8 A one-minute public commercial encouraging the frequent washing of the hands to avoid germs and getting sick is found in *Sweet Dream* (*Mimong*, 1936), one of the films recovered from the colonial period.

9 Bourdaghs, "The Disease of Nationalism, the Empire of Hygiene," 667.

10 On May 9, 2008, the Korean Film Archive premiered *Crossroads of Youth*, accompanied by a live *pyŏnsa* performance that was staged and directed by a young film director, Kim T'ae-yong, whose 2002 *Memento Mori* and 2006 *Family Ties* had received critical acclaim. The film was so popular that in 2008 and 2009, Kim staged several encore performances, including during a tour of the US East Coast.

11 Pak, *Mun Ye-bong kwa Kim Sin-jae*.

12 For a more detailed application of Nietzsche's *ressentiment* to a Korean film, see chapter 7.

13 Though considered a box-office failure when it was released because of its astronomical budget, Lee Si-myung's 2009 *Lost Memories*—based on a bestselling novel by Bok Kŏ-il—was one of 2002's most high-profile A-list film productions in South Korea. 2009 *Lost Memories* is predicated on the idea that Japan joined the United States in defeating Nazi Germany during the Second World War. As a consequence, the Japanese Empire remains intact in 2009 and still includes Korea. The JBI (Japanese Bureau of Investigation) is engaged in a "war against terror," targeting the Korean independence movement known as the *furei senjin*—a term derived from *futei senjin* (disobedient Korean) a derogatory term used by Japanese for Koreans.

14 So-young Kim, "In/Visible Cinema: Hollow Archive and National Cinema."

15 Baskett, *The Attractive Empire*, 7.

16 Ibid., 8.

17 Baskett quotes the Korean film historian Yi Yŏng-il's account of one such conflict. Merely two years after Japan's annexation of Korea in 1912, the screening of a short film that featured a match between a Western boxer and a Japanese judo wrestler led to mayhem when the Korean half of the audience cheered for the boxer and the Japanese half cheered for the wrestler. The film, which eventually concluded with the Japanese judo wrestler's victory, "sparked a violent exchange. From the balcony, Japanese hurled seat cushions and food at the Koreans, and the Koreans threw chairs back at the Japanese. The struggle spilled out into the main lobby where both sides beat each other with wooden sandals, walking sticks, and broken furniture until the colonial police were called to put an end to the violence." In the early 1930s, a similar instance occurred when the screening of the Hollywood silent film *Ben Hur* incited both Japanese and Korean audiences. The dramatic scene in which the film's subtitles read, "This moment for you Romans means one hundred years of trial for us Jews!" in particular was seen by audiences in Seoul as an obvious allegory of the conditions of the colonized Koreans, and "the film set off a near riot. The local colonial police put down the disturbance and *Ben-Hur* went back to the censor's office to be drastically recut." See ibid., 22.

18 K. Choi, "Impaired Body as Colonial Trope."

19 Kang O. et al., *Singminji sidae taejung yesurin sajŏn*, 80.

20 It is perhaps important to note that before Yutaka Abe became a prolific film director in Japan—his career spanned four decades (the 1920s to the 1950s)—he had acted in many Hollywood films, including Cecil B. DeMille's classic *The Cheat* (1915).

21 Baskett, *The Attractive Empire*, 24.

22 Sontag, *"Illness as Metaphor" and "AIDS and Its Metaphors,"* 69.

23 Ibid., 13.

24 Karatani, *Origins of Modern Japanese Literature*, 101.

25 "My Innocent Uncle" was written in first-person narrative, addressing the

readers as if they were a p'ansori (Korean peasant opera) audience. Ch'ae M., "My Innocent Uncle," in *My Innocent Uncle*, 7.

26 See K. Kim, *The Remasculinization of Korean Cinema*, 233–58. After reading that chapter in my earlier book, Martin Scorsese requested a 35 mm print of *The Housemaid*. He watched the film, fell in love with it, and proposed that his organization, the World Cinema Foundation, help restore the film. Eighty thousand euros were donated to the Korean Film Archive by the World Cinema Foundation for this restoration project. *The Housemaid* was in horrible condition because two original negative reels had been lost. With the aid of both the World Cinema Foundation and the Korean Film Archive, *The Housemaid* was analyzed and digitally restored, frame by frame. It premiered at the 2008 Cannes Film Festival. I then coproduced a remake of *The Housemaid*, directed in 2010 by Im Sang-soo—whose *The President's Last Bang* is prominently featured in the next chapter.

27 Paek Mun-im, *Wŏlha ŭi yŏgoksŏng*.

28 See the next chapter for a discussion of films that specifically deal with the death of Park Chung Hee.

29 K. Choi, "Impaired Body as Colonial Trope," 442.

30 During the workshop called "Korean Waves: Korean Popular Culture in East Asia and the World," which took place at Columbia University on November 16–17, 2007, *Epitaph* was screened with both of its directors, Jeong Beom-sik and Jeong Sik, present. During the question-and-answer period, Jeong Beom-sik discussed the importance of *sunŭng* (complicity) as the driving force behind the making of *Epitaph*.

31 It is not difficult to see that the hospital ward set in *Epitaph* pays tribute to the Bates Motel in Hitchcock's *Psycho*.

32 Quoted in Jameson, *Signatures of the Visible*, 91.

3. Virtual Dictatorship

1 *The President's Barber*, written and directed by first-time filmmaker Im Ch'an-sang, sold about two million tickets at the box office, and barely surpassed the break-even point (BEP).

2 First called Kyŏngmudae, the president's house changed its name to Chŏngwa-dae (the Blue House) in 1960 after the April 19th Student Revolution helped to oust the corrupt Syngman Rhee regime.

3 The sudden outburst of anger, the corporal punishment, and the acceptance of military-style push-ups by an ordinary citizen remind us of another Korean film released about a decade before these two films about the presidents. In Jang Sun-woo's (Chang Sŏn-u's) *To You, From Me* (*Nŏ ege na rŭl ponenda*, 1994), the writer protagonist (played by Mun Sŏng-gŭn) receives a humiliating punishment from a man wearing sunglasses in the middle of a bar after cynically responding to his right-wing views.

4 Foucault, *Discipline and Punish*, 135.

5 Ibid., 136.

6 Offering a long quote from a French law of the late eighteenth century that demonstrates how precise verbal commands dictate and regulate the movement of the body in order to mold an inept body into an awesome automaton, Foucault writes that the men move from "holding their heads high and erect; to standing upright, without bending the back, to sticking out the belly, throwing out the chest and throwing back the shoulders; and, to help them acquire the habit, they are given this position while standing against a wall in such a way that the heels, the thighs, the waist and the shoulders touch it, as also do the backs of the hands, as one turns the arms outwards, without moving them away from the body" (ibid., 135–36).

7 See Žižek, *Did Somebody Say Totalitarianism* (or one of his other books), to see how his critique of totalitarianism or dictatorship does not simply target the Soviet Union and the former Eastern bloc countries. He questions instead whether the current neoliberal, postmodern era truly can uphold values such as freedom of choice, and he finds that the choices we tend to privilege outside totalitarianism are largely fabricated.

8 For various looks at fascism and the definition of the term beyond historical fascism, see, for example, Laclau, *Politics and Ideology in Marxist Theory*; Reich, *The Mass Psychology of Fascism*; and Foucault, Preface.

9 The term "fascist investments" is invoked in an interview with Gilles Deleuze and Félix Guattari, who argue that there has been a rise of "comprehensive fascism" and suggest that there are a number of ways one can resist it—for example, through rechanneling of desire. See Deleuze, "Gilles Deleuze and Félix Guattari on *Anti-Oedipus*," in *Negotiations*, 18.

10 Ivy, "Foreword," viii.

11 Michael E. Robinson writes that Park Chung Hee's development "plan stressed South Korea's comparative advantage in cheap, educated labor as the basis for building an export-centered economy. Using US grants and guaranteed loans for its initial capitalization, Korea was, by the 1970s, itself successfully financing its economic expansion in the private global equities market. Given the ROK's strategic importance and the deep US commitment there, US banks willingly provided huge loans" (*Korea's Twentieth-Century Odyssey*, 132).

12 Cho, *Nae mudŏm e ch'im ŭl paet'ŏra*.

13 Jameson took the term "return of the historical repressed" from Freud in order to argue that the postmodern era conditions a waning of affect, so that history returns only in an unconscious, repressed form. This is one of the central terms in Jameson's famous "The Cultural Logic of Late Capitalism," in Jameson, *Postmodernism*.

14 Through the 1980s and 1990s, the buzzword in the Korean film industry was "realism," which was perceived to be the aesthetic trope through which dissent against the dictatorship could be voiced. During the 2000s, the new buzzwords were *wel-meidŭ* (well made) and *sijang jŏmyuryul* (domestic market share),

which insisted on an uneasy alliance between individual craftsmanship and protectionist nationalism against the Hollywood onslaught.

15 Baudrillard, *Simulations*, 2.

16 Chow, *Primitive Passions*, 22.

17 Ibid., 115.

18 Žižek, *The Sublime Object of Ideology*, 99.

19 Ibid., 97.

20 Bakhtin, *The Dialogic Imagination*, 169.

21 Because the film has an ensemble cast, arguably Chu (played by Han Sŏk-gyu) shares the lead with Kim Chae-gyu (played by Paek Yun-sik).

22 Žižek, *The Sublime Object of Ideology*, 82.

23 Sobchak, "History Happens," 3.

24 James, "Alternative Cinemas," 54.

25 Deleuze, *Cinema 2*, 82.

26 Chow, *Primitive Passions*, 8.

4. Mea Culpa

1 Hyundai Asan is one of the companies of Hyundai conglomerate, founded by Chung Ju-yung (1915–2001). Because Chung came from North Korea, he always had special affection for the North. Using his financial clout, he single-handedly engineered several North-South reconciliation projects—one of them being the Geumgangsan tour, described in this chapter.

2 Only twenty private vehicles a day driven by South Koreans were permitted to enter North Korea's Geumgangsan resort as of March 17, 2008, the time of my visit. This permission was withdrawn after July 11, 2008, when Park Wang-ja, a fifty-three-year-old South Korean female tourist, was fatally shot by a North Korean soldier at the resort.

3 As soon as Park Wang-ja was shot to death by a North Korean soldier at the Geumgangsan resort, South Korea suspended the North Korean tour. The suspension was indefinitely extended when the North refused to cooperate with the South on an investigation into the case and issued no apologies. In 2010 the continued stalemate between the North and the South led the North to declare it was seizing all South Korean properties in the Geumgangsan area and expelling all South Koreans still there.

4 Deleuze and Guattari, *A Thousand Plateaus*, 204.

5 Kwang-Tae Kim, "S. Korea Urges N. Korea to Retract Threat over Tourism," Associated Press, April 8, 2010 (http://www.businessweek.com/ap/financial news/D9EV9RD01.htm).

6 For years, Herculean efforts were made to vilify North Korea and its leader at the time, Kim Il-sung. The South Korean government even banned photographs of Kim from all South Korean publications.

7 *Seven Female Prisoners* focuses on a North Korean officer and his psychological

dilemma before he defects to the South during the war. Although it is neither a film that praises socialism nor criticizes the South, the film's director was prosecuted for not following the government's ideological line, which firmly stipulated "no film will positively represent any member of the People's Army."

8 The conservative Grand National Party won the presidency and the majority of the National Assembly in landslides in 2007 and 2008.

9 See chapter 10 in K. Kim, *The Remasculinization of Korean Cinema*.

10 All of the B-movies about North Korea made during this period relied on the conventions of comedy and produced a new stock character in the South Korean film industry: the naive and innocent North Korean, distinguished from the sinister North Koreans in films produced during the Cold War.

11 Replacing North Koreans as villains, surprisingly, were Americans, as evidenced by such blockbusters as *Welcome to Dongmakgol* (2005) and *The Host* (2006).

12 Of course, exceptions to this rule exist. *Crossing* focuses on a reluctant male t'albukja who escapes the North in order to find penicillin that his dying wife needs.

13 Linda Williams writes: "It might be more useful to consider how extensively race cards have been in play in the racial power games of American culture . . . To win at the 'game' of race is to lose the larger game of life in which unraced competitors already play with a full deck" (*Playing the Race Card*, 6–7). She argues that the wretched signs of racialized victims have appeared in every form of American melodrama.

14 Said, *Culture and Imperialism*, 184.

15 Said, *Orientalism*, 5.

16 Kim Jee-woon's *The Good, the Bad, the Weird* broke this record in 2008.

17 For a discussion of race in the Korean War, see K. Kim, *The Remasculinization of Korean Cinema*, 81–93.

18 See K. Kim, *The Remasculinization of Korean Cinema*, 77–106.

19 At the time of its production, Moon Geun-young, only eighteen, was arguably the biggest star in Korea. *Innocent Steps* was based on a script developed by producers to exploit Moon's popularity.

20 See K. Kim, *The Remasculinization of Korean Cinema*.

21 Prior to *Innocent Steps*, there was another high-profile South Korean film made about a fake marriage scheme, this one between a Korean man and a Chinese woman: Song Hae-sung's *Failan* (*P'ailan*, 2001). *Failan*, a realist film inspired by social issues, sold only about 400,000 tickets, but it did receive a lot of critical attention and its remake rights were sold in the United States. The opening sequence of *Failan* parallels that of *Innocent Steps*: Kang-jae (played by Choi Min-sik), the film's male protagonist, is first seen sleeping in a tawdry game room in Incheon, a Western port city about thirty miles from Seoul. Incheon is the site of the first Korean Chinatown, settled during the late nineteenth century. Kang-jae's drama begins on the day he receives a letter from Failan, a Chinese woman for whom he had signed a fake marriage document years ago

in exchange for cash and who is now dying. The letter from Failan (played by a Hong Kong star, Cecilia Cheung) moves Kang-jae, who begins to recollect his memories of her. Failan remembers Kang-jae as a generous man who helped her with the marriage scheme. In fact, unbeknownst to her, the scheme included Kang-jae's selling her to a pimp working at a seedy nightclub. But because she had tuberculosis, the pimp didn't want her. She eventually found work at a dry cleaning establishment in a small provincial town. Failan was so diligent with her work that at one point her employer declares her to be a "human washing machine." Though Kang-jae is killed at the very end of the film by members of the gang he belongs to, the film insists that he was able to repurify his soul through his love for Failan.

22 Pyong-gŏn Ch'ae and Kang-hyŏn Chŏng, "Ch'ehyŏng kyŏkch'a . . .'Injong'i talrajinda" [Gap in Body Size Leads to Change in Ethnic Group], *Joongang Ilbo*, November 21, 2006.

23 Quoted in Eagleton, *The Eagleton Reader*, 359.

5. Death, Eroticism, and Nationalism

1 During the latter part of the Japanese colonial era (1910–45), Japanese became the language normally used by Korean intellectuals as Japanese administrators pursued the naisen ittai policy that sought to combine two national bodies (Korea and Japan) into one.

2 Foucault, *The Birth of the Clinic*, 155.

3 For a discussion of Hong Sang-soo's first three films — *The Day a Pig Fell into the Well* (*Tweji ga umul e ppajin nal*, 1996), *The Power of Kangwon Province* (*Kangwondo ŭi him*, 1998), and *Virgin Stripped Bare by Her Bachelors* (*O! Sujŏng*, 2000) — see K. Kim, *The Remasculinization of Korean Cinema*, 203–29.

4 See Althusser's seminal "Ideology and Ideological State Apparatuses," in *"Lenin and Philosophy" and Other Essays*, 121–76.

5 Lippit, "Hong Sangsoo's Line of Inquiry, Communication, Defense, and Escape," 22.

6 Sontag, *"Illness As Metaphor" and "AIDS and Its Metaphors,"* 93.

7 Between *The Day a Pig Fell into the Well* (1996) and *Turning Gate* (2002), Hong made *The Power of Kangwon Province* (1998) and *Virgin Stripped Bare by Her Bachelors* (2000) — both of which were well received.

8 Deleuze, *Cinema 2*, 19.

9 This by no means suggests that Hong Sang-soo has no respect for the work of Ozu. On the contrary, in my private conversations with Hong, he has demonstrated the deepest respect for the work of the revered Japanese director. Hong has gone on record as saying that every aspect of Ozu's work is perfect. See Stephens, "Future Shock," 44.

10 Quoted in Jameson, *Marxism and Form*, 173.

11 Chuck Stephens reports that Hong had the following explanation for the title of his film: "As the future is yet to come, it means nothing, and if the future is

multiplied by man, the result is still zero. And if woman is the future of man, which is zero, woman is also nothing" (quoted in "Future Shock," 45).

12 Lippit also describes the typical Hong Sang-soo character as being in a psychic state of "aporia" or at the "end of the line" ("Hong Sangsoo's Line of Inquiry, Communication, Defense, and Escape," 26).

13 Jean Eustache is a French director who has made several films, including *The Mother and the Whore* (1973) and *Mes Petites Amoureuses* (1974). Hong Sang-soo had not been aware of these films until I loaned these films on video to him in 2003, right after he had completed *Turning Gate*.

14 Said, *Culture and Imperialism*, 184.

15 Agamben, *Homo Sacer*, 72.

16 Freud, *Beyond the Pleasure Principle*.

17 Benjamin, "On Some Motifs in Baudelaire," in *Illuminations*, 172.

18 Hannah Arendt, "Walter Benjamin: 1892–1940," 21.

19 *Turning Gate* is widely viewed as Hong's most commercially successful film. It was released in 2002 before the Korean film industry had introduced a computerized tally of national box office receipts, but it reportedly sold around 127,000 tickets in Seoul alone. Seoul usually comprises about half of the nation's total ticket sale, so we can estimate that the film sold around 250,000 tickets nationwide.

20 As Bill O'Reilly of *The O'Reilly Factor* frequently argues, the use of the word "noble" seems to occupy a special place in conservative pundits' rhetoric about the war.

6. Virtual Trauma

1 *Oasis* (2002) and *Secret Sunshine* (2007) each sold more than a million tickets in the local box office, passing the important break-even point for the investors.

2 *To the Starry Island* deals with the lives of a group of islanders who are traumatized after a massacre committed against them by the South Korean Army during the Korean War. Such depictions of atrocities by the nationalists were taboo in South Korea for many years. *A Single Spark* is a portrait of a famous union labor martyr, Chŏn T'ae-il, who at the age of twenty-two immolated himself in order to ignite the workers' struggle to unionize in Korea during the 1970s.

3 Miyoshi, "Against the Narrative Grain," 154.

4 Quoted in Jameson, *The Political Unconscious*, 110.

5 Ibid., 104.

6 Deleuze and Guattari, *Anti-Oedipus*, 10–11.

7 Quoted from the supplementary interview with the director on the DVD of *Oasis* (Seoul: CJ Entertainment, 2002).

8 Moretti, *Signs Taken for Wonders*, 162.

9 Earlier I wrote: "The last two decades, the 1980s and the 1990s, bracket South Korea's transformation from an insular, authoritarian society to one that is

more cosmopolitan, global and post-authoritarian. The dawning of a new modern era is normally punctuated by hope and optimism, but the weight of intense history and its attendant violence loomed so excessively large that it ended up traumatizing, marginalizing, and de-naturalizing men. Wrecked and disordered was the male subjectivity after the Korean War, the subsequent division, and the continuing legacy of colonialism through military dictatorship; the metaphor of the 'symbolic lack' was astutely installed as one of the primary thematic impulses in the postwar cinemas. The male lack was located in every field imaginable: of the accoutrements of power in sexual potency, paternal authority, communal function, historical legitimacy, and professional worth. The South Korean films of this period sought to reorient the subject back on its track into the Lacanian Symbolic where language could be reacquired, the Name of the Father reissued, and the castration anxiety disavowed" (K. Kim, *The Remasculinization of Korean Cinema*, 10–11).

10 Fantasy does seem to switch places with reality in *Peppermint Candy*, but only insofar as the linearity of time remains undisrupted. Though shot in a different style from the broodingly funereal *Green Fish*, *Peppermint Candy* projects the fantasy of recovering youth and purity by "turning back the clock." The film moves temporally in reverse order, beginning with a prologue that takes place in spring 1999 and ending with a segment that is set twenty years earlier, at the same place where the film began. With every turning back of the clock, Yŏng-ho, the protagonist, emerges younger, less corrupt, and more sincere. Right before he faces death in spring 1999, he yells, "I want to go back." The medium of cinema has allowed his wish to become true, and the Yŏng-ho of twenty years earlier is released from his sins and given back his youth and romantic ideals. But despite the fact that the film tells the story backward in time, it fails to challenge the absolute temporal linearity and the reality that is governed by time's tyrannical nature. In other words, the manipulation of time still functions within a temporal structure that neatly divides time into past, present, and future, without jumbling the eras together. The insistence on the rigid partitioning of time prevents for instance, the doubling of subjectivity (why can't the present Jong-du travel back in time to meet his younger self?) or the repetition of time that also produces splitting of the temporal path (as in Hong Sang-soo's films or in Akira Kurosawa's famous *Rashomon*). Imprisoned is not only the multiplicity of time, but also the bifurcation between fantasy and reality.

11 Rodowick, *Difficulty of Difference*, 96.

12 Freud, *The Uncanny*, 135.

13 Ibid., 150.

14 Deleuze and Guattari, *Anti-Oedipus*, 2.

15 Brooks, *Reading for the Plot*, 251.

16 For descriptive passages on Deleuze's "any-space-whatevers" concept and its application in the analysis of Buñuel's films, see Deleuze, *Cinema 1*, 123–33.

17 Ibid., 124.

18 Lars von Trier's *Dogville* (2003) may be one of the most subversive and controversial Westerns that even challenge its genre definition to have been made recently. The film is shot on a sound stage with a minimalist setting, reminding
the viewers of the film's artificiality. Most of the walls and streets are shown
only by painted outlines, and there are big labels like "door." The opening and
closing of the doors are indicated not by the actual doors moving, but by the
actors' miming and sound effects.

19 Widely known among Koreans is the rapid rise of marriages between rural
Korean men and Chinese, Vietnamese, and Thai women who seek better lives
in Korea. Only about two decades ago, most of the international marriages
held in Korea were between US military servicemen and Korean women. The
rising number of marriages between Korean men and foreign women show a
reverse in the trend.

20 Peattie, "The Japanese Colonial Empire," 264.

21 For a discussion on these Enlightenment films, see Chung, "The Scene of Development: Melodrama and Style in Sin Sang-ok's 'Enlightenment' Films,"
61–106.

22 Jameson, *The Political Unconscious*, 22.

23 Freud, "Mourning and Melancholia," in *The Standard Edition*, 14:243.

24 Ibid., 14:245.

25 Ibid.

26 Ibid., 14:246.

27 Kobayashi, *Literature of the Lost Home*, 53.

28 See the previous chapter on Hong Sang-soo's films, especially his emphasis on
sexual impotency and hypochondria.

7. "Unknowable" *Oldboy*

1 Both the *New York Times* and *LA Weekly*, enormously important publications
for any independent and foreign-language films opening in the United States,
printed harsh reviews of *Oldboy*. See Manohla Dargis, "The Violence (and the
Seafood) Is More Than Raw," *New York Times*, March 25, 2005; and Scott Foundas, "Oldboy Network: To: Quentin Tarantino From: Scott Foundas Re: Beware
of Imitations," *LA Weekly*, March 24, 2005.

2 Dargis, "The Violence (and the Seafood) Is More Than Raw."

3 *Oldboy* failed to gross $1 million in the United States, which is usually held to
be the benchmark of moderate success for limited release films. It eventually
reported selling $707,391 of tickets, which is not a bad figure for a Korean film
but is certainly well below the $2.38 million record set by a Korean film: *Spring,
Summer, Fall, Winter . . . and Spring. The Host* came close to beating that record,
with $2.2 million.

4 K. Kim, *The Remasculinization of Korean Cinema*.

5 Kinder, "Violence American Style," 67.

6 The Japanese manga version, first published in 1998, was written by Tsuchiya Garon and illustrated by Minegishi Nobuaki.

7 Both *Oldboy* and *Lady Vengeance* were blockbuster hits in Korea, although *Sympathy for Mr. Vengeance* was not as successful at the box office.

8 Weinstein, *Unknowing*, 253.

9 See particularly the chapter on "The Discovery of Landscape," in Karatani, *Origins of Modern Japanese Literature*.

10 In *Chilsu and Mansu*, Mansu's drunken bar brawl lands him at a police station, where he is detained overnight for additional questioning. A small misdemeanor that should have led to only a small fine results in far greater punishment because Mansu, the film reveals, has a father who is a long-term political prisoner. *The Day a Pig Fell into the Well* also includes a scene in which its protagonist—Hyo-seop—is sentenced to detention for three days after instigating a fight with a worker at a barbeque restaurant.

11 Joseph Jonghyun Jeon writes: "In contrast to Leonard Shelby in *Memento*, who is always waking up, refreshed and oblivious to what has immediately transpired, Dae-su is continually and repeatedly passing out. In public, in private, in a restaurant, in the middle of the woods, Dae-su suddenly and constantly loses consciousness, almost always for reasons outside of his control—through, for example, hypnosis, posthypnotic suggestion, and gassing." Though the gas that puts him to sleep does have a historical origin (it is the same gas used by the Russian army to suppress Chechen rebels), Dae-su's slumber, as Jeon notes, is an "ahistorical" one that separates him from the era of intense democratization and globalization achieved in modern Korean history. See Jeon, "Residual Selves," 723–24.

12 Freud, *The Uncanny*, 152.

13 It was widely reported that Steven Spielberg and Will Smith will be collaborating on a remake of *Oldboy*, despite Spielberg's intention to make the US version without the incest. The remake is complicated because Futabasha, the publisher of the Japanese manga from which *Oldboy* was adapted is suing the Korean production company, claiming that it never had the right to negotiate a remake. See Gavin J. Blair and Park Soo-Mee, "'Oldboy' Proceeds despite Legal Scuffle," *Hollywood Reporter*, June, 25, 2009.

14 See chapters 3 and 4 in K. Kim, *The Remasculinization of Korean Cinema*.

15 Deleuze, *Nietzsche and Philosophy*, 119.

16 Ibid., 122.

17 Derrida, "Plato's Pharmacy," in *Dissemination*, 61–84.

18 Girard, *Violence and the Sacred*, 8.

19 On the "Kafkan uncanny," see Weinstein, *Unknowing*, 101–6.

20 Jackson, "Borrowing Trouble."

21 In *Sympathy for Mr. Vengeance*, Ryu's girlfriend, Cha Yeong-mi (played by Bae Doona), orders a bowl of jajangmyeon from a Chinese restaurant. When Park Dong-jin arrives, she mistakes him for the restaurant's deliveryman. Instead of getting jajangmyeon, she receives torture.

22 Yang, "*Jajangmyeon* and *Junggukjip*."

23 Park Chan-wook began experimenting with voice-over narration in *Oldboy*. In *Lady Vengeance*, he employed a sixty-year-old female narrator, Kim Se-won, with long experience in radio and television narration; her voice nostalgically reminded the viewers of radio dramas and popular television documentary programs such as *Ingan sidae* (*Human Life*) from the 1970s and the 1980s.

24 Chion, *The Voice in Cinema 1*.

25 Deleuze, *Cinema 2*, 249.

26 Ibid.

8. The End of History

1 Fukuyama, *The End of History and the Last Man*.

2 Slavoj Žižek argues that in the first decade of the twenty-first century, Fukuyama's Utopian dream died twice: first, when 9/11 precipitated the collapse of the liberal-democratic political agenda, and second, when the financial market crashed in 2008 (*First as Tragedy, Then as Farce*, 5). In Korea, however, the 2008 global meltdown of the housing market not only consolidated the New Right's power, but it also allowed the national economy to grow because of continuing foreign demand for Korean goods.

3 Jameson, *Signatures of the Visible*, 84.

4 Žižek, *Welcome to the Desert of the Real!*, 5.

5 Joseph Jonghyun Jeon writes: "Through the focus on newspapers, [*Memories of Murder*] expands its query of the fact to the scale of history, and an implicit preoccupation that emerges is the status of history in a milieu where facts are not only scarce, but also underwhelming. So one might ask then, does the paucity of fact in this film also mark the end of history? As mentioned above, the film is based on the true story of Korea's first serial killer, who was never caught. The lack of closure in the investigation becomes an occasion in the film to consider deeper failures of historical memory. But *Memories of Murder* does more than simply register the frustrations of investigation, and instead transforms this story of failed detection into a parable of epistemological uncertainty, expanding its scope such that it becomes a historical parable" ("Memories of Memories"). By paring the failure of detection (the killer in Bong's film is never caught) with a failed mode of historiography, Jeon seems to suggest that Bong's work is a rare modernist film that critiques the end of history, a postmodern symptom.

6 One of the most oft-quoted passages in film studies is the following from Bazin's article "The Ontology of the Photographic Image": "now, for the first time, the image of things is likewise the image of their duration, change mummified as it were" (15).

7 Kwanghwa Gate, one of the most sublime architectures built during the Chosun Dynasty, and the symbol of its era, precipitated a public outcry from Yanagi Muneyoshi, a Meiji-era intellectual, who protested the Japanese governor-

general's office's planned demolition during the colonial era. Despite that its demolition was then halted, Kwanghwa Gate nevertheless suffered from various setbacks over the past one hundred years: partial damage from public neglect, fires from the war, removal and relocation, and even authorized vandalism ordered by the military dictator Park Chung Hee (his unimpressive calligraphy was displayed on the gate for years). Only on August 15, 2010, did Kwanghwa Gate, after years of reconstruction that spanned several presidential changes, reopen. See Yanagi, "For a Korean Architecture About to Be Lost."

8 A local conglomerate, Samsung, is one of the largest investors in the Korean film industry. Its subsidiary, CJ Entertainment, makes direct investment, produces films, distributes local and imported films, operates the CGV multiplex theater chain, and sells the distribution and broadcasting rights of its products on the foreign market.

9 K. Kim, *The Remasculinization of Korean Cinema*, 177.

10 Deleuze, *Cinema 1*, 123.

11 Norimitsu Onishi, "Gay-Themed Film Gives Closet Door a Tug," *New York Times*, March 31, 2006.

12 The other four films that have sold more than ten million tickets are Kang Woo-suk's *Silmido* (2003), Kang Je-gyu's *The Brotherhood of War* (*Tae Guk Gi*, 2004), Bong Joon-ho's *The Host* (*Koemul*, 2006), and Yun Che-gyun's *Haeundae* (2009).

13 A recent investigative article on the front page of the *Hanguk ilbo* (*Korea Times*) reported that the national income distribution in Korea reached unprecedented heights of inequality in 2010. See Yi Yŏng-t'ae, "Yanggŭkhwa, taehanmin'guk i kalrajin'ta" (Polarization, the Republic of Korea Is Splitting in Two), *Hanguk ilbo*, July 12, 2010.

14 Baudrillard, *America*, 6.

15 See Deleuze, *Cinema 2*, 126–55.

16 See Bergson, *Creative Evolution*.

17 Abbas, *Hong Kong*, 11.

18 The writer-director Kim Dae-woo has repeatedly mentioned in interviews how difficult it was for him to look up primary historical accounts of Chosun-era servants and slaves while conducting research for his film, *The Servant* (*Pangjajŏn*). See P. Kang, "'Chunhyangjŏn ŭn kot'ong ija kippŭm ija chongyŏngsim iŏtta."

19 *Hwang Chin-i*, based on the novel with the same title by Hong Sŏk-jung, a North Korean writer, is the only South Korean film that was shot in the Geumgangsan (Diamond Mountain) Special Tour Region.

20 Latour, *We Have Never Been Modern*.

Abbas, Ackbar. "Cosmopolitan De-Scriptions: Shanghai and Hong Kong Public Culture." *Public Culture* 12, no. 3 (Fall 2000): 769–86.

———. *Hong Kong: Culture and the Politics of Disappearance*. Minneapolis: University of Minnesota Press, 1997.

Abelmann, Nancy, and Kathleen McHugh, eds. *South Korean Golden Age Melodrama*. Detroit, Mich.: Wayne University Press, 2005.

Agamben, Giorgio. *Homo Sacer: Sovereign Power and Bare Life*. Translated by Daniel Heller-Roazen. Stanford: Stanford University Press, 1998.

Althusser, Louis. *"Lenin and Philosophy" and Other Essays*. Translated by Ben Brewster. New York: Monthly Review Press, 1971.

Andreotti, Libero. *Theory of the Dérive and Other Situationalist Writings on the City*. Barcelona: Museu d'Art Contemporani de Barcelona, 1996.

Arendt, Hannah. "Walter Benjamin: 1892–1940." In Walter Benjamin, *Illuminations: Essays and Reflections*, edited by Hannah Arendt and translated by Harry Zohn, 1–55. New York: Schocken, 1968.

Bakhtin, Mikhail M. *The Dialogic Imagination: Four Essays*. Edited by Michael Holquist. Translated by Caryl Emerson and Michael Holquist. Austin: University of Texas Press, 1981.

Baskett, Michael. *The Attractive Empire: Transnational Film Culture in Imperial Japan*. Honolulu: University of Hawaii Press, 2008.

Baudrillard, Jean. *America*. Translated by Chris Turner. London: Verso, 1988.

———. *Simulations*. Translated by Paul Foss, Paul Patton, and Philip Beitchman. New York: Semiotext(e), 1983.

Bazin, André. "The Ontology of the Photographic Image." In *What Is Cinema? Volume I*. Edited and translated by Hugh Gray, 9–16. Berkeley: University of California Press, 1967.

Benjamin, Walter. *The Arcades Project*. Edited and translated by Howard Eiland and Kevin McLaughlin. Cambridge: Harvard University Press, 1999.

———. *Illuminations*. Edited by Hannah Arendt. Translated by Harry Zohn. New York: Schocken, 1969.

Bergson, Henri. *Creative Evolution*. Edited by Keith Ansell Pearson, Michael Kolkman, and Michael Vaughan. Translated by Arthur Mitchel. New York: Palgrave Macmillan, 2007.

Berry, Chris. "Full Service Cinema: The South Korean Cinema Success Story (So Far)." In *Text and Context of Korean Cinema: Crossing Borders* (conference proceedings), edited by Young-Key Kim Renaud et al., 7–16. Washington, D.C.: Sigur Center for Asian Studies, George Washington University, 2003.

———. "What's Big about the Big Film?" In *Movie Blockbusters*, edited by Julian Stringer, 217–29. London: Routledge, 2003.

Bourdaghs, Michael. "The Disease of Nationalism, the Empire of Hygiene." *positions: east asia cultures critique* 6, no. 3 (1998): 637–73.

Brooks, Peter. *Reading for the Plot: Design and Intention in Narrative*. Cambridge: Harvard University Press, 1984.

Ch'ae, Man-shik. *My Innocent Uncle*. Translated by Bruce and Ju-Chan Fulton, Kim Vhong-un, and Robert Armstrong. Seoul: Jimoondong, 2003.

Chion, Michel. *The Voice in Cinema*. Translated by Claudia Gorbman. New York: Columbia University Press, 1999.

Cho, Kap-che. *Nae mudŏm e ch'im ŭl paet'ŏra* [Spit on My Grave]. Vols. 1–8. Seoul: Chosŏn ilbo sa, 2001.

Choe, Youngmin. "Affective Sites: Hur Jin-Ho's Cinema and Film-Induced Tourism in Korea." In *Asia on Tour: Exploring the Rise of Asian Tourism*, edited by Tim Winter, Peggy Teo, and T. C. Chang, 109–26. London: Routledge, 2009.

Choi, Jinhee. *The South Korean Film Renaissance: Local Hitmakers, Global Provocateurs*. Middletown, Conn.: Wesleyan University Press, 2010.

Choi, Kyeong-Hee. "Impaired Body as Colonial Trope: Kang Kyŏng'ae's 'Underground Village.'" *Public Culture* 13, no. 3 (2001): 431–58.

Chŏn Pong-gwan. *Kyŏngsŏng kidam: kŭndae Chosŏn ŭl twihŭndŭn sarin sakŏn kwa sŭk'aendŭl* [Horror Stories of Keijo: Murders and Scandals That Shook Modern Korea]. P'aju, Kyŏnggi-do: Sallim, 2006.

Chow, Rey. *Primitive Passions: Visuality, Sexuality, Ethnography, and Contemporary Chinese Cinema*. New York: Columbia University Press, 1995.

Chua, Beng Huat, and Koichi Iwabuchi, eds. *East Asian Pop Culture: Analysing the Korean Wave*. Hong Kong: Hong Kong University Press, 2008.

Chung, Steven. *Sin Sang-ok and Postwar Korean Mass Culture*. Ph.D. diss., University of California at Irvine, 2007.

Deleuze, Gilles. *Cinema 1: The Movement-Image*. Translated by Hugh Tomlinson and Barbara Habberjam. Minneapolis: University of Minnesota Press, 2003.

———. *Cinema 2: The Time-Image*. Translated by Hugh Tomlinson and Robert Galeta. Minneapolis: University of Minnesota Press, 1989.

———. *Negotiations, 1972–1990*. Translated by Martin Joughin. New York: Columbia University Press, 1995.

———. *Nietzsche and Philosophy*. Translated by Hugh Tomlinson. New York: Columbia University Press, 1983.

Deleuze, Gilles, and Félix Guattari. *Anti-Oedipus: Capitalism and Schizophrenia*. Translated by Robert Hurley, Mark Seem, and Helen R. Lane. Minneapolis: University of Minnesota Press, 1983.

———. *A Thousand Plateaus: Capitalism and Schizophrenia*. Translated by Brian Massumi. Minneapolis: University of Minnesota Press, 1987.

Derrida, Jacques. *Dissemination*. Translated by Barbara Johnson. Chicago: University of Chicago Press, 1981.

Eagleton, Terry. *After Theory*. New York: Basic, 2003.

———. *The Eagleton Reader*. Edited by Stephen Regan. Oxford: Blackwell, 1998.

Eisenstein, Sergei M. *Nonindifferent Nature*. Translated by Herbert Marshall. Cambridge: Cambridge University Press, 1987.

Foucault, Michel. *The Birth of the Clinic*. Translated by A. M. Sheridan Smith. New York: Vintage, 1973.

———. *Discipline and Punish: The Birth of the Prison*. Translated by Alan Sheridan. 2nd ed. New York: Vintage, 1995.

———. Preface to *Anti-Oedipus: Capitalism and Schizophrenia*, xi–xiv. By Gilles Deleuze and Félix Guattari. Translated by Robert Hurley, Mark Seem, and Helen R. Lane. Minneapolis: University of Minnesota Press, 1983.

Freud, Sigmund. *Beyond the Pleasure Principle*. Edited and translated by James Strachey. New York: Norton, 1975.

———. *The Standard Edition of the Complete Psychological Works of Sigmund Freud*. Translated and edited by James Strachey, in collaboration with Anna Freud, and assisted by Alix Strachey and Alan Tyson. 24 vols. London: Hogarth, 1953–74.

———. *The Uncanny*. Translated by David McLintock. New York: Penguin, 2003.

Fujitani, Takashi. "Right to Kill, Right to Make Live: Koreans as Japanese and Japanese as Americans during WWII." *Representations* 99 (Summer 2007): 13–39.

———. "Total War at the Movies: Lessons for Archiving National Histories?" In *Panhwan hogŭn yŏnghwa yusan ŭi nanum: Tong Asia ŭi yusil yŏnghwa sujip kwa yŏksa kisul* [Repatriation or Share of Film Heritage: Lost Film Collection and Description of the History in East Asia] (conference proceedings), 93–111. Seoul: Han'guk Yŏngsang Charyowŏn, 2008.

Fukuyama, Francis. *The End of History and the Last Man*. New York: Free Press, 1992.

Gateward, Frances, ed. *Seoul Searching: Identity and Culture in Korean Cinema*. Albany, N.Y.: State University of New York Press, 2007.

Girard, René. *Violence and the Sacred*. Translated by Patrick Gregory. Baltimore: Johns Hopkins University Press, 1977.

Howard, Chris. "Contemporary South Korean Cinema: 'National Conjunction' and 'Diversity.'" In *East Asian Cinemas: Exploring Transnational Connections on Film*, edited by Leon Hunt and Leung Wing-Fai, 88–102. London: I. B. Tauris, 2008.

Ivy, Marilyn. "Foreword: Fascism, Yet?" In *The Culture of Japanese Fascism*, edited by Alan Tansman, vii–xii. Durham: Duke University Press, 2009.

Jackson, Earl, Jr. "Borrowing Trouble: Interasian Adaptations and the Dislocutive Fantasy." Paper presented at the Asia/Cinema/Network: Industry, Culture and Technology Conference, Pusan, Korea, October 12, 2005.

James, David E. "Alternative Cinemas." In *Contemporary American Independent*

Film: From the Margins to the Mainstream, edited by Chris Holmlund and Justin Wyatt, 50–58. New York: Routledge, 2005.

————. "Im Kwon-Taek: Korean Cinema and Buddhism." In *Im Kwon-Taek: The Making of a Korean National Cinema*, edited by David E. James and Kyung Hyun Kim, 47–83. Detroit, Mich.: Wayne State University Press, 2002.

James, David E., and Kyung Hyun Kim, eds. *Im Kwon-Taek: The Making of a Korean National Cinema*. Detroit, Mich.: Wayne State University Press, 2002.

Jameson, Fredric. "Notes on Globalization as a Philosophical Issue." In *The Cultures of Globalization*, edited by Fredric Jameson and Masao Miyoshi, 54–77. Durham: Duke University Press, 1998.

————. *Marxism and Form: Twentieth-Century Dialectical Theories of Literature*. Princeton: Princeton University Press, 1971.

————. *The Political Unconscious: Narrative as a Socially Symbolic Act*. Ithaca: Cornell University Press, 1981.

————. *Postmodernism, or, The Cultural Logic of Late Capitalism*. Durham: Duke University Press, 1991.

————. *Signatures of the Visible*. New York: Routledge, 1992.

Jeon, Joseph Jonghyun. "Memories of Memories: Historicity, Nostalgia, and Archive in Bong Joon-Ho's *Memories of Murder*." *Cinema Journal*, forthcoming.

————. "Residual Selves: Trauma and Forgetting in Park Chan-Wook's *Oldboy*." *positions: east asia cultures critique* 17, no. 3 (2009): 713–40.

Jeong, Kelly Y. *Crisis of Gender and Nation in Korean Literature and Cinema: Modernity Arrives Again*. Plymouth, UK, 2011.

Kang Ok-hui et al., eds. *Singminji sidae taejung yesurin sajŏn*. [The Dictionary of Popular Artists of the Colonial Era]. Seoul: Sodo, 2006.

Kang, Pyŏng-jin. "'Chunhyangjŏn' ŭn kot'ong ija kippŭm ija chonkyŏngsim iŏtta [*Chunhyangjon* Was a Pain, a Happiness, and a Tribute]." *Cine 21* (http://www.cine21.com/Article/article_view.php?article_id=61041&page=3&mm=005002002).

Karatani Kōjin. *Origins of Modern Japanese Literature*. Edited and translated by Brett de Bary. Durham: Duke University Press, 1993.

Kim Chin-song. *Sŏul e ttansühol ŭl hŏhara* [Grant a Permit in Seoul to Dance Hall]. Seoul: Hyŏnsil Munhwa Yŏng'gu, 1999.

Kim, Kyung Hyun. *The Remasculinization of Korean Cinema*. Durham: Duke University Press, 2004.

Kim, Pil Ho, and Hyunjoon Shin. "The Birth of 'Rok': Cultural Imperialism, Nationalism, and the Glocalization of Rock Music in South Korea, 1964–1975." *positions: east asia cultures critique* 18, no. 1 (2010): 199–230.

Kim, So-young. "In/Visible Cinema: Hollow Archive and National Cinema." In *Panhwan hogŭn yŏnghwa yusan ŭi nanum: Tong Asia ŭi yusil yŏnghwa sujip kwa yŏksa kisul* [Repatriation or Share of Film Heritage: Lost Film Collection and Description of the History in East Asia] (conference proceedings), 41–66. Seoul: Han'guk Yŏngsang Charyowŏn, 2008.

Kim Sung-ok. "A Journey to Mujin." Translated by Moon Hi-kyung. In *Modern*

Korean Literature: An Anthology 1908–65, edited by Chung Chong-wha, 348–72. London: Kegan Paul International, 1995.

Kinder, Marsha. "Violence American Style: The Narrative Orchestration of Violent Attractions." In *Violence and American Cinema*, edited by J. David Slocum, 63–100. New York: Routledge, 2001.

Klein, Christina. "Why American Studies Needs to Think about Korean Cinema, or, Transnational Genres in the Films of Bong Joon-Ho." *American Quarterly* 60, no. 4 (2008): 871–98.

Kobayashi Hideo. *Literature of the Lost Home: Kobayashi Hideo—Literary Criticism, 1924–1939.* Edited and translated by Paul Anderer. Stanford: Stanford University Press, 1995.

Korean Film Council (KOFIC). *Hanguk yŏnghwa yŏngam* [Korean Film Annals]. Seoul: Korean Film Council, 2000–2010.

———. *2007-nyŏn Han'guk yŏnghwa kyŏlsan* [2007 Korean Film Industry Summary]. Seoul: Korean Film Council, 2007.

———. "Best 5 Korean Films of Last 10 Years." *Korean Cinema Today* 5 (November–December 2009): 8–19.

Kwŏn Podŭrae. *Yŏnae ŭi sidae: 1920-yŏndae ch'oban ŭi munhwa wa yuhaeng* [Age of Dating: Culture and Trends of the Early 1920s]. Seoul: Hyŏnsil Munhwa Yŏng'gu, 2003.

Laclau, Ernesto. *Politics and Ideology in Marxist Theory*. London: Verso, 1979.

Lamarre, Thomas. "Bacterial Cultures and Linguistic Colonies: Mori Rintaro's Experiments with History, Science, and Language." *positions: east asia cultures critique* 6, no. 3 (1998): 597–635.

Latour, Bruno. *We Have Never Been Modern*. Translated by Catherine Porter. Cambridge: Harvard University Press, 1993.

Lee, Hyangjin. *Contemporary Korean Cinema: Identity, Culture, Politics*. Manchester, UK: Manchester University Press, 2001.

Lefebvre, Martin. "Introduction." In *Landscape and Film*, edited by Martin Lefebvre, xi–xxxi. New York: Routledge, 2006.

Lippit, Akira. "Hong Sangsoo's Line of Inquiry, Communication, Defense, and Escape." *Film Quarterly* 57, no. 4 (2004): 22–30.

Maliangkay, Roald. "Supporting Our Boys: American Military Entertainment and Korean Pop Music in the 1950s and Early 1960s." In *Korean Pop Music: Riding the Korean Wave*, edited by Keith Howard, 21–33. Folkestone, Kent: Global Oriental, 2006.

———. "When the Korean Wave Ripples." *IIAS Newsletter* 42 (Autumn 2006): 15.

Marx, Karl, "Capital, Volume Three." In *The Marx-Engels Reader*, 2nd ed., edited by Robert C. Tucker, 439–42. New York: Norton, 1978.

McLaughlin, Kevin. "Virtual Paris: Benjamin's 'Arcades Project'" In *Benjamin's Ghosts: Interventions in Contemporary Literary and Cultural Theory*, edited by Gerhard Richter, 204–25. Stanford: Stanford University Press, 2002.

Miyoshi, Masao. "Against the Narrative Grain: The Japanese Novel and the 'Postmodern' West." In *Postmodernism and Japan*, edited by Masao Miyoshi and H. D. Harootunian, 143–68. Durham: Duke University Press, 1989.

Moretti, Franco. "Planet Hollywood." *New Left Review* 9 (May–June 2001): 90–102.

———. *Signs Taken for Wonders: On the Sociology of Literary Forms*. London: Verso, 2005.

Nancy, Jean-Luc. *A Finite Thinking*. Edited by Simon Sparks. Stanford: Stanford University, 2003.

Nichols, Bill. *Representing Reality*. Indianapolis: Indiana University Press, 1991.

Nietzsche, Friedrich. *On the Genealogy of Morals and Ecce Homo*. Translated by Walter Kaufmann and R. J. Hollingdale. New York: Vintage, 1967.

Paek Mun-im. *Wŏlha ŭi yŏgoksŏng: Yŏgwi ro ilnŭn han'guk* [Scream under the Moon: Korean Horror Film History through Female Ghosts]. Seoul: Ch'aeksaesang, 2008.

Pak Hyŏn-hŭi. *Mun Ye-bong kwa Kim Sin-jae, 1932–1945*. Seoul: Sŏnin, 2008.

Parquet, Darcy. *New Korean Cinema: Breaking the Waves*. London: Wallflower, 2009.

Peattie, Mark. "The Japanese Colonial Empire, 1895–1945." In *The Cambridge History of Japan*, edited by John W. Hall et al., vol. 6, *The Twentieth Century*, edited by Peter Duus, 217–23. Cambridge: Cambridge University Press, 1988.

Reich, Wilhelm. *The Mass Psychology of Fascism*. New York: Noonday, 1970.

Robinson, Michael E. *Korea's Twentieth-Century Odyssey: A Short History*. Honolulu: University of Hawaii Press, 2007.

Rodowick, D. N. *Difficulty of Difference*. New York: Routledge, 1991.

Said, Edward. *Culture and Imperialism*. New York: Vintage, 1994.

———. *Orientalism*. New York: Vintage, 1979.

Shim, Doobo. "Hybridity and the Rise of Korean Popular Culture in Asia." *Media, Culture, and Society* 28, no. 1 (2006): 25–44.

Shin, Chi-Yun, and Julian Stringer, eds. *New Korean Cinema*. Edinburgh: Edinburgh University Press, 2005.

Sobchack, Vivian. "History Happens." In *The Persistence of History: Cinema, Television, and the Modern Event*, edited by Vivian Sobchack, 1–14. New York: Routledge, 1996.

Sontag, Susan. *"Illness as Metaphor" and "AIDS and Its Metaphors."* New York: Picador, 2001.

Stephens, Chuck. "Future Shock: Hong Sang-Soo's Lady in Red." *Film Comment* 40, no. 6 (November–December 2004): 43–45.

Suh, Serk-bae. "Empire and Nation: The Debates of Japanese and Korean Intellectuals on Nation and Culture from the 1930s through the 1950s." Ph.D. diss., University of California, Los Angeles, 2006.

Virilio, Paul. *The Art of the Motor*. Translated by Julie Rose. Minneapolis: University of Minnesota Press, 1995.

———. *The Vision Machine*. Bloomington: Indiana University Press, 1994.

Weinstein, Philip. *Unknowing: The Work of Modernist Fiction*. Ithaca: Cornell University Press, 2005.

Williams, Linda. *Playing the Race Card: Melodramas of Black and White from Uncle Tom to O. J. Simpson*. Princeton: Princeton University Press, 2002.

Yanagi Muneyoshi. "For a Korean Architecture about to Be Lost." In *Sources of Japanese Tradition, Volume 2, Part 2*. Edited by William Theodore de Bary et al., 145–47. New York: Columbia University Press, 2006.

Yang, Young-Kyun. "*Jajangmyeon* and *Junggukjip*." *Korea Journal* 45, no. 2 (2005): 60–88.

Yi Sang. "Lingering Impressions of a Mountain Village—a Few Paragraphs from a Journal of Travels to Sŏngch'ŏn." Translated by John Frankl. *Azaleas* 2 (2008): 331–46.

Yi, Yŏng-il. *Han'guk yŏnghwa chŏnsa* [Complete History of Korean Cinema] Seoul: Sodo, 2004.

Žižek, Slavoj. *Did Somebody Say Totalitarianism: Five Interventions in the (Mis)Use of a Notion*. New York: Verso, 2002.

———. *First as Tragedy, Then as Farce*. London: Verso, 2009.

———. *The Sublime Object of Ideology*. London: Verso, 1989.

———. *Welcome to the Desert of the Real! Five Essays on 11 September and Related Dates*. London: Verso, 2002.

box office. *See* Korean film industry

Bresson, Robert, xiii, 221n35

Buddhism, 28, 30–31, 76

Buñuel, Luis, 169, 229n16

capitalism, xii–xiii, 1–17, 26–28, 47, 67, 70–71, 73–74, 83–84, 99, 103, 107, 110, 119, 165, 180, 190–92, 200–12, 215n17, 220n23. *See also chaebŏl* (conglomerate); class and occupation; Korean film industry; "late capitalism"; Marxism

castration, 19, 63, 161, 162, 229n9

cellphones, 42, 50, 101, 143, 145, 205

censorship and bans, 61, 66, 76–77, 104, 195, 214n6, 215n6, 222n17, 225n6, 225n7

CGV. *See* multiplexes

chaebŏl (conglomerate), xii, 5, 225n1, 233n8

"change mummified" (André Bazin), 221–22, 232n6

children, 40, 45–46, 76–79, 85–89, 123, 145, 162, 165, 167, 170, 185. *See also* "primitivizing 'China'"

China, xiii, 1, 15, 51, 55, 60–61, 107, 213n1, 214–15n6, 226n21; Mao Tse-tung and, 96. *See also* Chinese diaspora and immigrants in Korea; May Fourth Movement; national cinema: Chinese; "primitivizing 'China'"; Yanbian

Chinatown, 115–22, 140, 226n21

Chinese diaspora and immigrants in Korea, 84, 109–10, 115–22, 139–40, 226–27n21. *See also* race and ethnicity

Cho, Kap-che, 84

Choe, Youngmin, 29, 214n3

Choi, Dong-hun, 12, 51–53, 210–22, 218n41

Choi, Jae-won, ix

Choi, Kyeong-Hee, 57, 61, 76–77

Choi, Min-sik, 182, 226n21

Chŏn, Pong-gwan, 58

Ch'ŏnbyon p'unggyŏng (*Landscape of Ch'ŏnbyon*, Pak T'ae-won, 1936), 38

Chŏn U-ch'i-jŏn (*Tale of Chŏn U-ch'i*), 51, 212

Chosun Dynasty, 126, 200–202, 207–12, 232n7

Chow, Rey, 85–86, 100

Christianity and church, 150, 163, 168–76, 185, 197, 211

chronotopes, 28, 90–91, 97

Chunhyang, 55, 58, 66–68, 71, 74, 178, 210, 221n1

"cinematic affect" (Youngmin Choe), 29

cinematography. *See* film style

city/countryside. *See* urban/rural divide

CJ Entertainment, xii, 218n44, 233n8

class and occupation: anarchists, 199; barbers, 82–92, 176; bargirls and courtesans, 17, 30, 66–67, 73–74, 108–11, 115, 118, 122–23, 212, 226n21; bourgeoisie, 3, 11, 26, 169; capitalists, 67, 70–73, 136, 187, 190–92, 199–200; doctors, 4, 6, 57, 73, 75–79, 92, 160, 209; film directors, 65, 68, 129, 138–39, 143–45, 148; intellectuals, 6, 38, 57, 64–65, 69–72, 83, 84, 121–50, 203, 227n1; landlords, 62–64, 71, 84, 121; land speculators, 170; loan sharks, 63, 74, 79; middle managers, 49–50, 92; migrant workers, 24–25, 31, 43, 46, 62–64, 106, 108–10, 115–22, 140; peasants and servants, 24, 61, 63, 82, 233n18; pimps, 6, 92–93, 99, 118, 226–27n21; restaurant workers, 132, 137–39, 154, 193–94, 231n10; *sajang* (company president), 123–24, 167–76; salary men, 6, 183–85; sex workers, 30, 108, 111, 118, 122–23;

vagabonds, 49–50; widening gap, 200, 210, 233n13; workers, 30, 33, 61, 83, 103, 192, 194, 228n2; *yangban*, 64, 209–12

claustrophobia, 36, 41

coffee shops, 15, 143, 147

colonialism. *See* Japan

comedy. *See* genre

communism, 2, 88–90, 104, 112. *See also* anti-communism

complicity (*sunŭng*), 18, 57, 71–73, 77, 78, 80, 82, 223n30

computer graphics (CG). *See* film style

conservative politics, 4, 33, 42, 81–84, 150, 228n9, 228n20

conservative presidents: Chun Doo Hwan (1980–87), 19, 152, 168–69, 186; Chung Hee Park (1961–79), 18, 76, 81–100, 117, 119, 224n11, 233n7; Lee Myung-bak (2008–present), 3, 200, 215n13; Syngman Rhee (1948–60), 223n2. *See also* liberal presidents

corporeality, 7, 30, 41, 43, 45, 55–80, 81–84, 89–90, 92, 99, 111, 121, 123–24, 140, 178–80, 190–92, 223n3. *See also* corpse; crime and misdemeanor: organ sale; defecation; sex

corpse, 41, 69, 75, 78, 91, 123–24, 220n26

cosmopolitanism, 13, 15, 19, 31, 42, 125, 127, 129, 147

credit market crash (2008–9), 27, 232n2

crime and misdemeanor: adultery, 131, 134, 137, 141–43, 148; DUI, 154; embezzlement, 55, 67, 74, 181, 229n10; harassment, 142–44; kidnapping and ransom, 171–72, 183, 185, 188; murder and assassination, 18, 38, 42, 62, 75–76, 78, 92–95, 97–99, 106, 141, 171–76, 183, 232n5; narcotics, 128–29, 142; organ sale, 190–92; public lewdness, 141; public obscenity, 132, 137, 142; smoking,

145–46, 163. *See also* violence: rape; North Korea: terrorism and

Crossroads of Youth (*Chŏngch'un ŭi sipjaro*, An Chong-hwa, 1934), 58–63, 74–75

Cut the Chain (*Swesasŭl ŭl kkŭnŏra*, Lee Man-hŭi, 1971), ix

dame in distress. *See* genre

Dargis, Manohla, 178–79, 230n1

Day a Pig Fell into the Well, The (*Tweji ga umul e ppajin nal*, Hong Sang-soo, 1996), 128, 141, 148, 182, 227n3, 231n1

death. *See* corpse; crime and misdemeanor: murder and assassination; suicide

Debord, Guy, 32

decolonization, 14, 68, 126. *See also* postcolonialism

"defamiliarization of the familiar" (Karatani Kōjin) 6, 26, 38

defecation, 87, 90–91, 98, 196

deindustrialization, 30, 42–44, 49, 117

Deleuze, Gilles: on any-space-whatevers, 169, 229n16; on becoming, 8, 97, 130, 136, 138, 141, 161, 165, 196; on body-without-organs, 7; on cliché, 85, 97–99, 137, 198; on desire-recording, 45; on desiring machine, 8, 153; on deterritorialization, 45–49; on faciality, 16; on lines of flight, 49, 104, 120; Nietzsche and, 187–89; on nomad, 7–8, 25, 47–48, 112, 150; on originary world, 20, 205, 207; on peaks of present/ sheets of past, 16, 128, 135, 215n20; on power, 8, 82, 189, 211–12; on power of the false, 7–8, 20, 211–12; on schizo (Anti-Oedipal), 6–8, 19, 38, 45, 161–66, 177; on smooth and striated, 49–50, 147; on virtual and actual, x, 6–9, 30, 33–36, 42–54, 85,

illness, 17, 57, 65, 75, 78, 87, 114, 121, 141, 146, 160, 190, 196, 221n8; Alzheimer's, 157; hypochondria, 19, 23, 129, 133–34, 138, 143, 148, 230n28; liver disease, 92, 190; schizophrenia, 6, 60, 78, 162, 165, 194; speech impediment, 18, 68–71, 76–77, 157, 160, 195; tuberculosis, 6, 18, 55–57, 68–71, 75, 108, 111; venereal disease, 148. *See also* "impaired body as colonial trope" (Kyeong-Hee Choi); triangulated archetype (colonial and post-colonial eras)

"illness as metaphor" (Susan Sontag), 69

Im, Sang-soo, 84, 92–100

"IMF crisis," 1, 16, 26, 27, 169, 194, 218n44. *See also* Korean economy

Im Kwon-Taek, 17, 23–31, 38, 40, 53, 132–33

"impaired body as colonial trope" (Kyeong-Hee Choi), 57, 61, 76–77

incarceration, 66, 68, 111, 129, 162–63, 166, 172, 175, 183–85, 190, 193, 196–98, 231n11

incest, 183–87

industrialization, 3, 18, 27, 30–31, 38, 43–44, 49, 121, 214n6. *See also* deindustrialization

infecundity and barrenness, 30, 48, 53, 123–24

Innocent Steps (*Taensŏ ŭi sunjŏng*, Pak Yŏng-hun, 2005), 108, 116–18, 226n21

insanity, 61–63, 77–79, 164, 195

inter-ethnic marriage, 70, 79, 113–22, 195, 230n19

Internet and e-mail, 5, 15, 27, 119, 182, 192, 198, 215n7, 218n47

"inversion of consciousness" (Karatani Kōjin). *See* tenko (inversion of consciousness, Karatani Kōjin)

Ito, Hirobumi, 61

jajangmyŏn and Chinese food, 137, 154, 183–84, 192–93

James, David E., 28–29, 35, 96

Jameson, Fredric, 4, 42, 79, 84, 135, 153, 200, 214n8, 215n17, 220n23, 224n13

Jang, Sun-woo (Chang Sŏn-u), 44, 150, 179, 186, 203–6, 223n3

Japan: annexation of Korea and, xiii, 1, 13, 16, 18, 28, 55–64, 109, 121, 125–26, 170; collaboration with, 60–80; colonial-era films and, 17–18, 55–72, 78–80, 121, 205, 222n17; colonial modernity and, 17–18, 38, 58–60, 79–80; Korean film exports to, x–xi, 1–2, 9–11, 15–16, 33, 215n8; films set in colonial era, ix, xi, 28, 59–60, 72–80, 201, 205–8, 212, 222n13; Imperial and Kwantung Army and, 75–76, 84, 221n4, 221n5; invasion of Korea (1592) by, 9, 209–10. *See also* complicity (*sunŭng*); decolonization; *naisen ittai*; post-colonialism

Jeon, Ji-hyun, 2, 11, 16

Jeon Woo-chi: The Taoist Wizard (Choi Dong-hoon, 2009), 12, 51–53, 210, 218

JSA: Joint Security Area (Park Chanwook, 2000), 105, 107

Jung, Woo-sung, ix–x

Kang, Woo-suk, 13, 233n12

Kang Je-gyu, 2, 105, 233

Kant, Immanuel, 9, 37

Karatani, Kōjin, 25–26, 34, 47, 69, 220n34

KBS, 13, 15, 214

Kim, Dae-jung. *See* liberal presidents

Kim, Dae-woo, 209, 233n18

Kim, Hae-il, 65

Kim, Jee-woon, ix, 14–15, 59, 201

Kim, Patti, 13

"supersensible" (Immanuel Kant), 37
Sweet Dream (Mimong, Yang Chu-nam,
    1936), 60, 221n8
Sympathy for Mr. Vengeance (Park Chan-
    wook, 2002), 178–79, 187–90, 199,
    231n21

Taejanggŭm (Jewel in the Palace), 14, 209
t'albukja (North Korean defectors). See
    North Korea
Tale of Cinema (Kŭkjangjŏn, Hong Sang-
    soo, 2005), 128, 132, 143–48
taste culture, xii, 10, 13–15, 58–59, 65,
    79, 93, 193–94
telephone. See mobile phones
television. See mass media
tenko (inversion of consciousness,
    Karatani Kōjin), 26, 34, 36, 47
terrorism. See North Korea
To the Starry Island (Kŭ sŏm e kago-
    sip'ta, Park Kwang-su, 1993), 105,
    151–52, 228n2
tour, 1, 3–4, 27–29, 34, 61, 101–4, 118–
    20, 130–31, 147, 151, 214n3, 225n1,
    225n2, 225n3, 233n19
trains, 58, 63, 130
translatability, ix–xi, 112–13, 129–30,
    144, 164, 196. See also han'gŭl
trauma, 16, 19, 27, 72, 80, 152, 156, 162,
    168, 170, 176–77, 184, 186, 194, 205,
    211–12, 229n9
trees, 23, 42, 51, 155, 168
triangulated archetype (colonial and
    post-colonial eras), 17–18, 62–65,
    70–71, 73–74, 76–77
Tsui, Hark, xii, 79
tuberculosis. See illness
Turning Gate (Saeghwal ŭi palgyŏn,
    Hong Sang-soo, 2002), 129–36, 145,
    149, 228n13
Two Cops (Kang Woo-suk, 1993), 13
Typhoon (T'aep'ung, Kwak Kyŏng-t'aek,
    2005), 106, 108–12, 114

Ubermensch. See Nietzsche, Friedrich
Ugetsu monogatari (Mizoguchi Kenji,
    1953), 76
"uncanny" (Sigmund Freud), 30, 35, 73,
    79, 139, 160–61, 166, 192
"unknowable" (Philip Weinstein), 181–
    82, 194
urbanity, 14–16, 31–37, 58–60, 70, 127,
    129–31
urbanization, 3, 12–15, 18–19, 28,
    32, 116, 126, 130, 226n21. See also
    cosmopolitanism; genre: film noir;
    youth culture
urban/rural divide, 6, 19, 25, 31–37, 70,
    116–18, 131–34, 167–69, 205, 230n18
US military occupation, 13, 54, 115, 120,
    217n36, 220n26, 230n19; American
    servicemen and women, 13–14,
    220n26, 230n19
utopia. See Marxism

violence: with acupuncture needles,
    38; "discipline and punish" and, 48,
    82–83, 146; with guns, ix, 94–95,
    98, 102, 112, 185, 205; human rights
    violation and, 13, 42, 229n9; with
    knife, 38, 141, 178, 188, 190, 199;
    with poison, 73, 231n11; police and,
    31, 42, 66, 75, 166, 181–83, 186, 194,
    222n17, 247n10; rape, 62–63, 70,
    73–74, 155, 157, 162, 177; representa-
    tion of, 20, 63–64, 157, 179–80, 188,
    199, 222n17; with sickle, 62–63, 65,
    69–70, 74; torture, 81, 88, 231n11;
    war, 17–18, 55–56, 60, 71, 79, 104,
    152, 179, 222n13, 228–29n9, 233n7.
    See also crime and misdemeanor
Virgin Stripped Bare by Her Bachelors
    (O! Sujŏng, Hong Sang-soo, 2000),
    127, 134, 136, 147–48, 150, 227n3
virtual-actual. See Deleuze, Gilles
virtuelle (Walter Benjamin), 21, 219n52
voice, 88, 98, 196–99, 232n23

KYUNG HYUN KIM is associate professor of East Asian languages and literatures at the University of California, Irvine.

Library of Congress Cataloging-in-Publication Data

Kim, Kyung Hyun, 1969–
Virtual hallyu : Korean cinema of the global era / Kyung Hyun Kim.
p. cm.
Includes bibliographical references and index.
ISBN 978-0-8223-5088-0 (cloth : alk. paper)
ISBN 978-0-8223-5101-6 (pbk. : alk. paper)
1. Motion pictures—Korea—History—21st century.
2. Cultural industries—Korea—History—21st century.
3. Popular culture—Korea—History—21st century.
I. Title.
PN1993.5.K6K52424 2011
791.4309519—dc23
2011021955

Virtual Hallyu